Praise for *From Co*

"The book is very well researched about a great team and some of the most talented players who ever played the game. Not only great champions but true gentlemen."
—Dick Cunningham

"I enjoyed going back in time while reading this book. It brought back good memories of a great season leading up to the NBA championship. I was blessed to experience such a great season with a great team!
—Jon McGlocklin

"The Milwaukee Bucks resume should lead with this glossy fact: 'From expansion team to NBA world champs in 3 years. An unparalleled achievement in any pro sport.' The magical run was culminated during the 1970-71 season and is captured in this game-by-game recall of author Rick Schabowski. Join him for this detailed recollection of the greatest year in Bucks history. Enjoy the memories!"
—Eddie Doucette, the Original Voice of the Bucks

"This book chronicles the Bucks' historic 1970-71 championship season in compelling detail. It was an era of all-time great players with eye-popping statistics. A must-read for Bucks fans and NBA junkies. What struck me most was the numbers those guys put up; not just Kareem and Oscar, but Wilt, Unseld, all the other stars who played in the league at that time: points, rebounds, assists."
—Bob Greacen

FROM COIN TOSS TO CHAMPIONS

1971: THE YEAR OF THE MILWAUKEE BUCKS

FROM COIN TOSS
TO CHAMPIONS

1971: THE YEAR OF THE
MILWAUKEE BUCKS

Rick Schabowski

HenschelHAUS Publishing, Inc.
Milwaukee, Wisconsin

Published by
HenschelHAUS Publishing, Inc.
www.henschelHAUSbooks.com
Email: info@henschelHAUSbooks.com

ISBN: 978159598-719-8
E-ISBN: 978159598-720-4
LCCN: 2019933920

Printed in the United States of America.

*A portion of the proceeds from the sale of this book goes to the
MACC Fund (Midwest Athletes Against Childhood Cancer).*

To all Milwaukee Bucks fans

CONTENTS

FOREWORD

I STARTED WORKING AS A SPORTS anchor at WITI TV in Milwaukee in 1987, the last year the Bucks played at MECCA. A solid veteran core (Sidney Moncrief, Jack Sikma, Paul Pressey, and "The Deuces," Ricky Pierce) constituted a squad that won far more than they lost, but could never bring a second NBA championship to Brew City.

A lifelong sports fan who grew up in Philadelphia, I was certainly familiar with the Bucks' world champion team of 1971, but outside of the legendary exploits of Lew Alcindor and Oscar Robertson, didn't know much about other members of the team and the franchise's back story when I arrived here.

I heard stories from my co-workers about Bobby Dandridge, Lucius Allen, and Dick "The Cement Mixer" Cunningham, had the pleasure of working with Jon McGlocklin at Fox Sports Wisconsin, and read extensively about the '71 season but never got a true sense of the team until I read this terrific book by Rick Schabowski.

From Coin Toss to Championship is a wonderfully researched, richly detailed, game-by-game history of that magical season. It is in effect "1971 Milwaukee Bucks All Access," taking the reader onto that unforgettable golden-hued court and into the locker room as the team battled the likes of Wilt Chamberlain, John Havlicek, Walt Frazier, and Wes Unseld on their journey to the game's ultimate prize.

What follows in the pages ahead represents a treasure trove of game stories, player interviews, and vintage photos from Rick's personal collection (an impressive array from the pre-cellphone era of photography!) that will both trigger great memories and provide fresh insight for Bucks fans who experienced that remarkable run and create an important historical reference for younger fans who came in at "Fear the Deer" and future generations of Bucks supporters.

Mark Concannon

Four time Emmy Award-winner

Author, *Mettle & Honor*

MettleandHonor.com

INTRODUCTION

A FTER THE 1965 BASEBALL SEASON, when the Braves moved to Atlanta, Milwaukee was no longer "home" for a major sports franchise. Not many people would ever conceive that a mere five-and-half years later, Milwaukee would have not only a professional team but a world champion. The Milwaukee Bucks accomplished this winning the 1970-71 National Basketball Association championship.

Allan H. ("Bud") Selig worked tirelessly to get major league baseball back in Milwaukee, and his efforts succeeded when the Seattle Pilots were purchased out of bankruptcy court and moved to Milwaukee late in the evening of March 31, 1970.

While this process was taking place, another person was working to bring a major sports franchise to Milwaukee—Marvin Fishman.

Fishman was a successful realtor in the Milwaukee area. His initial effort to get a team was to get a franchise in the American Football League. He was making great progress until someone named Vince Lombardi changed things.

The Packers had a lease to play at Milwaukee County Stadium, and when it came up, Lombardi demanded a clause stipulating that the Packers would be the only team to use the stadium, which was granted.

After several meetings with NBA commissioner Walter Kennedy, who liked the idea of a team in Milwaukee, Fishman decided to pursue that route. Local businessman Wesley Pavalon joined the effort, and on January 22, 1968, Milwaukee was awarded a franchise. After a local contest to name the team, Bucks was selected.

The 1968-69 NBA season ended with the Bucks posting an impressive record for an expansion team, 27-55, but they still had the worst record in the Eastern Conference of the NBA. This earned them the opportunity to participate in a coin flip with the Phoenix Suns for the first pick of the upcoming draft, which would give the winner the NBA's negotiating rights to Lew Alcindor. (This book will use Lew Alcindor. Even though he converted to Islam while attending UCLA, his name wasn't legally changed until after the 1970-71 season.)

The Bucks won the flip and signed him to a contract. They immediately became a contender and improved their record to 56-26 but lost in the Eastern Conference finals to the New York Knicks, four games to two.

A trade that brought All-Pro guard Oscar Robertson to the Bucks helped them improve their record to 66-16 and a 12-2 mark in the NBA playoffs, earning them the championship.

I was a freshman in college, and, like most sports fans in Wisconsin, I caught Bucks fever. I missed only five regular season and playoff games that were played at the Milwaukee Arena, and also went to Madison for the playoff games held at the University of Wisconsin Fieldhouse. When the Bucks returned to Milwaukee the afternoon after winning the championship, I went to the airport to welcome and congratulate them.

In 2011, the 40th anniversary of the championship season, Bucks Vice President of Business Operations John Steinmiller sent a letter to the players that really summarizes the season.

> *"Celebrate your accomplishments and never forget.*
> *NO major league sports expansion franchise has*
> *ever won a league championship in just its third*
> *year of existence. Many still feel that the 1971*
> *Bucks team was the MOST dominant team and*
> *NBA Champion ever. It's been established statisti-*
> *cally and objectively. The most important thing is*
> *that for one great season, you were part of a*
> *Championship effort—a melding of talent, charac-*
> *ter, perseverance, and personalities. You did it!"*[1]

I hope you enjoy reading about an unforgettable season.
—Rick Schabowski

---

1) John Steinmiller, personal letter to team members, April 29, 2011.

CHAPTER 1

A TOSS OF THE COIN

WITHOUT QUESTION, THE BIG EVENT that made the Bucks become an instant contender was the coin flip that resulted in the upstart club winning the first pick of the 1969 NBA draft, which meant the opportunity to bid for UCLA senior Lew Alcindor.

The two teams that won the right to take part in this event—the Milwaukee Bucks and the Phoenix Suns—did so by losing the most games in their divisions. In the previous season, the Bucks posted a 27-55 regular season record, while the Suns went 16-66.

The coin toss was a relatively new procedure for the NBA. Up until 1966, teams drafted in the reverse order of their won-lost record, with the only exception being a special territorial pick allowing a team to draft a player from its local area which, if used by a team, would result in a forfeiture of their first-round pick. The territorial pick rule was eliminated for the 1966 draft; instead, a coin toss between the worst teams in each division was introduced to determine who would obtain the overall first pick.

On the morning of March 19, 1969, the Bucks' general manager, John Erickson, and board chairmen Wes Pavalon and Marvin Fishman were in the Bucks office on 7th Street and Wisconsin Avenue, ready for the phone call from NBA Commissioner Walter Kennedy from his office, located on the 23rd floor of 2 Pennsylvania Plaza in New York. The third party, representing the Suns, was their team president, Richard Bloch.

People deny being superstitious, but three people in the Bucks office had their good luck items on their person. John Erickson was wearing a kibbutz medal his wife had brought back from Israel, Wes Pavalon was wearing a St. Christopher medal, and Marv Fishman had a Winston Churchill silver dollar in his left shoe.

At 9:57 a.m., Erickson picked up the phone and told the media gathered to cover the event, "It's some babe in New York."[1]

The ground rules of the flip were presented to both teams by Kennedy's two secretaries, Helenmarie Burns and Constance Maroselli, who took places on each side of him, and the process started. At 10:01, technical difficulties broke the three-way connection. The group in Milwaukee got very excited when the phone rang a minute later, but the call was from a fan who wanted to know who won the flip.

Five minutes later, with all parties back on the line, Kennedy began,

> *"I have two cards on my desk. One has Phoenix written on it, one has Milwaukee. I will pick one, and that team will have the privilege of calling the flip or passing and allowing the other team to call. Understood? The card says Phoenix. What is Phoenix's pleasure?"[2]*

Bloch responded that Phoenix would make the call.

Reflecting on Bloch's choice, Fishman recalled,

> *"Fine, I thought. Let Phoenix call. The old gambler's adage is to never choose on an even bet. The house*

never makes a choice. It is always safer to let the other guy choose against himself."[3]

The process moved to the final step. Kennedy said,

"I have a 1964 Kennedy half dollar. I will flip it with my right hand, catch it in my right hand, and turn it over on the back of my left hand."[4]

After concluding the flip, Kennedy asked Phoenix to make the call. The Suns knew they would be involved in the coin flip process, so they asked their fans to make the choice by voting at Suns games. Bloch now gave Kennedy their decision, following their orders were: "Call it heads." Kennedy immediately informed both parties the coin had come up tails.

When the Bucks won the flip, bedlam erupted in the Bucks office. Pavalon jumped up and turned to hug Erickson, forgetting about the lit cigarette in his mouth and leaving Erickson with a burn in his ear. Everyone was

Board member Wes Pavalon seems a little excited about the Bucks' winning the NBA rights for Lew Alcindor. (Author's collection)

elated, walking around in circles, happy and relieved, while Erickson was in pain. Erickson later said,

> *"We are doubly happy about this for our Bucks fans who have been patient and understanding. They also have been going to church regularly, judging from today."*[5]

The situation was very different for the Suns. Bloch sat down and reflected about the loss of the flip and its financial effects to the club. His wife came in and asked him how he would like his eggs for breakfast.

> *He said, "We have just lost the coin flip. We have just lost the greatest basketball player there is."* And she said, *"Oh, I'm sorry. How would you like your eggs? Scrambled or over?"*[6]

Phoenix Coach Johnny Kerr expressed disappointment, commenting,

> *"We lost a great one. Alcindor will do more things in the NBA than Elvin Hayes has. He absolutely can't miss. He does many things that don't show up in the box scores. He does a tremendous job of hitting the open man and he gets the ball out on the fast break as well as anybody in basketball. Losing him is going to make things that much tougher for us. We have been looking at our team two ways—with Alcindor and without him. Now we have to concentrate on doing the best we can without him."*[7]

Suns all-star guard Gail Goodrich said,

> *"I think it's an injustice that they had to flip a coin at all. We obviously have the worst team in the league, so we should have first choice. That's the way it is in football and baseball; why not basketball? I understand the thinking behind the rule.*

> *They don't want anybody trying to finish with the worst record. At the same time, though, they are questioning the integrity of the players. It's a big loss to us. There are other fine college players, but nobody like Alcindor."[8]*

The page-one headline of *The Phoenix Gazette* summed it up well: *Cindor Dream Turns to Ashes.*

The Bucks now had visions of Alcindor playing on their team and the positive things he would bring to the court. Coach Larry Costello said,

> *"I've said a hundred times that you can't win without a good big man, and Alcindor is definitely a good big man. At 7 foot 2½ or 7 foot 3, he would be good if he just stood there and didn't jump."[9]*

Bucks' guard Jon McGlocklin predicted,

> *"He's going to make us a powerful team. He can take some of the pressure off Flynn Robinson and me, and we in turn can take some off him. The defenses won't be able to sag on him very much."[10]*

Flynn Robinson looked forward to an Alcindor addition to the team.

> *"Having him at center will give me more opportunity to drive in, and the way he gets the ball off the board will help the whole club. Defense is his biggest asset of all. Just knowing he's there means a lot."[11]*

The coin flip was only the first battle in a war. The Bucks were victorious in obtaining the rights to bid for the services of Alcindor, but the next battle would be signing him to a contract. Wes Pavalon noted,

> *"The NBA has proved to be the acme and zenith of
> pro basketball because it doesn't alter its draft to
> meet special circumstances. I can't foresee the
> league making any alterations now in favor of one
> club at the expense of others."*[12]

Indeed, Pavalon was referring to a sense that some of the
powers in the NBA might be involved in a power play to
prevent a fledgling team in a small market from getting
such a player. As late as November of 1968, there were
rumors of changing the rules of trading first-round
choices. The rule changes didn't go through, so Milwaukee
represented the NBA in the negotiations for Alcindor.

The negotiation team representing Alcindor in his
contract talks was composed of UCLA benefactor Sam
Gilbert and a Los Angeles brokerage executive, Ralph
Shapiro, both of them unpaid volunteers.

Alcindor explained the negotiating process in *Giant
Steps*, his autobiography:

> *"I've never been a very patient negotiator, and I
> was even less so then. We told both sides that,
> rather than get involved in a build-you-up/tear-you-
> down bidding war between the leagues, we would
> hear only one blind bid each and make our decision
> firmly. There were a number of benefits to this plan.*
>
> *First, it eliminated a lot of agonizing and anxiety;
> we figured I should get the best contract ever
> offered to a player coming into the league, but none
> of us was certain how much that was or how far
> we could push it.*
>
> *Second, we assumed that, rather than risk losing
> me, each team would put more money on the table
> than they might otherwise part with. We'd get the
> top dollar without having to worry about whether, if*

we'd only held out, more might have been forthcoming. Third, Sam and Mr. Shapiro felt that heated bidding might cause a lot of animosity, particularly from the side that lost, and in the long run that might not be good for my career. And fourth, it seemed to me the honorable thing to do." [13]

Alcindor's collegiate career ended on Saturday, March 22, 1969, with a 37-point, 20-rebound performance in a 92-72 rout of Purdue in the NCAA championship game, giving UCLA its third consecutive title. When asked after the game about his choice of league, he responded,

> *"The decision is very much up in the air. There are a whole lot of things involved, a lot of variables."* [14]

Little time was wasted as the Bucks met with Alcindor's negotiating team and his father, Ferdinand Lewis Sr., at a midtown New York hotel on Monday, March 24. The meeting was arranged by NBA commissioner Walter Kennedy. The Bucks were represented by Wes Pavalon, team president Ray Patterson, and John Erickson.

Erickson was happy to meet Alcindor.

> *"This was the first opportunity we had to talk to Lew, and I was very impressed with him. He's a fine person, very knowledgeable, a truly warm person. He was very friendly and very attentive throughout our meeting."* [15]

Erickson also observed,

> *"The only feeling I got was that Lew is anxious to conclude his negotiations at the earliest possible time. Remember, he still has to talk with the American Basketball Association representatives, probably this week."* [16]

Alcindor was very pleased with the meeting.

> *"They made an extremely good five-year offer. I left that meeting knowing, for the first time, what the numbers were. I could forget about holes in my pants or saving pennies at the gas pump; however these negotiations came out, I was solid on the bottom line."*[17]

Tuesday, March 25, was a busy day. The Bucks' John Erickson called Walter Kennedy, confirming that the Bucks would select Alcindor with the first pick of the draft. Erickson said,

> *"We presented the Milwaukee picture to him, as far as what we thought we could do, and he presented his picture to us. Now we know the area of each other's thinking. His area included things he was looking for apart from money. This gave us a starting point. He will contact us when he is ready to negotiate. We don't know where he is going to play, but we're going to try to sign him. It may be a long, hard job, but we're going to try."*[18]

Meanwhile, Alcindor and his negotiating team spent their Tuesday talking to representatives of the ABA. New York Nets owner Arthur Brown and ABA Commissioner George Mikan presented their offer, which was also for five years. Alcindor's group was shocked about how low the offer was in comparison to that of the Bucks. They were under the assumption that with the ABA being a less-established league, they would offer more money to overcome the prestige of the NBA. There were also rumors that a number of ABA owners were willing to contribute money to offer as a signing bonus. When Sam Gilbert asked Mikan if that was the extent of their offer, Mikan said that was it.

Although it meant not playing in New York, Alcindor chose the Bucks' contract, commenting,

> *"I loved New York but I would have to pass up a great deal of money to live there. Basketball was a business; that fact was brought home to me my first day on the job. My first professional compromise: I chose Milwaukee."[19]*

The ABA had blown it! Mikan had a check for one million dollars in his suit pocket and did not present it at the time of the contract offer. Mikan said,

> *"We decided that it wasn't necessary to give him our best offer. We figure when he comes back to us, then we'll use the check for the second round of talks."[20]*

The negotiating ground rules put in place by Alcindor and his team had been totally ignored. Two ABA owners stopped Sam Gilbert in a hotel lobby with another offer. Gilbert was offended.

> *"We were the ones who established the ground rules in the beginning. We feel Lew is being fair. He gave both parties every chance to make their offers under this rule. I'm sure that if the first ABA offer had been greater, he would have accepted it."[21]*

Alcindor spoke further about the ground rules.

> *"We told each of them to make me a one-shot deal. I saw the Milwaukee people Monday, and the ABA people Tuesday, and I told the ABA people their bid was low. The ABA people came back Tuesday night and wanted to make another offer, but I told them I wasn't interested. It was my decision and nobody else's not to get into a bidding war because it*

Alcindor with Bucks General Manager
John Erickson. (Author's collection)

*degrades the people involved. It would have made
me feel like a flesh peddler, and I'm not that."[22]*

League strength was another issue Alcindor considered.

*"With all things being equal, it would have been
easier playing in New York. It would have been
different if the ABA had a better offer, but things
not being the same, I went to the NBA. The quality
of the NBA can be measured in terms of organization and in its established record of sound
organization. That is not the case of the ABA."[23]*

The ABA's last offer, as spelled out by Mikan in a Minneapolis press conference, included:

- A five-year, $1 million contract, collateralized by $1 million in cash deposit.
- A $500,000 cash bonus.
- Five percent of the New York Nets stock.
- A $62,500-a-year annuity payment starting at age 41 for 20 years.
- Ten percent of the ABA national television contract during the five-year period, equaling at least $500,000.

Everything came to a conclusion on Wednesday, April 2, 1969, at a signing ceremony/press conference at Los Angeles' Beverly Hilton Hotel. John Erickson didn't reveal the terms of the contract but pointed out it was a

"...multiyear pact. It was very fair for Lew and fair for Milwaukee."[24]

When asked what he would do with the money, Alcindor answered,

"I'm just going to use it to make myself financially stable."[25]

Endnotes to Chapter 1

1) Gene Graff, "Bedlam Marks Local Triumph," *Milwaukee Sentinel*, March 20, 1969, pt. 2, p. 1.

2) Robert Lipsyte, "Flipping," *New York Times*, March 20, 1969, p. 58.

3) Marv Fishman and Tracy Dodds, *Bucking the Odds: The Birth of the Milwaukee Bucks.* (Milwaukee, WI: Raintree Publishers, 1978), p. 109.

4) Cleon Walfoort, "Bucks Win Coin Flip, 1st Draft Choice," *Milwaukee Journal*, March 19, 1969, pt. 2, p. 19.

5) *Ibid.*

6) Fishman and Dodds, p. 110.

7) "Suns Disappointed at Loss of Alcindor," *Milwaukee Journal*, March 19, 1969, pt. 2, p. 19.

8) Bob Wolf, "Phoenix Players Say Flipping Coin in Draft Unfair, Slur to Integrity," *Milwaukee Journal*, March 20, 1969, pt. 2, p. 15.

9) *Ibid.*

10) *Ibid.* p. 18.

11) *Ibid.*

12) Cleon Walfoort, "Next Task: Sign Alcindor," *Milwaukee Journal*, March 19, 1969, pt. 2, p. 26.

13) Kareem Abdul-Jabbar and Peter Knobler, *Giant Steps: The Autobiography of Kareem Abdul-Jabbar* (New York, NY: Bantam Books, 1983), p. 191-192.

14) "Lew's Gone, but Memory Lingers On," *Milwaukee Sentinel*, March 24, 1969, pt. 2, p. 1.

15) "Bucks Meet Lew, Get No Promises," *Milwaukee Journal*, March 25, 1969, pt. 2, p. 14.

16) Ray Grody, "Bucks Talk to Alcindor in New York," *Milwaukee Sentinel*, March 25, 1969, pt. 2, p. 1.

17) Abdul-Jabbar and Knobler, p. 192.

18) "Guess Whom Bucks Will Pick?" *Milwaukee Journal*, March 26, 1969, pt. 2, p. 17.

19) Abdul-Jabbar and Knobler, p. 193.

20) Terry Pluto, *Loose Balls: The Short, Wild Life of the American Basketball Association* (New York, NY: Simon and Schuster, 1990), p. 192.

21) Fishman and Dodds, p. 113.

22) "Lew Cool to New ABA Bid," *Milwaukee Journal*, March 30, 1969, pt. 3, p. 1.

23) Lou Chapman, "Alcindor Agrees to Sign With Bucks," *Milwaukee Sentinel*, March 29, 1969, pt. 2, p. 1.

24) Lou Chapman, "Alcindor Accepts Nest Egg," *Milwaukee Sentinel*, April 3, 1969, pt. 2, p. 1.

25) *Ibid.*

CHAPTER 2

TRYING TO GET AN OSCAR

O N MONDAY, APRIL 20, 1970, the Bucks' quest for the NBA title ended in New York's Madison Square Garden. The Knicks and their center, Willis Reed, manhandled them. Lew Alcindor fouled out in a 132-96 defeat. As Alcindor walked to the bench after drawing his sixth foul, the fans serenaded him with a chorus of *Good Night, Louie*.

The Bucks' first general manager, John Erickson, recalled the moment.

> *"All I can remember was we were walking out and we could hear them singing. Lew looked over at me, and he said, 'We'll be back, Mr. Erickson.' That's all he said. And we did come back. I remember going into the locker room and telling Lew we were going to get him some help."*[1]

Who would've thought that the very next day, the major addition to a young Bucks squad was the acquisition of Oscar Robertson?

For reasons unknown, Bob Cousy didn't care for Oscar Robertson. Before Robertson's rookie season in 1960, a national sports magazine asked Cousy about the incoming rookies for the upcoming season. Cousy responded,

> *"West could be the best, and Oscar could be a Royal letdown."*[2]

17

Little did these two realize that before the 1969 NBA season began, Cousy would be Robertson's coach with the Royals.

Cousy wanted to abandon the Royals' pattern offense, which consisted of Robertson bringing the ball up and either passing to Jerry Lucas for a shot, driving for a shot of his own, or passing to an open teammate. Cousy thought was to use a fast-breaking offense similar to the ones he helped run when he was a guard with the Boston Celtics during their many championship seasons. He considered Lucas too slow to play the up-tempo game, and Lucas expressed his dissatisfaction.

> "I asked to be traded because I felt I wasn't going to fit in with their style of play. It had nothing to do with my feelings for Bob. I felt I would be better somewhere else."[3]

Lucas was traded to the San Francisco Warriors for Jim King and Bill Turner. Robertson was puzzled by the trade.

> "In order to fast break, you got to get the ball and we don't have anyone here big enough to get the ball."[4]

The season became a nightmare for Robertson, and Lucas sensed potential discord in the first meeting with their new coach.

> "Cousy had a meeting with Oscar and myself and said to us we'd be the key to anything that would happen in Cincinnati. That's the way things began, but they deteriorated from that point. A short time after he was there and we got into training camp, I think he wanted a certain type of play, a different type. I don't sense any jealousy between Cousy and Oscar, but I did sense that Cousy wants to be

*the boss, he has to be the boss, he is the boss. I
don't know, maybe he feels Oscar has too much
influence over the players." [5]*

The situation had so deteriorated that after a loss to the
Celtics on January 30, 1970, a game in which Robertson
had to leave with six minutes remaining because of a
pulled groin, a reporter asked him how he felt about the
trade. The reporter was asked to leave, but Robertson
called up his business agent, J.W. Brown, and found out
he had been traded to the Baltimore Bullets for forward
Gus Johnson.

The Royals' management was in for a surprise. Later,
at a meeting held in J.W. Brown's office, the agent
informed management,

*"Well, unfortunately Oscar doesn't want to go to
Baltimore. And I guess you haven't read his contract lately. Oscar has the right of veto over any
trade."[6]*

This prompted the Royals' front office to call Baltimore and
express the terms for Robertson's contract: three-years for
$700,000. The deal did not go through.

Cousy elaborated further about the negotiations:

*"We sat down with Oscar and he told us he wants
$700,000. I'd like to give it to him because he's a
superstar, but he is not attracting fans into our
stadium. Although Oscar draws terrific on the road,
we are going to lose between $200,000 and
$300,000 this year unless we sell every seat in our
remaining eight home games, and that's rather
unlikely. We cannot offer a quarter of a million
dollars a year."[7]*

The groin injury kept Robertson out of the lineup until February 22, when he played 44 minutes, scoring 28 points, 14 rebounds, and 11 assists, a triple-double. About a month later, on March 20, he played his last game with the Royals.

It was made clear that Robertson's playing days for the Royals were over. Robertson commented,

> *"I wanted to play the remainder of my years in Cincinnati, but I feel that I cannot play for the Royals under any circumstances after this year. It's to the point now that I have to leave."*[8]

Robertson had a number of suitors for his services: the Bullets, Knicks, Lakers, Suns, and the ABA Indiana Pacers, to name a few. All made offers for him. Robertson consulted former Royals teammate Wayne Embry, who spent his final season playing in Milwaukee. Embry gave not only the city, but also the Bucks' organization, very high marks. Robertson recalled,

> *"I wanted to know the organizational structure, and the general situation, besides the finances, of course. Wayne has a lot of respect for the people there, and Jack Twyman (also a former teammate of Robertson's) told me the same thing."*[9]

There were many factors to consider in Robertson's final decision. He wanted good schooling for his children, he liked the Midwest because of its change of seasons, and he wanted to live in a good neighborhood. Accordingly, he told his agent,

> *"I might just like to play in Milwaukee."*[10]

Brown inquired, looking for an asking price from the Bucks,

> *"If I can get you a three-year contract for $700,000, is that a deal?"*[11]

The negotiations were finished quickly with no issues. Bucks owner Wes Pavalon told J.W. Brown,

> *"We want to pay Oscar what we think he is worth. Milwaukee had a fine season, used lots of young players, and all they need is Oscar to join with those kids."*[12]

Brown was amazed with the contract talks.

> *"There was no dickering. Oscar quoted a figure. Milwaukee said it was going to pay it because he deserved it. That was the end of the discussion on money."*[13]

The contract also included a no-cut clause, an injury clause, and approval on trades.

The contract was in place, but compensation from the Bucks to the Royals had to be worked out. The Bucks were considering offering All-Rookie Team forward Bob Dandridge to the Royals as part of the deal, replacing him with Bob Greacen, but Robertson and Brown wanted a deal where both Dandridge and the other starting forward, Greg Smith, would remain with the Bucks. Milwaukee ended up parting with guard Flynn Robinson ("The Electric Eye"), a former Royal, and Charlie Paulk, a power forward who had been the Bucks' first round choice in the 1968 NBA draft.

Oscar Robertson was elated and looking forward to joining the Bucks.

> *"I can help the team. I feel pretty good about the trade. It's a very good situation as I see it. I had my choice of several teams I could go with because of a stipulation in my contract—New York, Phoenix, San Diego, and Milwaukee in the NBA, and several teams in the ABA. I chose Milwaukee because I can fit in there well. They're going places. They've got a fine young team with Lew Alcindor. It's true they're kids, but they got some valuable experience in the playoffs against a team like the New York Knicks. I know a little about that. It's like a fistfight. You learn your way around. That's where I can help them."*[14]

A lot of potential trade rumors came out after the deal with Milwaukee. The Knicks were willing to give up Cazzie Russell and Dave Stallworth. The Suns were willing to deal Gail Goodrich, center Jim Fox, and 6-foot-9 forward Greg Howard, who played the season in Italy. The Lakers offered center Mel Counts and a high draft choice.

Alcindor had nothing but good to say about the acquisition of Robertson.

> *"I was ecstatic. We had been good but young, quick but lacking in the on-court presence that could command deference not only from our opponents, but from ourselves. Last year every game had been a toss-up. Now, even before the Big O walked on the court for our first practice, we all had the feeling that this was our year."*[15]

Even though Robertson was 32 years old, this was no concern for Bucks Coach Larry Costello.

> *"I'd say Oscar has two or three great years left. And with Alcindor around to get him the ball, he may decide he wants to play longer. Oscar will be great for us. He creates situations and he drives to*

the basket. With Robertson around, other teams won't be able to sag on Lew now and forget everybody else. I figure Oscar and Alcindor will complement each other's talents beautifully."[16]

Bucks assistant coach Tom Nissalke recalled Costello's comments to him.

"When we made the Oscar trade, the first thing Larry said was, 'There are two things we're going to get from him. We know he can score, obviously, but we're going to get leadership and our defense is going to get much, much better because he won't let it be as bad as it was."[17]

On Friday, May 1, the Bucks held a press conference at the Pfister Hotel in downtown Milwaukee, welcoming Robertson and his wife, Yvonne, to their city. Robertson

Oscar Robertson and his wife Yvonne are introduced at the Pfister Hotel after signing a contract with the Bucks. Coach Larry Costello is on the left. (Author's collection)

was elated to play with an outstanding center for the first time in his NBA career.

> *"I thought this would be an opportunity I had wanted since the beginning of my career. Before I didn't think I'd have the chance to play on an NBA championship team before retiring. But now I'm in Milwaukee and we have Alcindor."*[18]

When asked about how long a period of adjustment would be needed to fit into an offense with a quality center, Robertson replied,

> *"I don't think that will be the case. There's an adjustment when you come into pro ball with the long schedule and all the contact. It's like a jungle compared with college ball, and it takes time to adjust to that. But I've been in pro ball and you learn to adjust. You're adjusting to your teammates all the time."*[19]

Bucks board chairman Wes Pavalon remarked,

> *"I don't think Oscar realizes how good Lew is, and I don't think Lew realizes how good Oscar is. Until they play together, they won't be able to realize how great this thing can be."*[20]

One minor situation that came about as a result of Robertson's trade to Milwaukee was his uniform number. Bucks' starting guard Jon McGlocklin had worn Robertson's number 14 since joining the Bucks in the expansion draft, commenting,

> *"I have had the number since I came to Milwaukee, you know, and it's been good to me. I'm superstitious, I guess, you don't like to change. I didn't know what was going to happen. A few weeks ago I was in Milwaukee and I met Oscar. I said to him,*

> *'Say, if you want that number 14, it's yours.' But he
> said, 'No, when I left Cincinnati, I left the number
> 14 in Cincinnati. That's all behind me.'"*[21]

Oscar decided to wear the number one after considering wearing the letter "O," referring to his first name. Robertson told Bucks president Ray Patterson,

> *"A couple of years from now, I won't be going so
> good, I'll be slowed up, and the fans may yell at
> me, 'Hey, Oscar, you're a big zero.'"*[22]

Players, coaches, writers, and experts had their opinions on how the addition of Robertson would benefit all the parties involved, but after a few exhibition games, Robertson gave his thoughts.

> *"With Lew Alcindor at center, you don't have to
> drive in as deep to help the forwards on the boards.
> You can play your own position—you can play
> guard."*[23]

Reflecting later on playing with Robertson, Alcindor observed,

> *"Oscar took the game seriously. All season long if
> someone screwed up or didn't seem to want to play,
> he would chew them out for not doing his job.
> People who weren't rebounding, guys who weren't
> playing defense, they were in trouble around Oscar.
> You had to respect him; you were playing with a
> legend, and he was still doing all his job; how could
> you not do yours?"*[24]

Bucks fans couldn't wait for the opening of the regular season.

Endnotes to Chapter 2

1) Tom Oates: "Forty years later, Milwaukee Bucks' lone title a ride to remember." *Wisconsin State Journal*, D1, May, 22, 2011.

2) Oscar Robertson, *The Big O: My Life, My Times, My Game* (Emmaus, PA: Rodale Inc., 2003), p. 137.

3) Milton Richman, "Bob Cousy Versus Robertson: No Room for Both in Cincy?" *Washington Afro-American*, February 10, 1970, p. 16.

4) John Devaney. *Alcindor and the Big O* (New York: Lancer Books, 1971), p. 15.

5) Richman, p. 16.

6) Robertson, p. 233.

7) "Robertson Trade Falls Through As Bullets Refuse Demands, Too," *Toledo Blade*, February 2, 1970, p. 16.

8) Bob Wolf, "Unhappy Big O here to Meet Bucks Today," *Milwaukee Journal*, March 1, 1970, pt. 3, p. 3.

9) Bob Wolf, "Big A Plus Big O Equals Buck Brilliance Unlimited," *The Sporting News*, November 7, 1971, p. 31.

10) Robertson, p. 242.

11) *Ibid,* p. 242.

12) *Ibid*, p. 243.

13) *Ibid.* p 243.

14) Rel Bochat, "Big O Sure He'll Raise Bucks," *Milwaukee Sentinel*, April 22, 1970, pt. 2, p. 10.

15) Kareem Abdul-Jabbar and Peter Knobler, *Giant Steps: The Autobiography of Kareem Abdul-Jabbar* (New York: Bantam Books, 1983), p. 209.

16) Phil Elderkin, "Big O Far From Finished," *The Sporting News*, May 16, 1970, p. 49.

17) Oates, p. D7.

18) Terry Bledsoe, "Oscar Sees No Problems, Pavalon See Great Things," *Milwaukee Journal*, May 2, 1970, pt. 2, p. 8.

19) *Ibid.*

20) *Ibid.*

21) Devaney, p. 46.

22) *Ibid.*

23) Phil Elderkin, "NBA Basketball," *The Sporting News*, October 30, 1970, p. 28.

24) Abdul-Jabbar and Knobler, pp. 213-14.

CHAPTER 3

CHAMPIONSHIP SEASON
TIP-OFF

GAME 1—SLOW-STARTING BUCKS WIN OPENER:
BUCKS 107, HAWKS 98

The Bucks' opening game for the 1969-70 season was nationally televised by ABC, showcasing the debut of then-rookie Lew Alcindor, and the 1970-71 opener was also shown nationally featuring two debuts: Atlanta Hawks rookie Pete Maravich, who broke Oscar Robertson's collegiate scoring record while playing at Louisiana State University, and the debut of a Bucks team featuring Robertson in the backcourt. Many predictions of greatness were forecast for the Bucks, but you wouldn't believe it the way they played the first half.

The game was played on Saturday, October 17, 1970, in tiny Alexander Memorial Coliseum on the Georgia Tech campus. More than 7,000 people saw the Bucks come out very flat, falling behind in the first half by as many as 16 points. The game was tied at 14 in the first quarter, but the Hawks went on a huge run and ran up a 43-27 lead. Bucks coach Larry Costello remarked that their first half performance was easily worse than in any of the previous ten exhibition games. Costello said,

> *"I don't know how we did it. They outrebounded us, 41-21, and Bill Bridges alone got 19, yet we some-*

how stayed close. We were actually lucky to be in the ball game, but that shows you the value of defense. If you play good defense, no matter how bad you are on offense, you can hang in the game."[1]

Costello's defensive adjustments, putting Bob Dandridge on Lou Hudson and switching Robertson to Jim Davis, helped. Hudson had 18 points at half but only had nine in the second half, none of them in the fourth quarter. Hawks coach Richie Guerin blamed the Atlanta offense for contributing to the lack of Atlanta scoring.

The Bucks still trailed 64-52 midway through the third quarter. An angry Costello called a time-out and got on the team.

"This isn't an exhibition. We got to clear those boards, no more two and three shots for them."[2]

The time-out worked. The Bucks went on a tear, outscoring the Hawks, 13-1, tying the game at 65 with three minutes and 44 seconds left in the third quarter. The fourth quarter started with the Hawks ahead, 75-74.

The Bucks grabbed control of the game in the fourth quarter, outscoring the Hawks, 33-23. Alcindor was the game's leading scorer with 32 points and grabbed 17 rebounds. Robertson had an off-game, hitting just five of 21 shots, ending up with 15 points. The Hawks double-teaming of him contributed to his offensive woes. Robertson commented,

"I was surprised they double-teamed me, but I knew they couldn't keep a sustained effort that way, and they couldn't, because I knew our free man would start to hit, and that was what happened."[3]

After the game, Costello said the Bucks were "just fortunate"[4] to be behind only nine points at halftime.

> "We just couldn't hit a shot in the first half, but after the half we did a better job on the floor and under the boards."[5]

Maravich had a tough afternoon in his NBA debut, scoring just seven points on three of 13 shooting in 22 minutes of playing time coming in for Walt Hazzard and Lou Hudson. Maravich said,

> "I made a lot of mistakes. One of the big mistakes was taking some shots I shouldn't have taken, but at least most of them were the kind I can cure with more playing time and playing more with the team."[6]

Despite an off-performance by Maravich, Costello was very impressed.

> "He's a good, hard-working kid. He's quick and handles the ball well. He may have to slow down his tempo a bit though, but that's something you just don't change overnight."[7]

After the game, Robertson talked to Wayne Embry, who had been hired by the Bucks to help with coaching and scouting. Embry attributed the lackluster performance to opening-day jitters, the national TV, the big crowd, and other factors.

Robertson countered,

> "I didn't see any jitters in the clubhouse before the game."[8]

Embry showed Robertson the post-game statistics sheet and told him he could see it there.

Bucks	FG-FGA	FT-FTA	Rebs.	Pts.	Hawks	FG-FGA	FT-FTA	Rebs.	Points
Alcindor	13-23	6-8	17	32	Bellamy	10-20	1-4	12	21
Allen	1-7	0-0	3	2	Bridges	5-14	5-7	24	15
Boozer	5-13	3-4	6	13	Chambers	1-8	3-5	3	5
Cunningham	1-1	1-2	1	3	Davis	7-16	2-3	15	16
Dandridge	7-18	7-8	10	21	Hazzard	3-11	1-1	3	7
McGlocklin	4-13	3-4	0	11	Hudson	11-27	5-5	4	27
Robertson	5-21	5-5	5	15	Maravich	3-13	1-1	3	7
Smith	3-6	0-0	7	6					
Zopf	2-2	0-1	1	4					

Game 1 Box Score

GAME 2—DUNKED IN DETROIT:
PISTONS 115, BUCKS 114

When the Bucks met the Pistons on October 20 at Detroit's Cobo Hall, the Pistons were in first place with a one-game lead over the Bucks in the NBA Midwest Division, with three road-game victories over San Francisco, Phoenix, and Seattle.

A big reason for the Pistons' resurgence was center Bob Lanier. He had helped lead St. Bonaventure to the 1970 Final Four, and who knows how far the team might have advanced if Lanier hadn't torn ligaments in his right knee midway through the second half in the East Regional Final versus Villanova on March 14, 1970. St. Bonaventure's opponent in the National Semifinals was Jacksonville. Lanier was unable to play due to the surgery he had the day after the injury. What a match-up it would have been, Lanier versus Jacksonville's Artis Gilmore, and if the Bonnies would've won, UCLA would've provided the competition for the title game. Lanier was the number-one pick of the 1970 NBA draft.

There was more to the Pistons than Lanier. He averaged 21 points a game for the first three games, but the strong point of their team was their guard play, with

Dave Bing leading the team in scoring at 25 points a game and Jimmy Walker adding 20 a game. Coach Costello considered the Pistons the Bucks' main threat for the division title.

> *"They were always a guard-oriented team, weak at forward and center in the past. Bing is still the key man, the one we have to stop. He makes 'em move, scores, sets things up. We have to hold their guards down. But Lanier is a great player, and he gives them what they needed to become a real contender."*[9]

A crowd of 11,316, the first sellout since the Pistons' 1968 playoff appearance, saw an exciting offensive battle. The game was tied 11 times in the first period, which ended in a tie at 33. The Bucks took a 63-56 lead to the locker room at halftime. The Bucks came out strong in the third period and extended their lead to 10 points on two occasions, but could deliver the knock-out punch by getting the ball in to Alcindor more often.

Lanier's knee, in his opinion, was at 80-percent capability, so he concentrated on his outside game, hitting five of his six field goals from there. Bing really hurt the Bucks, knocking down 16 of 29 shots, ending up with 37 points, and Walker added 20.

Despite the great showing by the Pistons, the game looked to be in hand for the Bucks, who held a 112-105 lead with a minute and a half left, but it was not to be. With 32 seconds left, Detroit cut the lead to 113-111, with the Bucks having possession. Robertson had the ball stolen by Walker, and the Pistons called time out with 14 seconds remaining. The ball went to the hot shooter, Bing, who had his shot go in and out, but reserve forward Bob

Quick tipped in the rebound to tie the score. To make matters worse, Alcindor fouled Quick on the play, and Quick sank the free throw, putting Detroit ahead 114-113 with five seconds left.

The Bucks still had a chance. Guard Lucius Allen, bringing the ball up court, called time-out. The only problem was the Bucks didn't have any left, resulting in a technical foul. Walker sank the foul shot, making the score 115-113 with three seconds remaining.

Allen was aware the Bucks had no time-outs left, but the Bucks were in a predicament, which Allen explained.

> *"There wasn't anything else I could do. By the time we would have got the ball to midcourt, the clock would have run out. I saw the big fellow (Alcindor) was being double-teamed underneath, and I saw Oscar Robertson was covered, so I called time-out."*[10]

Costello agreed that the time-out call by Allen was a great decision.

> *"I knew we didn't have any time-outs left, but it was a good play, the only thing we could do. I was happy to see Lucius call it almost immediately after Quick's free throw. Otherwise we'd never have a chance to get a shot. This way we had a chance to tie it up."*[11]

The Bucks did get the ball to Alcindor as time ran out. He was fouled before the shot, giving him two free throws, one for the foul, and the other for the bonus. He missed the first, effectively ending the game. He made the second, resulting in the final score of Detroit 115, Milwaukee 114.

Alcindor led all scorers with 38 points on 16 out of 20 from the field, along with 16 rebounds. Bob Lanier was very impressed with Alcindor.

"He was everything I expected. He beat me laterally too many times coming across in front of the basket. When I leaned on him, I got in trouble. If I tried to take him outside, he shot over me. I'll have to learn more about him, I guess."[12]

It was a tough loss to take, prompting Costello to comment,

"There was no way we should have lost that game. Too many mistakes, just careless play, that's all. Leads can be blown, sure, but you're not supposed to blow them without even getting down the floor to get off a shot."[13]

Pistons' coach Bill Van Breda Kolff noted that

"Milwaukee's a great team, but now the Bucks know they've got some competition."[14]

Robertson also expressed his disappointment:

"Basketball is a funny game. One little call here, one little call there and everything is turned around. I can't say anything about the officiating, but I thought I was fouled on that last steal by Walker. We had three or four calls in a row go against us, and that can take you right out of a game."[15]

The Bucks announced before the game that they had trimmed their roster to ten players, assigning forward Bob Greacen and guard Jeff Webb to their farm club in the Continental Basketball League, the Milwaukee Muskies.

Both the Muskies' and Bucks' next games were scheduled for Saturday, October 24, at the Milwaukee Arena.

Game 3—Double Overtime Thriller:
Bucks 122, Bullets 120

The Bucks' loyal fans were excited about the first home game of the regular season on Saturday evening, October 24, against the Baltimore Bullets. Coach Larry Costello observed,

> *"We're in great spirits, a home floor sellout, new faces in our lineup and we know we've got to be up. The opposition is tough. Baltimore's a run and shoot club. They don't hesitate too long to get off shots. They're not deliberate like the Chicago Bulls or Cleveland, for example."*[16]

The sellout Milwaukee Arena crowd of 10,746 saw the Bucks come out hot in the first period, ending the period with a 36-26 lead. The Bucks opened the lead up to 42-28 and ended up with a 60-54 advantage at halftime. Hot shooting by the Bullets drew them even with the Bucks at 67-67 midway through the third period. The game stayed competitive with the score tied at 76, 78, 90, 92 and 94.

The Bucks scored six straight at that point, before the Bullets had their shooting return, grabbing a 104-101 lead with one minute 15 seconds remaining. A pair of free throws by Robertson narrowed the lead to one, but Jack Marin's free throw gave the two-point lead back to the Bullets. Alcindor sent the game to overtime, scoring on a rebound of his missed shot with six seconds left.

Robertson and McGlocklin had hot hands in the overtime, scoring eight of Milwaukee's ten points, and the situation seemed under control with the Bucks leading,

115-111, with under a minute to go. Two free throws by Marin cut the lead to two with 38 seconds left, and the Bucks hoped to use up much of the clock and score. Instead, McGlocklin was called for an offensive foul, giving the Bullets the ball. Earl Monroe hit a jump shot as time ran out, sending the game to a second overtime.

Neither team could find the basket in the second overtime, the Bucks missing their first five shots, the Bullets missing four. Robertson hit a basket, and Bob Dandridge added a free throw and a follow-up basket on a missed shot. The Bullets added three charity tosses to stay close. Bob Boozer came through with a 10-foot jumper with 56 seconds remaining that gave the Bucks some breathing room at 122-118.

Wes Unseld fouled out of the game with three minutes remaining in the second overtime, but his replacement, Jim ("Bad News") Barnes, hit a jump shot from the corner, slicing the lead to two. The Bucks held onto the ball as long as they could but missed an opportunity to put the game away when Robertson missed a shot with 14 seconds left. The Bullets called time out to set up a possible third overtime. It was not to be. Kevin Loughery missed a 15-footer, a tip-in failed, and Alcindor grabbed the rebound and the game ended with the Bucks victorious, 122-120.

Alcindor, despite being in foul trouble for most of the second half, scored 39 points and grabbed 18 rebounds, while Robertson chipped in with 24. Wes Unseld had a great game also, leading the visitors with 27 points, snaring 22 rebounds, Monroe adding 25 points.

Ironically, the Continental Basketball Association game, a preliminary game between the Milwaukee Muskies and Waukegan (IL) Wizards before the NBA game, also went to double-overtime. The only difference was that with the pro teams waiting to take the floor, the affair was decided in a sudden-death overtime with the Wizards winning 124-122 on a 25-foot jump shot by former Marquette player Blanton Simmons.

Bucks	FG-FGA	FT-FTA	Rebs.	Pts	Bullets	FG-FGA	FT-FTA	Rebs.	Pts.
Alcindor	14-24	11-16	17	39	Barnes	3-4	0-0	1	6
Allen	0-1	0-3	0	0	Carter	3-7	2-2	4	8
Boozer	7-9	0-0	4	14	Johnson	8-26	4-7	18	20
Cunningham	0-0	0-0	1	0	Marin	7-17	3-3	4	17
Dandridge	4-14	1-1	16	9	Miles	1-8	2-2	3	4
Freeman	0-0	0-0	0	0	Monroe	10-19	5-6	3	25
McGlocklin	9-15	2-2	4	20	Loughery	5-21	3-4	2	13
Robertson	8-25	8-9	6	24	Unseld	12-19	3-5	22	27
Smith	6-10	2-4	7	14					
Zopf	1-3	0-0	0	2					

Game 3 Box Score

GAME 4—BUCKS DELIVER SONIC BOOM TO SEATTLE: BUCKS 126, SONICS 107

A Milwaukee Arena crowd of 9,340 came out on Sunday evening, October 25, to watch the Bucks put away the Seattle Supersonics, 126-107. The Sonics were without their leading scorer, center Bob Rule, who had suffered a season-ending injury—a separated Achilles tendon—two days before against Portland.

The Bucks were physically and mentally tired after their double-overtime victory over Baltimore the previous evening. Jon McGlocklin noted,

> *"It was one of those times when a guy has to work on himself mentally. It's up to each individual to psych himself back up, and it isn't easy."*[17]

Bucks forward Greg Smith (4) shoots a baseline jumper as Earl Monroe (10), Wes Unseld (41), and Jack Marin (24) watch. (Author's collection)

With Rule out of the game, Sonics player-coach Lenny Wilkens started 6-foot-10½ Tom Black, a 29-year-old rookie from West Salem, Wisconsin, who had played amateur ball after splitting his collegiate career between the University of Wisconsin and South Dakota State. Alcindor took advantage of the mismatch, scoring ten first-quarter points while Black scored two, and the Bucks seized a 35-23 lead after the first quarter.

Wilkens decided to switch former Buck Don Smith from his forward position to center, and he responded by limiting Alcindor to only five points in the second quarter. The Bucks hot shooting, though, opened up a 66-48 halftime advantage.

Greg Smith came out hot in the third quarter with three quick baskets, and the Bucks opened up a 74-52 lead. Lethargic play by the Bucks caused the lead, to dwindle to nine at 96-87, and the third period ended with the Bucks on top, 100-89.

Costello was upset with the Bucks' performance:

> *"Too many turnovers. We had a tough game the night before, but when you let up after getting a good lead, the other team catches fire and it takes something to get going again. Clemens (Barry) and Snyder (Dick) kept throwing it up there and they were all going in. It can happen fast in pro basketball. We've got to do better on the defensive boards. They were getting too many second and third shots on us."*[18]

The Sonics cut the lead to eight early in the fourth quarter before the Bucks woke up. Balanced offense with Smith, Dandridge, and Alcindor's scoring propelled the Bucks to the 19-point margin of victory. Alcindor ended up with 37 points in 36 minutes, Dandridge added 24, Smith 21, and

Robertson 17. Snyder led Seattle with 24, and Don Smith added 20.

It had been a very emotional homecoming for Smith as the Bucks' fans gave him a great ovation when he was introduced before the game. Smith stated,

> *"I actually felt embarrassed out there. It was like the old days at Iowa State."*[19]

GAME 5—BUCKS COOL OFF ROCKETS:
BUCKS 126, ROCKETS 113

The Bucks got a well-deserved day off before their next game against the San Diego Rockets on Tuesday, October 27, at the Milwaukee Arena. The game featured the tallest and shortest players in the NBA, 7-foot-2 Lew Alcindor and the Rockets' 5-foot-9 rookie Calvin Murphy. Murphy had a big game in a losing effort in the Rockets previous game against Phoenix, scoring a career high 29.

Two other interesting match-ups were Alcindor going against "The Big E," Elvin Hayes, and Rockets coach Alex Hannum matching wits with Larry Costello, whom he had coached at Philadelphia and Syracuse.

The Rockets scored the first five points of the game, but the Bucks put together a string of ten unanswered points during the first period, which ended with the Bucks ahead, 34-19. The Bucks came out hot in the second period, opening up the lead to 46-24 midway through the period.

The Rockets came back on the hot shooting of Hayes and rookie Rudy Tomjanovich. Alcindor picked up his third foul, which helped Houston. Coach Costello noted,

> *"Lew got his third foul, and Cunningham (*Bucks back-up center Dick Cunningham) *went in for him.*

Hayes hits two shots in a row and comes alive.
They start dropping through for him.[20]

The Bucks took a 61-53 lead into the locker room at halftime.

The third quarter was competitive as the Rockets closed to within one point on two occasions at 73-72 and 76-75. Bob Dandridge had a hot hand, keeping the Bucks in the lead.

The turning point of the game came with 2:21 left in the third period, with the Bucks holding a precarious 82-75 lead when Alcindor was called for his fifth foul. Hayes had the ball and knocked Alcindor down driving to the basket. Hayes already had five fouls and a call against him would end his night. Referee Manny Sokol called the foul on Alcindor, igniting not only the 9,565 fans, but also the Bucks. Team co-captain Oscar Robertson called an immediate time-out and used the entire 90 seconds to make sure Sokol knew what he thought about the call.

Coach Costello was still upset about the call after the game.

> *"I can't comment on the refereeing. He (Hayes)*
> *didn't even come in from the side, he just came*
> *straight into him. Where was he (Alcindor) sup-*
> *posed to go? I can't afford a fine, but I can't wait to*
> *see that play on video tape."*[21]

The Bucks took out their frustration on the court, going on an 11-3 run fueled by baskets by Cunningham, Billy Zopf, Bob Dandridge, and two baskets and a free throw by Robertson, giving them a 93-78 advantage at the end of the third period.

Dandridge, who scored a game-high 39 points, sinking 14 of 22 shots in 39 minutes, talked about the foul on Alcindor.

> *"When we saw Lew go out, the kids came off the bench all fired up. Maybe San Diego slacked off because Lew was out, but we got running and never stopped."*[22]

Despite Hayes' 34 points and 21 rebounds, and Alcindor's fouling out with 20 points and ten boards, the Bucks won, 126-113. Rockets coach Alex Hannum observed,

> *"Tonight their big man didn't have a great game, but they had someone step into the breach for them. That's why Oscar is such a great plus for them. When the big man is down, Oscar can pick up the team and go to someone else, like he did to Dandridge tonight. You're not going to get a great game out of Alcindor every night and that's why getting Oscar is going to mean so much to Milwaukee."*[23]

Endnotes to Chapter 3

1)   Bob Wolf, "Bucks' Late Rally Crushes Hawks," *Milwaukee Journal*, October 18, 1970, pt. 3, p. 1.

2)   John Devaney, *Alcindor and the Big O: A Season's Diary* (New York: Lancer Books, 1971), p. 87.

3)   *Ibid.* pp. 88-89.

4)   "Lew, Dandridge Spark Buck Rally," *Wisconsin State Journal*, October 18, 1970, pt. 2, p. 5.

5)   *Ibid.*

6)   Wolf. p. 1

7)   *Wisconsin State Journal*, October 18, 1970.

8)   Devaney, p. 88.

9)   Rel Bochat, "Bucks Test Lanier, Hot Pistons Tonight," *Milwaukee Sentinel*, October 20, 1970, pt. 2, p. 1.

10) Bob Wolf, "Bucks Gain Time, Lose Point, Game," *Milwaukee Journal*, October 21, 1970, pt. 2, p. 19.

11) Rel Bochat, "Pistons Shock Bucks," *Milwaukee Sentinel*, October 21, 1970, pt. 2, p. 1.

12) Rel Bochat, "Pistons' Play Brings Bucks Down to Earth," *Milwaukee Sentinel*, October 22, 1970, pt. 3, p. 2.

13) Wolf. p. 19.

14) "Record Cobo Crowd Sees Pistons Nose Out Bucks," *The Sporting News*, November 7, 1970, p. 30.

15) Wolf. p. 19.

16) Rel Bochat, "Bucks, Bullets Clash Tonight," *Milwaukee Sentinel*, October 24, 1970, pt. 2, p. 1.

17) Bob Wolf, "Bucks Flat, but Win Easily," *Milwaukee Journal*, October 26, 1970, pt. 2, p. 15.

18) Rel Bochat. "Bucks Lower Boom On Sonics," *Milwaukee Sentinel*, October 26, 1970, pt. 2, pg. 7.

19) Wolf. p. 17.

20) Rel Bochat, "Bucks' Fury Cools Off Rockets," *Milwaukee Sentinel*, October 28, 1970, pt. 2, pg. 5.

21) Bob Hill, "Dandridge, Bucks Wheel Past Rockets," *Wisconsin State Journal*, October 28, 1970, pt. 3, p. 1.

22) Bochat. Oct. 28.

23) Devaney, p. 104-105.

CHAPTER 4

THE "BIG O" RETURNS

GAME 6—A ROYAL HOMECOMING:
BUCKS 121, ROYALS 100

FOR THE FIRST TIME EVER, OSCAR Robertson would be playing in Cincinnati wearing a visitor's uniform, and he was very psyched up.

Robertson hadn't left the Royals on very good terms, especially with Coach Bob Cousy. Rumor was that Cousy wanted to put in a running game much like the Celtics used to play and that Robertson wouldn't fit in. Robertson countered,

> *"That doesn't make much sense. How many different things can you do in pro basketball with the 24 second clock?"*[1]

After the trade to Baltimore for Gus Johnson fell through, Robertson commented,

> *"After I vetoed the trade, Cousy really flew off the handle, not to me directly; that would be beneath him. He sounded off in a two-column story in the paper. After that, there was no way I could go back to Cincinnati this season."*[2]

It appeared very unlikely that Robertson would play. He had suffered a groin muscle injury in a Thursday practice and on Friday, the day before the game, Coach Costello said,

"I don't see how he possibly can play. He didn't practice today, and from the way he was walking I'd say he may need some recuperation time. He's going on the trip, but I doubt he'll play. Fortunately, we've got three days off after this one before we play at Cleveland on Wednesday. We can't take a chance on aggravating it."[3]

Robertson's injury was so severe that they called up former West Milwaukee High School and Kansas State alumnus Jeff Webb from the Milwaukee Muskies to fill in for him.

At tipoff time at the Cincinnati Gardens on Saturday evening, October 31, the 9,634 fans still hoped to see Robertson play. Despite the injury, Robertson insisted on starting, and when he was introduced, he received a minute-long standing ovation. Robertson will always cherish that moment.

"When my name was introduced during the starting lineups, there was a roar. Everyone in the arena rose, and the sound got louder; it extended and welled. For more than a minute I stood there. The fans kept cheering. I swallowed my feelings, raised my hand. They cheered louder. It seemed they would never stop."[4]

Even though he was playing for the visiting team, the hometown crowd cheered for him every time he scored or was involved in a good play. Robertson was very appreciative of the reception he received from the fans, commenting,

"It felt great. I have nothing against the people here. They were great fans, and it gave me a great feeling."[5]

The Bucks took a 58-50 lead at halftime, and with four minutes gone in the second half, Robertson limped off the floor after a six-point, seven-assist, and four-rebound game. After the game, Robertson said,

> *"I could only labor around, I couldn't run, I couldn't push off to shoot, and I couldn't cut. We had a good lead, so I figured it was best to go out when I did. I don't think I aggravated it, so I should be okay for the next game."*[6]

The Bucks opened up a big lead in the third period, outscoring the Royals, 36-20, taking a 94-70 lead. Coach Costello said,

> *"We started running in the last half. That's all we talked about at halftime."*[7]

Bob Boozer had a great game, scoring 23 points on 10 out of 15 from the field and adding nine rebounds. Costello was very pleased with Boozer's performance:

> *"That's the best Boozer played since joining us. He took his good shots, didn't throw the ball away and played a solid game all around."*[8]

Alcindor led the Bucks, who won 121-100, with 28 points and 22 rebounds. Rookie guard Billy Zopf scored 10 points, connecting on four out of five from the field, scoring 10 points.

The game also featured former Bucks' Charlie Paulk and Flynn Robinson facing their former team for the first time. Paulk scored 13 points and grabbed 10 rebounds in 32 minutes of playing time. Robinson, who had been a holdout until a week earlier, scored 12 points in 20 minutes. This was the most extensive playing time he got for the season so far, the main reason being the ejection of Norm Van Lier on a pair of technical fouls late in the third period. Tom Van Arsdale led the Royals with 23 points, and Nate Archibald added 19.

Cousy was very impressed with the Bucks,

> *"That was the best Alcindor ever played against us, and that's saying something because he killed us last year. He was more alert on defense."*[9]

He also was pleased that the Cincinnati fans gave Robertson a good ovation.

> *"Oscar was a great hero here for a long time, and he deserved it."*[10]

Endnotes to Chapter 4

1) Bob Wolf, "Big O Eager to Renew Feud with Cousy, Royals," *Milwaukee Journal*, October 29, 1970, pt. 2, p. 24.

2) *Ibid.*

3) Rel Bochat, "Bucks, Minus 'Big O,' Seek 4th in Row," *Milwaukee Sentinel*, October 31, 1970, pt. 2, p. 1.

4) Oscar Robertson, *The Big O: My Life, My Times, My Game* (Emmaus, PA.: Rodale Inc., 2003), p. 257.

5) Bob Wolf, "Robertson Returns, Helps Bucks Romp," *Milwaukee Journal*, November 1, 1970, pt. 3, p. 6.

6) *Ibid.*

7) Bob Wolf, "Lew 'Too Much,' Says Bucks Rival," *Milwaukee Journal*, November 2, 1970, pt.2, p.11.

8) Rel Bochat, "Boozer's Play, Lew's Defense Spark Bucks," *Milwaukee Sentinel*, November 1, 1970, pt. 2, p.1.

9) Wolf, p. 11.

10) John Devaney, *Alcindor and the Big O: A Season's Diary* (New York: Lancer Books, 1971), p. 106.

"The Big O," Oscar Robertson. looking forward to a championship season for the Bucks. (Lulloff collection)

CHAPTER 5

THE STREAK CONTINUES

GAME 7—CLOSE CALL IN CLEVELAND:
BUCKS 110, CAVALIERS 108

The Bucks had only one game scheduled the first week of November, so it made a lot of sense to give Oscar Robertson some time off to heal his groin injury. Costello commented about the schedule:

> *"I don't know if we'll even take him along to Cleveland for Wednesday night's game. It might be better if he stayed here all week for treatments and was back in good shape for Phoenix next Sunday. That would be the best thing for it. It'll never heal this way. Rest and treatment is what it needs. Heck, we've got 76 regular season games to go. We have a break in the schedule right now, with one game in seven days, so it's a good time for him to mend."*[1]

The matchup on Wednesday, November 4, featured one of the best NBA teams, the Bucks, versus the worst, the 0-11 Cavaliers. Cleveland coach Bill Fitch would do anything for a victory.

> *"I look under the rug for a victory, then under the table, but I'll win even if I have to wrestle my five-year old daughter. You do everything you can to keep away from pushing the panic button."*[2]

Everything favored the Bucks except for one thing. You have to play the game. One would think that if you had

Lew Alcindor score 35 points in the first half, which he did, you'd have a commanding lead, yet the Bucks found themselves down 62-51 at halftime. They still trailed 75-63 midway through the third quarter. The Bucks outscored Cleveland 19-4 during a third-quarter stretch and led 84-81 at the end of the third quarter. Alcindor already had 49 points as the game went into the fourth quarter.

There was an issue that Costello had to deal with; Alcindor had four fouls and sat out the beginning of the quarter. Cleveland seized the opportunity and regained the lead. Two minutes into the fourth quarter, Costello put Alcindor back into the game, and the Bucks led 103-96 after Alcindor scored his 51st point. What proved to be his 52nd and 53rd and final points of the game gave the Bucks a 105-100 lead.

The Bucks scored only one point on a free throw by Bob Dandridge before a layup by the Cavaliers' McCoy McLemore and a jumper by former Milwaukee Messmer High School star John Johnson made the score 106-104 with 1:10 left to go. The pace continued fast and furious when, after Lucius Allen hit two free throws, the Cavs' John Warren hit a jumper making the score 108-106.

Dandridge scored on a goal-tending call against Walt Wesley with 48 seconds remaining, but Bobby Smith's jumper with 38 seconds left made it 110-108. The Bucks tried to run off the clock, but to no avail, which gave Johnson a shot to tie the game with eight seconds left. He missed, and Alcindor grabbed the rebound with six seconds left. Dandridge was fouled, but he missed both free throws. The Cavs had the ball with a chance to tie, but a crucial steal by Greg Smith sealed the victory.

Alcindor's 53 points came on 20 for 32 shooting from the field, and he made 13 of 14 free throws. Dandridge scored 24, while Johnson led Cleveland with 27.

After the game, Alcindor commented about his all-time high (at this point of his career) scoring effort.

> *"That doesn't mean too much to me, my personal high. Winning the game was the big thing."*[3]

Coach Costello was not happy with the team's play.

> *"We weren't always hustling. Lew Alcindor shouldn't have to do it all for us. This isn't a one-man or a two-man team. This is a team. We got other guys that are paid to play this game, damn it. Where were they?"*[4]

GAME 8—BUCKS DIM SUNS:
BUCKS 125, SUNS 105

The Bucks' schedule was very light in the beginning of the season and they played only seven games in the first 25 days. Coach Costello didn't like it.

> *"I don't think it's good. We play one game, then we're off three days. Then we play another game and we're off three more days. You can't get into a groove with a schedule like that."*[5]

Indeed, the Bucks had three days off before their next game, a home contest against the Phoenix Suns on Sunday, November 8. The Suns, on the other hand, came off games on Friday at Chicago, and on Saturday at Atlanta.

The Bucks got their fast break in high gear, seeking to take advantage of the situation and took a 125-105 win in front of a sellout crowd of 10,746. Despite playing with an upset stomach that Bucks trainer Arnie Garber treated with antacid tablets, Bob Dandridge had a great night, scoring a game-high 32 points on 14 out of 22 shooting. He also added 14 rebounds and five steals in 31 minutes. Alcindor chipped in with 26 and Bob Boozer added 19. Oscar Robertson came off the injured list and scored eight, the layoff affecting him as he sank only two of 17 shots, but he did have nine assists. The Suns' leading scorers were Dick Van Arsdale with 23, Connie Hawkins with 22, and Neal Walk with 20.

After leading 33-27 at the end of the first quarter, the Bucks extended their lead to 63-50 at halftime. They scored the first eight points of the third quarter, making the score 71-50. The lead swelled to 100-73 after the third quarter, and after a six-point run to open the fourth quarter, the Bucks were in command, up 106-73.

Costello praised the Bucks on another point.

> *"Defense had as much as anything to do with it. Dandridge did a helluva job all around, Greg Smith was fine on Hawkins, and McGlocklin played himself a game. We got their forwards out from the lanes and they had nothing underneath."*[6]

Dandridge added,

> *"We took it away from them in the first half with our running."*[7]

Game 9—Green Versus Green:
Bucks 123, Celtics 113

The Bucks made a visit to historic Boston Garden on Wednesday, November 11. The game featured the NBA's top two scorers, Alcindor and John Havlicek. After winning 11 NBA titles in 13 years with Bill Russell in the pivot, things had been tough for Boston last season. Russell had retired, and the Celtics had slipped to sixth place. This season was going well for the Celtics, who brought in an 8-5 record for this evening's game, and one of the big reasons was Dave Cowens.

The 6-foot-9 rookie out of Florida State came into the game averaging 19.5 points and 17 rebounds a game. Celtics coach Tommy Heinsohn was very impressed with Cowens.

> *"The amazing thing about him is that he's a natural forward playing center, and even though he's playing out of position, he's doing a whale of a job. By midseason, he will make them forget Pete Maravich and the rest of the rookie crop. He means more to the Celtics than Maravich does to the Atlanta Hawks. At least at the moment he does."*[8]

Luckily for the Celtics, their running game was working great in the first half. They needed it. Alcindor scored 25 in the first half, but the game was tied at 58. The Bucks fell behind 75-65, in the third, but then got hot, taking an 84-83 lead into the fourth quarter.

A big reason for the Bucks' lead was the way they adjusted to the Celtics' defense. Costello noted,

> *"Lew was the cause of everything that happened to turn it our way. They were sagging on him, and we*

compensated for it because somebody else was always open. We got better shots as we went along, 12- to 15-foot jumpers, and Lew was getting the rebounds and getting our fast break going."[9]

With the Bucks ahead 92-88, and nine minutes left, the Bucks kept hitting the open man. Boozer got hot, and baskets by Robertson and McGlocklin gave the Bucks a 107-97 lead, which they maintained in a 123-113 victory.

John Havlicek, who paced the Celtics with 31 points, eight rebounds, and nine assists, was impressed with the addition of Robertson to the Bucks.

"He's unbelievable the way he takes charge. He stands out there with the ball and waits until Alcindor and the corner men make their cuts and then he hits the open man. The Bucks were tough enough to defend against before Robertson. Now they're just about impossible."[10]

Alcindor led the Bucks with 44 points, 15 rebounds, six blocked shots, and four steals; Robertson scored 26 on 10 out of 15 shooting from the field with 10 assists, and Bob Boozer scored 18.

GAME 10—BUCKS BEST BRAVES:
BUCKS 116, BRAVES 107

The Bucks were shooting for a club record—eight straight wins—on Saturday, November 14 against the Buffalo Braves in a game played at Buffalo's Memorial Auditorium. There was a big disparity in the number of games they had played. In comparison to the other 16 NBA teams, the Bucks had played four fewer games. The scenario would change dramatically the next 16 days as the Bucks would play 12 games, seven of them on the road.

The Bucks scored a 116-107 victory in a game in which, whenever the starters were given a rest, the Braves would make a comeback. The Bucks led by eight points at half, 55-47, and built the advantage up to 85-67 late in the third quarter. The Bucks had a scare in the middle of the fourth quarter when Alcindor limped to the bench after colliding with Herman Gilliam. Alcindor commented,

> *"His knee went into my knee. I had a little pain, but it was no injury, just a bruise."*[11]

Costello was unhappy with the Bucks' play:

> *"We need a lot more consistency if we're going to be champions, and we've got to be more aggressive on defense. We made it too easy for them to get shots. Why, they were even shooting over Lew Alcindor. We don't put our hands up on defense. We're too nice. We've got to get tougher, put some hands on those guys, make them know they're in a ball game."*[12]

Alcindor led the Bucks, scoring 27 along with 20 rebounds, and Jon McGlocklin followed closely with 25 points. The Bucks sank 23 layups, prompting Costello to note,

> *"That's the easiest basket in basketball, and that's why we run. With Lew to get the fast break started, and Oscar Robertson to make it go, we should be able to run all night."*[13]

Bob Kaufmann led Buffalo with 23 points and 13 rebounds.

Alcindor at the charity stripe. (Author's collection)

GAME 11—BUCKS DODGE BULLETS, GET VICTORY:
BUCKS 105, BULLETS 90

The Bucks returned home to the Milwaukee Arena for a Sunday evening game on November 15 against the Baltimore Bullets. A sellout crowd of 10,746 watched the Bucks offense in high gear, coupled with a smothering defense *en route* to their ninth straight victory, 105-90.

The game didn't start well for the Bucks. The visitors turned a 6-6 tie into a 20-12 lead and enjoyed a 31-22 advantage at the end of the first quarter. Early in the second quarter with the Bullets on top, 33-24, the Bucks scored 18 unanswered points on hot shooting by Alcindor and McGlocklin. The Bullets came back with a streak of their own led by Jack Marin and Wes Unseld, making it 42-41 Bucks. At halftime the Bucks led, 52-47.

The Bucks were on top, 77-69, after three quarters, but they had something going against them. Alcindor picked up his fourth foul late in the third quarter and went to the bench, not returning until three minutes were gone in the fourth quarter.

Defense was the name of the game, prompting Coach Costello to comment.

> *"As far as that goes, everybody played defense like you hope to see it played. If you hold a team like that down to 90 points it's really something. The guys were switching, talking out there, helping each other out. We were digging and coming up with everything."*[14]

With three minutes left, the Bucks were clinging to a 93-87 lead. The Bucks sealed the deal with a 12-3 run to end the game. Costello had high praise for Robertson.

> *"Oscar was fantastic. He was great on Monroe, and he came out shooting. He was driving, rebounding, shooting, running, leading our offense—and he must have made four or five steals. He just did everything."*[15]

Monroe in 38 minutes ended up with seven points on two for 15 on field goal attempts.

Bullets coach Gene Shue commented on his team's play after the game.

> *"Our defense was excellent. We wanted to hold them close to 100 points and we did, but who ever thought we'd only get 90? You know, we can't win unless our guards are scoring. We hit a real cold*

spell in the second quarter and they took control right there."[16]

Alcindor and Robertson had very similar stats, each going 11 for 19 from the field and adding five free throws for 27 points. Robertson added 12 assists, while Alcindor had 21 rebounds. Jack Marin led the Bullets with 20 points, with Wes Unseld not far behind with his 19-point, 20 rebounds performance.

GAME 12—TEN WINS IN A ROW!
BUCKS 119, WARRIORS 100

The scheduler made it very difficult for the Bucks as they played their third game in three days on Monday, November 16 at home against the San Francisco Warriors. A Milwaukee Arena crowd of 10,247 watched the Bucks put away the stubborn Warriors in a 119-100 victory, giving the Bucks their tenth win in a row and a two-game lead in the Midwest Division.

The Warriors, who led, 34-29 after one quarter, opened up an eight-point advantage in the second quarter and held a 55-53 lead at halftime. The Bucks came out hot in the third quarter, outscoring the Warriors, 21-6, behind the torrid shooting of Robertson and McGlocklin, grabbing a 74-61 lead with less than seven minutes left in the quarter. Alcindor's fourth foul sent him to the bench with the Bucks up 83-73, a lead that would quickly evaporate. A 9-1 Warriors run sparked by Joe Ellis, Lucas, and Thurmond cut the Bucks' lead to 84-82 at the end of the third quarter.

The fourth quarter proved Oscar Robertson's observation:

"It's just a matter of time. No team can hold us for a full game. We're playing mostly in spurts, but that's the way you do it. The Warriors were up for this one. They played great ball for a while, but they couldn't keep it up."[17]

With 6:40 left and the Bucks ahead 97-92, Alcindor delivered the knockout punch. He scored three baskets on a stuff, a short hook, and a baseline hook, and McGlocklin added a backhanded layup for a 13-point lead.

Thurmond led the Warriors with 25 points, and Lucas was close behind with 23. Usually hot-shooting Jeff Mullins was held in check by Robertson's defense, hitting only four of 17 shots, scoring 12 points.

Alcindor paced the Bucks with 31 points. Dandridge was right behind with 30 points, and he added a game-high 14 rebounds. Warriors' coach Al Attles had high praise for Dandridge.

"Dandridge made the difference. I personally think we've got the best defensive center in the league in Nate Thurmond, but with Alcindor out there, Nate can't help out any of the other guys on defense. He left Alcindor once or twice, and each time Lew dunked the ball. That's where Dandridge takes advantage. He moves all the time and he always has good position. The mark of any good basketball player is to move without the ball, and Dandridge exemplifies that."[18]

Indeed, Dandridge was constantly moving and driving as he went to the foul line for 15 free throws, sinking 12 of them. Bob Boozer led the bench scoring with 11 points. Boozer was getting some decent playing time and having fun. He reflected,

"I've been on some stumble-and-flutter ball clubs. It feels great to be with an outfit that goes like this one does."[19]

GAME 13—ROCKETS FALL:
BUCKS 117, ROCKETS 111

After an off day, the Bucks left for the West Coast for four games, three of them in three nights. Costello observed,

"They're all tough, and even tougher when it's on the road."[20]

The Bucks had an 11-1 record but only had a two-game lead over the Pistons in the NBA's Midwest Division.

On Wednesday, November 18, 8,958 fans made the trip to the San Diego Sports Arena to watch Coach Alex Hannum's Rockets take on the Bucks. This was the fourth season the Rockets were in the league, and it would prove to be their last in San Diego, as the franchise relocated to Houston for the 1971-72 season.

The game stayed close. Hot shooting by Bob Dandridge kept the Bucks even at 13. A jumper by Bob Boozer gave the Bucks a 33-25 lead after the first quarter.

Despite having two players with four fouls, Alcindor and Smith, the Bucks opened up a 61-47 lead at halftime.

Two baskets by Dandridge, along with jumpers by McGlocklin, Cunningham, and Robertson, helped the Bucks maintain the lead, which grew to 15 points early in the third quarter. The Rockets whittled it to 76-68 with five minutes left in the quarter. Smith scored six points, helping the Bucks build an 89-77 advantage going into the fourth quarter.

Rockets' rookie Calvin Murphy scored his first basket with ten minutes left, but the Bucks still led, 92-81. Billy Zopf scored two baskets, but Stu Lantz and Larry Siegfried got hot and narrowed the lead to 97-90 with seven minutes left.

A Rockets fourth-quarter surge was led by Don Adams, a rookie forward from Northwestern. Coach Hannum, commenting on Adams' performance, said,

> "He turned a disaster into a good basketball game."[21]

Adams scored 23 points in the game, 16 of them in the fourth quarter. The Rockets went on an eight-point run. Adams scored four of them, and a stuff shot by Elvin Hayes cut the Bucks lead to 108-104 with two and a half minutes left. Bob Boozer hit a jump shot stopping the run. The deciding play of the game took place with the Bucks up 110-106. Dandridge intercepted a pass and set up Alcindor for a three-point play. The Bucks held on for a 117-111 victory, their 11th in a row.

Reflecting after the game, Costello noted,

> "We played well when our starters were in there, but we lose a lot of speed when we have Smith and Dandridge out at the same time, which happened tonight because of foul trouble. We aren't a strong rebounding team, so we've got to utilize our speed. The big thing is that we keep getting the basket when we need it. Someone always comes along to pick the others up."[22]

Coach Hannum was impressed by the Bucks' defense.

> "They made us take bad shots and do things we aren't used to doing. That's the essence of good

defense, and at the same time it sets up easy shots for them. Alcindor alone is a big factor on defense. He covers so much area around the basket that he allows them to use the principle of a zone defense. It's almost impossible to combat something like that."[23]

The Rockets were led by Adams with 23 points, connecting on 10 of 14 from the field. Alcindor led the Bucks with 25, adding 16 rebounds, besting Hayes' 16 points and ten rebounds.

GAME 14—GREEN VERSUS GOLD:
BUCKS 117, LAKERS 100

On November 20, the stars were shining bright at The Forum in Los Angeles. Two of the big match-ups were Oscar Robertson versus Jerry West and Lew Alcindor versus Wilt Chamberlain. This would be only the second time the two great centers had played against each other in a regular season game due to Chamberlain's missing a majority of the previous season with a knee injury.

Another star, Lakers' forward Elgin Baylor, would be unable to play because of an Achilles tendon injury, which had sidelined him since the beginning of the season. Costello was excited about the game.

"These guys respond to opponents like Jerry West and Wilt Chamberlain. Oscar Robertson will be on West and he makes you come up with your best. Lew not only likes the challenge of facing Chamberlain, but Lew also has a lot of fans here from his UCLA days. I think there's plenty to get us up."[24]

Alcindor and Dandridge each scored a pair of baskets, giving the Bucks an early 12-6 lead. Happy Hairston and

West, along with Chamberlain, countered, and the score was tied at 14. There were two ties before the Bucks ended the quarter with baskets by Alcindor and Dandridge, giving the Bucks a 22-18 advantage.

Alcindor sat out almost half of the first two quarters because of three fouls. The game was tied at 24 after baskets by West and Gail Goodrich, but Dick Cunningham and Lucius Allen came off the bench to help lead the Bucks to a 32-26 lead. Cunningham was ready for the challenge.

> *"I got mentally psyched up to play against Wilt. If Lew gets in trouble, I've got to be there."*[25]

Alcindor sat out the last ten minutes of the second quarter, but Cunningham came up big off the bench, sinking five of six shots and a free throw for 11 points, and he also grabbed six rebounds. Dandridge chipped in with six baskets in the second quarter, giving the Bucks a 47-37 advantage at halftime.

Alcindor returned to the floor to start the second half, and the Bucks did well. In the first five minutes of the third quarter, Alcindor scored four baskets, helping the Bucks open up a 59-44 lead. The rest of the team not only played great defense but also shot well. After a Jon McGlocklin jump shot with 1:40 left in the third quarter, the Bucks led, 74-55, and took a 79-61 lead into the fourth quarter.

The onslaught continued in the fourth quarter as the Bucks' fast break was in high gear. Allen and Robertson scored off the break, and Cunningham and Gary Freeman had layups, giving the Bucks a 99-75 lead. After a Lakers basket, Alcindor's field goal was followed by a three-point play by Boozer, giving the Bucks their biggest lead, 104-77.

The Lakers cut the lead by way of the hot, under-handed free-throw shooting of Chamberlain. One of the NBA's worst foul shooters was on a tear, sinking 14 of 16 free throws and finished the game making 12 straight. The lead was cut to 108-92 with 2:13 remaining. Alcindor fouled out with nine seconds left, but the Bucks had won their 12th in a row, 117-100.

In defeat, Chamberlain had played a great game, scoring 28 points, snaring 23 rebounds, and blocking 10 shots, including six of Alcindor's. Chamberlain was very impressed by the Bucks.

> "You can't add guys like Oscar and Bob Boozer and
> Lucius Allen and not be a better ball club, and
> they've got guys who are exceptionally quick—Lew,
> Dandridge, Greg Smith. Quickness is what does it
> for you."[26] ... I thought I played well against Lew.
> He didn't beat us, they beat us." [27]

Alcindor complimented Wilt.

> "Chamberlain played an excellent game."[28]

GAME 15—THIRTEEN A LUCKY NUMBER:
BUCKS 127, WARRIORS 102

On Saturday, November 21, in front of 8,224 fans at the Cow Palace in San Francisco, the Warriors hosted the Bucks. Alcindor would be going up against Nate Thurmond, who up to that point in Alcindor's career, was the best center he ever played against.

In the duel between the two centers, Alcindor scored 14 points and finished off an eight-point run with a dazzling, driving stuff shot. Thurmond would not be denied, scoring 12 points, many of them medium and long-range jump shots. With the game tied at 26, the Bucks scored six straight to end the first quarter with a 32-26 lead.

The Bucks held a 36-32 lead a minute and a half into the second quarter, then scored nine straight points, four of them by Bob Boozer. The rest of the half, the teams traded baskets. Alcindor only had one basket in the quarter, giving him 16 for the game, but Robertson had 14 points at the half. Thurmond helped keep the Warriors in the game, adding three baskets, which gave him 18 points at the half. The Bucks led 56-42 at halftime.

The Bucks' front line scored big time in the third quarter. Greg Smith had ten points, and Dandridge and Alcindor each added eight, giving the Bucks a 90-72 lead after three quarters. The Bucks opened the lead up to 29 points in the fourth quarter, and Costello cleared his bench.

The Bucks had balanced scoring in a runaway, 127-102 victory. Alcindor had 28 points with 15 rebounds, Robertson added 25, Smith 23 on 11 of 16 from the field, and Boozer and Dandridge each scored 18. The Warriors were led by Thurmond with 30 points and 14 rebounds. The win gave the Bucks a 13-game winning streak.

GAME 16—MILWAUKEE PULVERIZES PORTLAND: BUCKS 126, TRAILBLAZERS 104

The last game of the murderous West Coast tour was against the Portland Trailblazers at the Memorial Coliseum on Sunday, November 22. The first-year expansion team's record of 9-13 included victories against Baltimore and Atlanta.

The Bucks came out flat while Portland came out energized, running up an early eight-point lead, and they led 31-28 after the first quarter. Portland maintained its great play and held a 40-32 lead early in the second quarter. Lucius Allen gave the Bucks a spark off the bench in the second quarter, and his two baskets helped the Bucks to a 55-50 halftime lead.

The third quarter belonged to the Bucks. Alcindor and Dandridge got hot as the Bucks outscored the Trailblazers 35-24, giving them a 90-74 advantage going into the fourth quarter. Costello played his bench extensively for the remainder of the game, and they played well in the 126-104 victory.

One player who didn't get much playing time for the Bucks was back-up center Dick Cunningham. He lost his uniform in San Francisco and wore number three, which had previously been worn by guard Sam Williams. Cunningham said,

"It was so tight, I couldn't move at all. I could hardly breathe."[29]

LeRoy Ellis and Shaler Halimon led Portland in scoring, each with 16, while Alcindor had 30, along with a season high 26 rebounds to lead the Bucks. Not far behind was Dandridge, who scored 28 points, connecting on 12 of 16 shots. He also had four steals, eight rebounds, and five assists.

Dandridge gave credit to the acquisition of Robertson for taking his game to a higher level.

"Oscar Robertson has made a big difference. He helps me especially when it comes to the fast break. When we ran last year, the guards weren't able to

*make the good bounce pass on the way down the
floor. Oscar can follow the flow of the fast break
and pick out the open man. He makes passes that
other guys can't make."*[30]

GAME 17—CLOSE CALL IN CHICAGO:
BUCKS 117, BULLS 108

The final game of the Bucks' road trip was closer to home,
Chicago. After an off day for travel, the Bucks played at
Chicago Stadium on Tuesday, November 24. Coach
Costello was looking forward to the game.

> *"The game with the Bulls is very important to us
> because it's in our division. We have five games on
> them in the loss column and a four and a half game
> lead. Chicago has always been trouble for us in the
> past."*[31]

Indeed, the Bulls had beaten the Bucks in four of six
meetings the previous season.

Things went badly for the Bucks in the first half. A
high-scoring first quarter saw them on the short end of a
35-30 score, and the Bulls increased the lead to 62-51 at
halftime. Hot shooting by Dandridge drew the Bucks even
at 65, but the Bulls maintained their lead, 86-83, after the
third quarter.

Two minutes into the fourth quarter trailing 89-84, the
Bucks made their run. In the next five and a half minutes,
they went on a 21-4 run to secure the victory. Everyone
played a role in the big spurt. Robertson drained three
straight jump shots, McGlocklin added two baskets,
Alcindor and Smith scored again, and the score was
105-93.

Chicago had a run of its own, slicing the score to 107-100 with two and a half minutes remaining, and even got the deficit as low as five at 109-104. Alcindor hit two free throws, and a huge steal and basket by Dandridge gave the Bucks a 113-104 lead. The Bucks held on, winning 117-108, for their 15th straight victory. Alcindor fouled out with 1:20 left in the game but led the Bucks with 37 points. Robertson had 24, and McGlocklin was right behind with 22. Jerry Sloan led the Bulls with 23, followed closely by Tom Boerwinkle with 21 and Chet Walker with 19.

All of the Bucks starters were red-hot from the field, each of them shooting over .500. Robertson hit nine of 12, Smith connected on seven of nine, McGlocklin 11 of 15, Alcindor 14 of 21, and Dandridge went six for 11. The Bucks set a club record with a sizzling .658 field goal percentage with 48 out of 73 attempts, sinking 20 of 28 in the first half.

Costello noted,

> *"Only 28 shots in a half must have been a record since the 24 second clock was put in. They didn't slow us down, though, we slowed ourselves down. Then we started running and playing more aggressive defense, but this was our toughest game since the double overtime with Baltimore."*[32]

Costello was proud of his team.

> *"The mark of a good team is to come back and we did it. In the past we had good leads and rode 'em out. This time we had to turn it on. We probably played too cautiously the first half, although the Bulls didn't make us change our game. We started*

to run the second half, and then Oscar came through as the super pressure player he is."[33]

After the game, Bulls coach Dick Motta said,

"We probably would have beaten most other teams. It was a good effort, but we made too many mistakes in that fourth quarter."[34]

Costello observed,

"Lew and Oscar are such winners, they won't let us have a letdown. It was a rough game tonight, but that's the way all the pro teams react to us. We found out in a hurry the Bulls wanted this one. They got control early and we had to come back. That's the mark of a good team."[35]

GAME 18—FINALLY, A HOME GAME!
BUCKS 113, PISTONS 87

The Bucks returned to the Milwaukee Arena for a game on Wednesday, November 24, against the only team to beat them—the Detroit Pistons. The Bucks had won 15 in a row since that defeat. How did the team feel about the streak?

Costello observed,

"They don't even talk about it. But they're certainly aware of it. They know that three more and we tie the Knicks' record. If we keep going, that game Saturday night in New York will be some pressure —the Knicks trying to keep us from doing it. But we aren't looking any farther ahead than the Pistons Wednesday night. If you look past somebody in this league, you get knocked off."[36]

Revenge was accomplished in a big way. The Bucks had their most lopsided win of the season, a 113-87 victory in front of a sell-out crowd of 10,746. After the game, Alcindor said,

> *"There were a lot of hungry guys out there tonight. It feels good to take care of them like that. We all wanted this one and we got it."*[37]

The game didn't start out as a blowout. During the first quarter, the teams were tied 10 times, and the quarter ended with the teams deadlocked at 31. The Bucks took control in the second quarter, outscoring the Pistons 37-18, giving them a 68-49 halftime advantage behind hot shooting from Greg Smith and Lucius Allen. The Pistons were sputtering with Dave Bing scoring six points and Bob Lanier five. There was no let-up as the Bucks built the lead to 94-72 after the third quarter.

Pistons coach Bill Van Breda Kolff rested his starters and played his bench for the fourth quarter. Costello followed suit after the Bucks were up 104-75 with eight minutes left.

The Bucks' defense was a big key to the rout. In the Bucks' loss to the Pistons in their first meeting, Pistons guards Jimmy Walker and Dave Bing combined for 57 points, 37 of them by Bing. This time, they only combined for 20.

Costello gave his team credit.

> *"We keyed on Bing. Oscar and the others who covered him didn't give him a good shot. He has to score for them to win."*[38]

Bing agreed with Costello's assessment.

> *"They doubled and triple-teamed us all the time. Over in Detroit, they didn't do it at all."*[39]

Lucius Allen driving on the Pistons' John Mengelt. (Author's collection)

Bing finished with 12 points on 5-18 from the field, while
Walker had eight points on three for 11 field-goal shooting.
The Bucks were led by Alcindor, who had 31 points and 17
rebounds, and Greg Smith chipped in with 21 points and
17 rebounds.

Endnotes to Chapter 5

1) Rel Bochat, "Boozer's Play, Lew's Defense Spark Bucks," *Milwaukee Sentinel*, November 2,1970, pt. 2, p. 1.

2) "Bucks Play Cavaliers in Likely Mismatch," *Milwaukee Journal*, November 4, 1970, pt. 2, p. 17.

3) Rel Bochat, "Lew Hits 53 in 110-108 Win," *Milwaukee Sentinel*, November 5, 1971, pt. 2, p. 1-4

4) John Devaney, *Alcindor and the Big O: A Season's Diary* (New York: Lancer Books, 1971), p. 107.

5) Bob Wolf, "Light Schedule Slows Bucks," *Milwaukee Journal*, November 6, 1970, pt.2, p. 14.

6) Rel Bochat, "Bucks' Fast Break Dims Suns," *Milwaukee Sentinel*, November 9, 1970, pt. 2, p. 3.

7) Bob Wolf, "Dandridge, Ailing at Start, Becomes a Pain to Suns," *Milwaukee Journal*, November 9, 1970, pt. 2, p. 11.

8) Bob Wolf, "Rookie Leads Celtics' Resurgence," *Milwaukee Journal*, November 11,1970, pt. 2, p. 19.

9) Rel Bochat, "Bucks Post 7th in Row, 123-113," *Milwaukee Sentinel*, November 12, 1970, pt. 2, p. 1.

10) Devaney, p. 108.

11) Bob Wolf, "Bucks Win, Set Record," *Milwaukee Journal*, November 15, 1970, pt. 3, p. 2.

12) *Ibid.*

13) *Ibid.*

14) Rel Bochat, "Bucks Blunt Bullets for 9th in Row," *Milwaukee Sentinel*, November 16, 1970, pt.1, p.1.

15) Bob Wolf, "Bucks Handcuff Monroe, Bullets," *Milwaukee Journal*, November 16, 1970, pt. 2, p. 15.

16) Alan Goldstein, "Bucks Whip Bullets in 105-90 Rout." *Baltimore Sun*, November 16, 1970, pt. C, p. 1.

17) Bob Wolf, " Waiting Game Ends; Bucks Keep Rolling," *Milwaukee Journal*, November 17, 1970, pt. 2, p. 13.

18) *Ibid.*

19) Rel Bochat. "Bucks Win 10th in a Row," *Milwaukee Sentinel*, November 17, 1970, pt. 2, p. 2.

20) Rel Bochat, "Bucks Seek 11th in Row at San Diego Tonight," *Milwaukee Sentinel*, November 18, 1970, pt. 2, p. 1.

21) Bob Wolf, "Smith Blossoms as Scorer and Bucks Win 11th in Row," *Milwaukee Journal*, November 19, 1970, pt. 2, p. 23.

22) *Ibid.*

23) *Ibid.*

24) Rel Bochat, "There's No Worry When You're Winning—Costello," *Milwaukee Sentinel*, November 20, 1970, pt. 2, p. 1.

25) Bob Wolf, "Lakers Swamped by Bucks," *Milwaukee Journal*, November 21,1970, pt. 1, p. 17.

26) *Ibid.*

27) Mal Florence, "Lakers Humbled, 117-100," *Los Angeles Times*, November 21, 1970, pt. 3, p. 1.

28) *Ibid.*

29) Bob Wolf, "Bucks' Dandridge Remains a Bargain," *Milwaukee Journal*, November 23, 1970, pt. 2, p 9.

30) *Ibid.*

31) Rel Bochat, "Bulls Threaten Bucks' 14 Game String Tonight," *Milwaukee Sentinel*, November 24, 1970, pt. 2, p. 1.

32) Bob Wolf, "Awesome Bucks Need Rally to Win," *Milwaukee Journal*, November 25, 1970, pt. 2, p. 10.

33) Rel Bochat, "Bucks Deck Bulls For 15th in Row," *Milwaukee Sentinel*, November 25, 1970, pt. 2, p. 1.

34) Bob Logan, "Bucks Escape Bull Upset, 117 To 108," *Chicago Tribune*, November 25, 1970, pt. 3, p. 1.

35) *Ibid.*

36) Bochat, November 25.

37) Rel Bochat, "Bucks Rip Pistons for 16th Straight, 113-87," *Milwaukee Sentinel*, November 26, 1970, pt. 1, p. 1.

38) Bob Wolf, "Pistons No Problem the 2nd Time Around," *Milwaukee Journal*, November 26, 1970, pt. 2, p. 17.

39) *Ibid.*

CHAPTER 6

THE NEMESIS KNICKS

GAME 19—THE STREAK ENDS:
KNICKS 103, BUCKS 94

After a day off for Thanksgiving, on the afternoon of November 27, in front of another sellout crowd at the Milwaukee Arena and a national television audience, it was a rematch of the previous season's conference finals. New York continued its dominance in the series, rallying to beat the Bucks, 103-94, ending the Bucks' 16-game winning streak.

The Knicks grabbed an early 14-8 lead, only to see the Bucks storm back, outscoring them 16-4, taking a 30-18 advantage on some big baskets by Jon McGlocklin and Lew Alcindor. It was time for the Knicks to make their comeback, and behind strong outside shooting, they outscored the Bucks the remainder of the quarter, 12-3, trailing 33-30 going into the second quarter. Willis Reed had a big first half, scoring 22 points. There were six ties in the second quarter, but Dave Stallworth hit the last two baskets of the half, giving the Knicks a 56-55 lead.

Midway through the third quarter, the Bucks had a scoring spree. It was a team effort. McGlocklin had a layup, Robertson hit a jumper, Alcindor had a dunk, a tip in and a pair of free throws, and Greg Smith had a layup. The Bucks led 83-74 at the end of the third quarter.

The fourth quarter belonged to the Knicks, who outscored the Bucks 11-4 to start the quarter, making it 87-85 with seven minutes left in the game. Things looked good for Milwaukee to take a four-point lead courtesy of an Alcindor hook shot. The Knicks missed a shot on their possession, and when Alcindor got the ball on offense, Reed fouled him, his fifth foul, sending him to the bench.

It was comeback time for the Knicks. After Alcindor missed both free throws, reserve Dave Stallworth hit two outside baskets, tying the score with 5:45 left. After the game, Red Holzman talked about Stallworth.

> "Dave was just great. We never would have made it without those big plays he made."[1]

With the game tied at 89, another reserve played a big role for the Knicks. Phil Jackson gave the Knicks the lead with a spinning layup on a fast break and hit a corner jump shot about a minute later. Jackson talked about the pair of baskets after the game.

> "That was the one that just had to go in. I've practiced that spinning layup before, although I've been too chicken to use it in a game, but I really wanted that shot from the corner to drop."[2]

Walt Frazier hit an outside basket, and the Knicks led 95-89 with 3:40 left.

Coach Costello called time out and was very upset with his team's play:

> "We acted a little tired out there. I don't know what it was. Maybe it's that they run us so hard. We were really sluggish at the end. We were terrible at the end. We didn't even play very smart. They played for three minutes without Willis Reed, and we never once got the ball into Lew."[3]

The Bucks narrowed the Knicks' lead to 97-94 with 1:40 left, but Stallworth hit a corner shot and Reed hit two shots, giving the Knicks a 103-94 win. The Bucks were held under the 100-point total for the first time of the season, and their 11-point total for the fourth quarter was the least scored in team history. In the final quarter, the Knicks shot a torrid 64 percent, while the Bucks shot just 27 percent.

After the game, Willis Reed reflected.

> *"It was a team victory and it proved to us that we've still got a great club. We've had problems getting started this season with injuries and little things, and this game gave us a chance to measure*

Dave DeBusschere (22) and Oscar Robertson going after a loose ball. (Author's collection)

ourselves. The Bucks are a fine team with great personnel and beating them, protecting our record, lifted us a lot. Beating them down the stretch, especially since they now have Oscar Robertson, really was impressive. I think Oscar is one of the greatest pressure performers in history."[4]

When Dave DeBusschere was asked if the Knicks played with more emotion because the record they hold for consecutive victories was in jeopardy of being broken, he answered,

"We were up emotionally, but not because of the record. We would be up for any team with Oscar and Lew and with the terrific start they've had."[5]

In the Bucks' locker room. Lew Alcindor said,

"They were in foul trouble with Reed on the bench but we stopped playing. It was a tough game, but we should have kept going. We had the lead."[6]

Coach Costello had high praise for the Knicks.

"Their outside shooting was too much. As a team, nobody in the league can compare with them in that respect. Every one of them can hit from the outside."[7]

Alcindor led the Bucks with 33 points and 16 rebounds, and Robertson and McGlocklin each had 18. The Knicks were led by Reed with 34 points and 10 rebounds, Walt Frazier had 20, and Dave Stallworth, who came off the bench, had 18. The Knicks' bench outscored the Bucks' bench, 24-0.

Bucks	FG-FGA	FT-FTA	Rebs.	Pts	Knicks	FG-FGA	FT-FTA	Rebs.	Pts.
Alcindor	14-25	5-9	16	33	Barnett	2-8	1-1	1	5
Allen	0-2	0-0	1	0	Bradley	3-8	0-0	1	6
Boozer	0-1	0-0	3	0	DeBusschere	7-14	0-1	8	14
Cunningham	0-0	0-0	0	0	Frazier	9-12	2-5	6	20
Dandridge	6-15	2-3	12	14	Jackson	2-2	0-1	2	4
McGlocklin	9-17	0-0	3	18	Reed	15-27	4-4	10	34
Robertson	7-14	4-5	3	18	Riordan	1-2	0-0	3	2
Smith	5-10	1-3	11	11	Stallworth	8-15	2-3	4	18
Zopf	0-0	0-0	0	0					

Game 19 Box Score

GAME 20—BUCKS NICKED IN NEW YORK:
KNICKS 100, BUCKS 99

Revenge and a new winning streak were possible just a little more than 24 hours later as a rematch with the Knicks took place at Madison Square Garden on Saturday evening, November 28, but the Knicks defeated the Bucks, 100-99 in front of a sellout crowd of 19,500.

The Bucks jumped to an early 12-3 lead, but the Knicks, as had been the case in the previous game, came back and trailed 28-24 at the end of the first quarter. They took a 52 -50 lead into the locker room at halftime.

Alcindor had a huge third quarter, scoring 16, and the Bucks took an 83-73 lead into the fourth quarter. The Bucks expanded the lead to 91-77 with eight minutes left, and it looked like the Bucks might gain revenge and begin a new winning streak.

With 5:31 left on the clock and the Bucks ahead, 96-84, the Knicks changed their defensive strategy. Willis Reed noticed that...

"...they were coming down at the same tempo,
setting up Alcindor or Robertson for easy baskets.
We had to break up that tempo."[8]

They used a press and confused the Bucks by showing them different defenses. Knicks' reserve forward Phil Jackson would chase the man with the ball, and his quickness and long arms paid off. Jackson commented,

> *"We were changing defenses so much that they didn't know what we were going to do."*9

The Bucks turned the ball over the next two times on offense. Alcindor lost the ball, and Dandridge was called for a three-second violation. The Knicks took advantage. Mike Riordan had a three-point play, narrowing the Bucks' lead to 96-87. The Knicks' defense continued to stymie the Bucks. Robertson and Smith made bad passes resulting in turnovers. The Bucks had committed four turnovers in a 70-second span.

After Bill Bradley scored off a steal, Riordan hit another jumper and the Knicks had scored seven straight, making the score 96-91. Robertson hit a basket with 3:44 left in the game to stop the bleeding, but the Knicks came back on a Stallworth bucket, and Bill Bradley hit a jump shot from the key, making the score 98-95. The Bucks worked the ball inside to Alcindor, who was fouled. He made one of the free throws, giving the Bucks a 99-95 lead with 2:34 left. The Knicks came right back when Bradley scored, making it a two-point game.

Costello called a time-out to settle the team down, but it was to no avail. They turned the ball over again, and after Alcindor committed a loose ball foul, his fifth personal with 1:21 left, Reed hit one of two free throws, making the score 99-98.

On the Bucks' next possession, Robertson missed a shot and the Knicks got the rebound. The Knicks worked

Jon McGlocklin watches as the Knicks' Walt Frazier goes to the basket. (Author's collection)

the ball around, looking for a decent shot. Bradley's shot was blocked by Alcindor. Reed got the loose ball and passed to DeBusschere, whose basket gave the Knicks the lead, 100-98, with 0:28 left. DeBusschere talked about the shot after the game.

> *"We pressed them and changed the whole flow of the game. I was lucky on that last shot. Everybody sloughed off to help out on Willis, and I had nothing to do but give a little fake and go up with the shot."*[10]

The Bucks called a time-out to set up the basket they hoped would let them retake the lead. The Knicks continued their tenacious defense. The Bucks hoped to run a play where Dandridge would get the inbounds pass and would drive to the basket. If Reed helped out on defense, he would pass to Alcindor; if Reed didn't come out and there wasn't a shot, he would look for Robertson. The way things worked out, Robertson got the ball and passed back to Dandridge. He missed an off-balance shot with 12 seconds left and Reed got the rebound. The Knicks managed to play keep away from the Bucks, who were unable to foul, and the game ended in a 100-99 New York victory.

Willis Reed said,

> "We beat the best ball club in the league. I got to say that they are the best because they are the best record-wise. The only difference between us tonight was that we are the more experienced ball club. You don't get experience overnight. They will be a better team 20 or 30 games from tonight."[11]

The Bucks were outscored 16-3 in the last 5:31, and Costello talked about his team's collapse.

> "We've had great luck against the press in the past, but this time we lost our composure. We dribbled, got trapped, and threw the ball away. If we could have just hit a basket toward the end, we might have eliminated the press, but we couldn't buy one."[12]

When Costello was asked if the consecutive victories by the Knicks were evidence that they would win in the playoffs, he responded,

> "No, sir. Neither loss was a convincing defeat. It would have been different if they had beaten us by 20 points, but we could have won both games; damn it, we should have won both games. Today was the same as yesterday. They shut us off in the fourth period. How many baskets did we score in the last three minutes after Oscar's basket? None.

Mistakes, we lost our composure. Mistakes, silly mistakes."[13]

Alcindor led the Bucks with 35 points along with 24 rebounds, and Robertson had 26 points. The Knicks had balanced scoring. DeBusschere had 21 points and 14 rebounds, Barnett was close behind with 19, and Reed had 18 points. Dave Stallworth came off the bench and added 12 points along with eight rebounds.

Endnotes to Chapter 6

1) Bob Wolf, "Knicks Rule From Bench, Put End to Bucks' Streak," *Milwaukee Journal*, November 28, 1970, pt. 2. p. 16.

2) Thomas Rogers, "Knicks Rally for 103-94 Victory and Snap Bucks' 16-Game Winning Streak," *New York Times*, November 28, 1970, p. 35.

3) Glenn Miller, "Knicks Bring Buck Streak to a Terrible End," *Wisconsin State Journal*, November 28, 1970, pt. 3, p.1.

4) Rogers, p. 35.

5) John Devaney, *Alcindor and the Big O* (New York: Lancer Books, 1971), p. 120.

6) Rel Bochat, "We Stopped Playing!" *Milwaukee Sentinel*, November 28, 1970, pt. 2, p. 1.

7) Wolf, pp. 16-17.

8) Devaney, p. 123.

9) Bob Wolf, "Rally by Knicks Topples Bucks," *Milwaukee Journal*, November 29, 1970, pt. 2. p. 2.

10) *Ibid.*

11) Devaney, p. 128.

12) Wolf. November 29. pt. 2, p. 2.

13) Devaney, pp. 128-129.

CHAPTER 7

STARTING A NEW STREAK —HOPEFULLY!

GAME 21—BUCKS BATTER BLAZERS:
BUCKS 124, TRAILBLAZERS 111

If the Bucks had won their two previous games versus the Knicks, November 29, 1970 would've been a historic night, as the Bucks would be going for their 19th straight victory, an NBA record. Instead it would be a very difficult game. Coach Costello noted,

> *"We had a tremendous emotional letdown. On top of that, this was our 12th game in 16 days, and the guys are tired. Everybody is looking forward to a day off. I knew it was tough getting excited about this game, but I warned the guys not to take it lightly, and I'm happy about the way it went."*[1]

The Bucks didn't disappoint the 9,489 who attended, getting a 124-111 victory.

The Bucks took a 33-22 lead after one quarter and opened it up to a 16-point lead, 39-23, early in the second quarter. Portland came back, and at halftime the Bucks led, 58-50.

A 42-point third quarter explosion by the Bucks gave them a 100-83 lead going into the fourth quarter. A switch in the starting lineup by Costello helped fuel the outburst. The Blazers were playing four guards and had fewer big men in the game. Costello countered by moving Jon McGlocklin to forward, replacing Greg Smith. Talking about the personnel change, Costello said,

> *"McGlocklin hit some shots after we started him at forward in the third quarter. They (Portland) were mixed up on their matchups. They didn't realize he was at forward and not at guard."*[2]

McGlocklin didn't mind the move, saying,

> *"I like moving up front. I can get free and move around more."*[3]

The Bucks were led in scoring by Alcindor, who scored 33 points in 35 minutes of action, on 14-21 field-goal shooting. They received balanced scoring from the rest of the team, McGlocklin with 20, Robertson with 17, and Dandridge with 15. Sharing scoring honors for Portland were Geoff Petrie and Leroy Ellis with 27. Ellis also grabbed a game-high 25 rebounds.

GAME 22—QUARTER POINT IN A GRUELING SEASON: BUCKS 107, BULLS 100

With the season a quarter completed, Costello was pleased.

> *"We've got a hell of a record (18-3) and I'm very happy with the way things are overall. Now we want to step up developing our bench, so we know what we can expect consistently from these guys coming into a game when we need help."*[4]

The practices went really well, and after Wednesday's session, Costello observed,

> *"We were passing instead of dribbling around today, and getting good movement. We spent the*

last three days mainly on offense. Our defense has been satisfactory, but we just weren't getting open for shots."[5]

Costello's words were prophetic. On December 3, the Bucks had both Alcindor and Greg Smith in foul trouble, and Dandridge had an off game, but the bench came through in a big way with a 107-100 victory in front of 9,759 hometown faithful.

The Bulls led 33-28 after the first quarter, and after Alcindor picked up his third foul early in the second quarter, they maintained their lead at halftime, 52-51. Things looked bleak when Alcindor went to the bench with his fifth foul with the Bucks behind 83-78.

The Bucks bench stepped up to rally the team. Lucius Allen came off the bench connecting on six of ten shots for 14 points, and Bob Boozer chipped in with eight points and 11 rebounds and did a great job defensively on Chet Walker, holding him to 13 points.

Boozer commented on his play,

"It's a matter of regaining my consistency. This is the first year since '65 that I haven't started, and that's a big adjustment to make. It's all in the head. You've got to get yourself in the proper frame of mind."[6]

The Bucks turned that 83-78 deficit into a 90-85 lead. They maintained the lead with great defense, the Bulls shooting only 23.3 percent in the fourth quarter, while the Bucks countered with a scorching 61.1 percent. It was still a tight contest, and after Jerry Sloan hit a pair of free throws, the Bulls trailed 95-94 with 2:38 left. Alcindor and Robertson came through with back-to-back baskets, and some free throws gave the Bucks some breathing room at

102-94 with 59 seconds left, ending up with a 107-100 win.

Costello had high praise for his bench:

> *"Allen and Boozer did a darn good job. Dick Cunningham battled harder, pushing and shoving, making it tough for them. We won with Lew in foul trouble, and that speaks a lot for the help we got from the bench."*[7]

Despite having his playing time limited to 32 minutes because of foul trouble, Alcindor had 22 points and 10 rebounds, Robertson had 22, and McGlocklin chipped in 18. Chicago's leading scorers were Bob Love with 22, Tom Boerwinkle with 21, and Jim Fox, who connected on eight of 14 shots, with 18.

The game also featured five technical fouls for heated disagreements concerning the officiating refs, two on Chicago (Coach Motta and Matt Guokas) and three on the Bucks (Alcindor, Boozer, and Assistant Coach Tom Nissalke).

GAME 23—BUCKS' BIG COMEBACK:
BUCKS 128, 76ERS 122

After the big win against Chicago, the Bucks played the next day, December 4, against Philadelphia. The Bucks won an exciting overtime thriller, 128-122, in front of a sell-out crowd of 10,746.

It was a tough game for the Bucks as the 76ers gave a great effort. The Bucks fell behind by 11 points in the first quarter but narrowed the gap to 31-29 after one quarter. The Bucks trailed at the half, 61-60, and were still on the short end of a 92-89 score at the end of the third quarter.

The teams exchanged five-point leads in the fourth quarter but were tied at 108 late in the quarter.

There was some exciting play to close out the regulation. Billy Cunningham went on a three-basket run, giving the 76ers what looked like an insurmountable lead, 114-110, with only 10 seconds left. The Bucks hoped to score quickly, looking for a basket by Alcindor and then, applying pressure defensively, hopefully, getting a steal. Instead, they got a 20-foot basket from Jon McGlocklin with three seconds left.

After the game McGlocklin noted:

> *"They weren't going to foul, but their pivotman came out to help put on the pressure and I had to throw it up high to get it over him."*[8]

Opening tipoff, Alcindor and Dennis Awtrey. (Author's collection)

All the 76ers had to do was get the ball in and run out the clock. Cunningham was the inbounder, with Greg Smith covering on defense. Commenting about the play, Smith said,

> *"I was going to pick up somebody and had my back to Cunningham. I turned around and couldn't help but catch it."*[9]

Smith took a dribble or two, launched a 15-foot jumper, the final horn sounded while the ball was in the air, and then it dropped through, tying the score at 114.

The 76ers were psychologically flat after losing the lead in regulation, and the overtime belonged to the Bucks. Alcindor, who was playing despite a bad case of the flu, sank three quick baskets and the Bucks were on their way. Alcindor said,

> *"I felt terrible, but I just had to put it all together. That shot by Greg sparked all of us."*[10]

Indeed, the Bucks scored on seven of their eight possessions in the overtime, hitting seven of their ten shots, ending the game with a shooting percentage of 60.7 percent. Alcindor led the Bucks with 35 points, while Cunningham led the 76ers with 33.

Cunningham was obviously unhappy after the game:

> *"I lost the game. Clark [Archie] started going down the floor and I saw Smith come between us. I shouldn't have even thrown the ball. I should have called time out."*[11]

Bucks	FG-FGA	FT-FTA	Rebs.	Pts	76er's	FG-FGA	FT-FTA	Rebs.	Pts.
Alcindor	14-19	7-17	18	35	Awtrey	7-11	0-0	6	14
Allen	6-9	0-1	0	12	Clark	5-17	3-4	4	13
Boozer	6-8	4-5	7	16	Crawford	3-5	0-0	0	6
Cunningham	0-0	0-0	3	0	Cunningham	13-29	7-7	14	33
Dandridge	9-13	6-7	8	24	Dierking	2-11	7-9	6	11
McGlocklin	6-12	4-4	1	16	Greer	8-15	2-3	7	18
Robertson	7-15	5-5	6	19	Howell	4-4	4-5	3	12
Smith	3-7	0-0	5	6	Washington	6-20	3-4	9	15
Zopf	0-1	0-0	0	0					

Game 23 Box Score

GAME 24—BUCKS HUMBLE THE HAWKS:
BUCKS 125, HAWKS 104

After three days off, the Bucks hosted the Atlanta Hawks on Tuesday, December 8. The Hawks were having a difficult season because of the defection of Joe Caldwell to the ABA's Carolina Cougars. Costello was high on Caldwell's abilities:

> "They miss Caldwell, period. They had a lot of flexibility with him. He can play forward or guard, he's a great jumper and he's quick as a cat, probably the quickest in the league when he was here. I'd sure like to have him."[12]

Bucks' forward Bob Boozer agreed:

> "It's amazing what a difference one man can make. They don't get that fast break going without him to throw the outlet pass."[13]

The Bucks led 32-27 after the first quarter and maintained the five-point lead, 58-53, at halftime. One of the reasons for the close game was Lou Hudson, who scored 22 points in the first half. Hudson really cooled off in the second half, scoring only eight. Trying to explain the lack of scoring in the second half, Hudson said,

"They didn't play me any tougher in the second half than they did in the first. I just wasn't getting the shots. I'll tell you one thing, though. That Alcindor makes a big difference. With him there, you can't go in. He keeps you outside, makes you take shots you don't want to take."[14]

The Bucks blew the game open in the third quarter, outscoring the Hawks 35-21 to take a 93-74 lead into the fourth quarter. What opened the game up for the Bucks? Costello had a theory:

"We got a lot of layups. We've been getting only 74 or 75 shots against teams like the Bulls and 76ers and had to shoot 65 percent to beat them. Tonight we got good percentage shots because of Lew, and we opened it up with better movement, some good passing on the fast breaks. It was the third period where we broke it wide open."[15]

Maravich only scored seven points in the first half but scored 22 in the second, ending up with 29, and Hudson leading the Hawks with 30. Balance was the word for the Bucks. Alcindor had 24 points and 13 rebounds, Dandridge scored 20, Smith and McGlocklin had 17 each, and Robertson added 11 points to go along with 13 assists as the Bucks rolled to a 125-104 romp.

Atlanta Coach Richie Guerin was very impressed with the Bucks:

"I know New York beat them twice, but they look like the best club to me. Their corner men (Bob Dandridge and Greg Smith) are much too quick for ours, and that guy in the middle (Alcindor) is just too much."[16]

Endnotes to Chapter 7

1) Bob Wolf, "Foe Not So Formidable, Bucks Return to Romping," *Milwaukee Journal*, November 30, 1970, pt. 2, p.13.

2) Rel Bochat, "Bucks Punish Portland, 124-111," *Milwaukee Sentinel*, November 30, 1970, pt. 2, p.1.

3) *Ibid.*

4) Rel Bochat, "Costello Checks 'Nicks," *Milwaukee Sentinel*, December 1, 1970, pt. 2, p. 1.

5) Rel Bochat, "Bucks Tuned Up For Bulls Tonight," *Milwaukee Sentinel*, December 3, 1970, pt. 2, p. 1.

6) Bob Wolf, "Bucks' Rally Beats Bulls With Power in Reserves," *Milwaukee Journal*, December 4, 1970, pt. 2, p.19.

7) Rel Bochat, "Boozer and Allen in Key Roles," *Milwaukee Sentinel*, December 4, 1970, pt. 2, p. 1.

8) Rel Bochat, "Impossible? Not to Greg Smith!" *Milwaukee Sentinel*, December 5, 1970, pt. 2, p. 1.

9) *Ibid.*

10) Bob Wolf, "Bucks' Spurt Defies Belief and Defeats Stunned 76ers," *Milwaukee Journal*, December 5, 1970, pt. 2, p. 17.

11) *Ibid.*

12) Bob Wolf, "Bucks' Big Artillery Outguns the Pistol," *Milwaukee Journal*, December 9, 1970, pt. 2, p. 21.

13) *Ibid.*

14) *Ibid.*

15) Rel Bochat, "Bucks Clip Hawks For 4th Straight," Milwaukee Sentinel, December 9, 1970, pt. 2, p.1.

16) Wolf. December 9.

CHAPTER 8

SPEED BUMPS

GAME 25—TAKING A BULLET:
BULLETS 127, BUCKS 97

After four straight home games, the Bucks went on the road for a contest against the Baltimore Bullets at the Civic Center on Wednesday, December 9. It was one of those games where everything went right for the Bullets, and the Bucks could only do wrong. Costello hoped that the team might learn a lesson from the 127-97 shellacking:

> *"These guys have to realize that the NBA isn't heaven. It's no cakewalk. There are other teams with talent in this league, and Baltimore is one of them. They've got a lot of go horses, and when we gave them life, everything fell into place for them."*[1]

The Bucks trailed 30-22 after the first quarter and came out with a good effort in the second quarter, narrowing the deficit to 36-32. Then the Bullets started their big run. They scored ten straight, and never looked back, opening up a 70-44 lead at halftime, a huge 98-59 advantage in the third quarter, and led 106-68 going into the fourth quarter. Knowing early on that the Bucks had zero chance of winning, Costello played the bench extensively. Gary Freeman played 24 minutes, Bob Boozer 23, Billy Zopf 20, and Lucius Allen 19.

Bullets' coach Gene Shue was philosophical about the rout.

"They were flat, but I don't want to take anything away from my players. They played a heck of a game. We were moving."[2]

Costello gave credit to the great defense played by Wes Unseld and Gus Johnson on Alcindor.

"We couldn't get the ball in to Lew. You're not going to win on outside shooting in this league. Hell, when you've got a seven-foot pivot man and you can't get the ball to him that's your problem."[3]

Indeed, Alcindor had a free throw in the first quarter for his only scoring, getting his first basket a minute into the second quarter. He still managed to lead the Bucks with 24 points, grabbing 15 rebounds, while the Bullets had many contributors. Unseld had 25 points and 18 rebounds, Jack Marin also had 25, and Earl Monroe added 24.

GAME 26—BUCKS CLOBBER THE CAVALIERS: BUCKS 134, CAVALIERS 92

The pasting by the Bullets woke up the Bucks. At least it did for their game against the Cavaliers on Friday, December 11, as the Bucks delighted a Milwaukee Arena crowd of 9,449 with a 134-92 victory.

There was no sense of a blowout win after the first quarter. The Bucks led 30-29, paced by 17 points from Alcindor. The Bucks bench ignited the team in the beginning of the second quarter. Lucius Allen scored three baskets, two of them on layups, giving the Bucks a 41-33 lead. Bob Boozer added two baskets during the quarter, and the Bucks led 57-44 at halftime.

Gary Freeman, who ended up the game with 14 points, added two quick baskets midway through the third quarter, making the score 68-58, and the Bucks were on their way. Costello had high praise for Freeman:

> *"I think the turning point, if there is one in a game like this, was when Freeman went in. He played very well offensively and defensively, using good judgment in one-on-one situations, going to the board, running, passing and picking good shots. Everybody seemed to pick up then."*[4]

Robertson, who missed his only field goal attempt in the first half, got hot in the second half, hitting on eight of his nine attempts, and the Bucks were up 93-69 after three quarters. Greg Smith and Freeman played a big role on defense, holding John Johnson to 15 points. The Bucks were led by Alcindor with 34 points and 17 rebounds, followed by Robertson and Greg Smith, who each added 22 points. Walt Wesley led the Cavaliers with 18 points.

GAME 27—BUCKS BLINDED BY SUNS:
SUNS 113, BUCKS 111

On Saturday, December 12, the Bucks lost their fifth game of the season, 113-111, in front of a near-capacity crowd of 11,002 at the Arizona Veterans Memorial Coliseum. The loss snapped a ten-game winning streak against the Suns.

Despite playing the night before and having to travel, the Bucks came out strong, building a 9-4 lead in the first three minutes. Phoenix came back with 11 straight points, which included a basket and a three-point play by Connie Hawkins and a layup by Dick Van Arsdale. Baskets by

Alcindor and Dandridge cut the lead to 15-13, but the Suns went on a run led by Paul Silas, Neal Walk, and Hawkins, and the first quarter ended with the Bucks trailing 36-26.

Robertson had three baskets early in the second quarter, but Mel Counts came back with three of his own as the Suns maintained their ten-point lead, 46-36, three minutes into the quarter. Two baskets by Greg Smith and one by Robertson narrowed the margin, but the Suns outscored the Bucks 6-1 in the last two minutes before halftime and took a 64-52 lead to the locker room.

Neal Walk was hot in the third quarter, hitting four straight baskets, three of them outside jumpers. The Bucks countered with 11 straight points, tying the game at 75. The game stayed close with a number of ties until Van Arsdale and Counts helped give the Suns an 89-83 lead. The Bucks ended the quarter with five straight points, a basket by Robertson and three points by Alcindor, making the score 89-88 at the end of the third quarter.

The Bucks took the lead early in the fourth quarter, their first since the three-minute mark of the opening period, on a basket by Dandridge. The Suns went on a ten-point run, six from Hawkins and four by Van Arsdale, giving them a 99-91 lead. The Bucks fought back, cutting the Suns' lead to three points on four different occasions, and after Dandridge hit a 20-foot jumper with 43 seconds left, the Bucks trailed, 113-111. Van Arsdale missed a shot with 20 seconds left, but Paul Silas got the rebound for the Suns. Costello begged his players to foul, but the Suns had such great ball movement the Bucks couldn't, and the Suns ran out the clock.

Alcindor led the Bucks with 36 points and 17 rebounds, Dandridge had 21 and Robertson had 19 to go along with 12 assists. The Suns had great balanced scoring, getting 26 from Van Arsdale, 25 from Hawkins, and 24 from Walk.

Game 28—Flying High in Seattle:
Bucks 124, Supersonics 107

The Bucks played their third game in three days, taking on the Seattle Supersonics in front of 12,627 fans at the Seattle Center Coliseum on Sunday, December 13.

The Sonics started the game hot and grabbed an early 16-9 lead. The Bucks came back, and a jump shot by Robertson gave them a 19-18 lead. The first quarter ended with the teams tied at 31. The Bucks had a huge second quarter, outscoring Seattle 35-18 to take a 66-49 halftime lead. The Bucks shot a sizzling 61 percent from the field in the first half.

The Bucks increased the lead to 20 early in the third quarter, but former Marquette star Don Kojis got hot, as Seattle closed the gap to 92-79 at the end of the third quarter. The Bucks put the Sonics away in the fourth quarter to take a 124-107 win.

Kojis led the Sonics with 29 points, connecting on 10 of 17 shots. Guard Dick Snyder added 25, going nine out of nine from the foul line, and Lenny Wilkens added 20 points. Alcindor led the Bucks with 40 points along with 22 rebounds; Dandridge had 24 points, hitting 12 of 16 shots, and Robertson scored 26, with 11 of 17 from the field.

Sonics player-coach Lenny Wilkens had high praise for Alcindor:

"He can go down the floor and score almost any time he wants to. And on defense, all he has to do is block a few shots and any time a guy goes to the hoop, he's got to be conscious of his presence. If you're not seven feet or six foot-11 and strong, he's almost impossible to stop. He gets the ball up high and shoots over people. He has improved tremendously in a year."[5]

Costello was proud of the Bucks' effort.

"We had to fight weariness as much as anything. Getting up at 5:30 Saturday morning after the Cleveland game and 8 o'clock Sunday morning after the Phoenix game is tough. The guys did a good job though and hustled. Seattle's a fast team, and if they'd built up a lead, Lenny Wilkens would have kept them running and might have worn us down."[6]

The Bucks got some much-needed rest with four days off. Workouts were planned for Tuesday and Wednesday at Concordia College, at the time located on the city's west side, with a workout at the Milwaukee Arena scheduled for Thursday.

GOING FOR THE RECORD

The Bucks' record for the season stood at 23-5. They were 16-12 at this point in the previous season. What were some reasons for the improvement?

Bucks' Publicity Director Jim Foley had some ideas:

"Defense, where the Bucks have been rising to the challenge. Last season Milwaukee scored 118.8 points per game but gave up 114.2 while winning 56 and losing 26. This season, through the first 28 games, the Bucks have been averaging nearly 117

points while giving up only 106 a game, and by virtue of those figures lead the league in point difference."[7]

Another factor Foley pointed out was the Bucks' field goal percentage. Last season, the Bucks set an NBA shooting record with a .488 percentage. This season they were at .502, and the starters were connecting at a .522 percentage.

With the Bucks' great start, a question arose. Would the Bucks be able to beat the best-ever NBA season record of 68-13 set by the 1966-1967 Philadelphia 76ers, a team that had Larry Costello on its roster?

When Costello was asked, he said,

"I'd say our chances were slim. The season is only one-third over and we have already lost five. It would be difficult to avoid losing less than 13."[8] ...

"Actually, I have not been thinking about the record. The big thing is to have the best record in the league, so you can open each playoff series at home and always have the odd game."[9]

GAME 29—BUCKS BASH BOSTON:
BUCKS 124, CELTICS 114

After four days off, the Bucks hosted the Celtics at the Milwaukee Arena on Friday, December 18.

Costello was pleased with the practice held at the Arena on Thursday. Alcindor missed the practice because of a migraine headache. After resting on Tuesday and Wednesday, Bob Dandridge's ailing right ankle was doing much better. After Thursday's practice, Costello commented:

*"We really ran today, showing speed and a lot of
movement. It's what we need, what we haven't had
consistently. Boston is a good running club and
very tough on offensive rebounding."*[10]

The game was close. The Bucks, after enjoying a 27-25
advantage after the first quarter, opened the lead to 11 a
number of times during the second quarter before taking a
62-55 lead at halftime.

The Bucks built the lead to 95-81 early in the fourth
quarter when Boston made a comeback. Costello commented on playing against the Celtics:

*"You have to be in shape to play them. No mental
lapses or it's two points. They're tough off the
boards and they go and go. Sure, we got a 14-point
lead and had some 10-point leads, but Boston is an
explosive outfit and can reel off 10 on you just like
that."*[11]

Celtics' forward Don Nelson had a hot shooting hand in
the fourth quarter. The Celtics pulled to within one point,
103-102, with 6:12 left in the game, and the score was tied
at 109 with two minutes and 41 seconds left. Now it was
time for a Bucks run.

Dandridge sank two free throws and Alcindor had a
dunk, putting the Bucks ahead 113-109. Robertson came
up with a huge steal, went three-quarters of the court and
dropped in a layup. Alcindor blocked a shot by Havlicek,
and Celtics guard Art ("Hambone") Williams lost the ball
out of bounds. The Bucks took advantage, getting a dunk
by Alcindor, followed by a three-point play by Dandridge.
In a one minute and 32 second span, the Bucks had
scored 11 straight points, putting the game out of reach.
The final score was 124-114.

Boston's coach Tom Heinsohn summed up the frustration of having to play against the Bucks, and in particular, Alcindor.

> *"It's awfully nice to have a guy 7-2 to go to with the score tied and two minutes to play. Either he makes a basket or gets two free throws."*[12]

GAME 30—ROYAL UPSET:
ROYALS 119, BUCKS 110

After a big win against the Celtics the night before, giving your team a 24-5 record, going to play a 12-18 team you had routed by 21 points earlier in the season, should be a cake walk. But on Saturday, December 19, in front of

Bucks' forward Bob Dandridge looking for an open man in a game against the Celtics. (Author's collection)

5,071 fans at the Cincinnati Gardens, the Bucks lost to the Royals 119-110, dropping the Bucks' record to 24-6. It was their third loss in the last six games and their first loss of the season to a team with a sub-.500 record.

Costello had no excuses for the Bucks' loss.

> *"We just weren't mentally prepared to play the ball game. We came out there and threw the ball away four times and got behind 10-1 and we let them outrun us. Give them credit. They played a great ball game, but we didn't take them seriously enough. Mental preparation is so important in this game. On paper, there was no excuse to lose to these guys."*[13]

The Bucks led 24-23 after one quarter and only trailed 50-49 at halftime. The fourth quarter started tied at 82 and the first three minutes belonged to the Royals as they opened up a 94-84 lead. The closest the Bucks came in the remainder of the game was closing the deficit to six points before losing, 119-110.

Tom Van Arsdale, who had a good game for the Royals with 17 points and 12 rebounds, noticed the Bucks' lethargy.

> *"I don't think they were up for the game, and you can't change your attitude once the game starts. They tried to change it in the second half but they couldn't."*[14]

Alcindor led the Bucks with 35 points and grabbed 20 rebounds. Royals rookie Sam Lacey scored a career high 23, hauled in 17 rebounds, and blocked nine shots, five by Alcindor. When Alcindor was asked after the game about the blocked shots, he commented about the officiating of Manny Sokol and Richie Powers.

"When you're able to crawl on somebody's back, you can do a lot of things."[15]

Endnotes to Chapter 8

1) Bob Wolf, "Bucks' 127-97 Misery Has Company in TV Audience," *Milwaukee Journal*, December 10, 1970, pt. 2, p. 19.

2) Rel Bochat, "Bullets Flatten Bucks, 127-97," *Milwaukee Sentinel*, December 12, 1970, pt. 2, p. 1.

3) *Ibid.*

4) Rel Bochat, "Cavaliers Bombed By Bucks," *Milwaukee Sentinel*, December 12, 1970, pt. 2, p.1.

5) Bob Wolf, "Super Job by Super Lew," *Milwaukee Journal*, December 14, 1970, pt. 2, p. 13.

6) Rel Bochat, "Things Fair 'n' Foul for Weary Bucks," *Milwaukee Sentinel*, December 15, 1970, pt. 2, p. 1.

7) John Devaney, *Alcindor and The Big O.* (New York, New York: Lancer Books, 1971), 135.

8) *Ibid.* p. 134.

9) Bob Wolf, "Costello Reflects on Record," *Milwaukee Journal*, December 16, 1970, pt. 2, p. 23.

10) Rel Bochat, "Bucks Duel Celts At Arena Tonight," *Milwaukee Sentinel*, December 18, 1970, pt. 2, p. 1.

11) Rel Bochat, "Bucks Hold Off Celtics," *Milwaukee Sentinel*, December 19, 1970, pt. 2, p.1.

12) Bob Wolf, "Lew's Cramming Teaches Celtics a Lesson in Rallies," *Milwaukee Journal*, December 19, 1970, pt. 2, p. 7.

13) Bob Wolf, "Bucks Play It Cool, Royals Get Red Hot," *Milwaukee Journal*, December 20, 1970, pt. 2, p. 1.

14) *Ibid.*

15) *Ibid.*

Bucks' starting forward, Greg Smith. Eddie Doucette, the "Voice of the Bucks," nicknamed him "Captain Marvel:" (Lulloff collection)

CHAPTER 9

STRONG FINISH
FOR THE FIRST HALF

GAME 31—BRAVES SCALPED:
BUCKS 131, BRAVES 101

After their humiliating loss in Cincinnati, the Bucks returned home on Sunday evening, December 20. They overcame poor play in the first half to beat the expansion Buffalo Braves, 131-101, in front of 10,174 fans.

The first quarter ended with the Bucks ahead, 36-25, but the second quarter was different. Buffalo came back, taking the lead, 53-52, and on a Nate Bowman tip-in at the buzzer, they took a 59-57 halftime advantage. The Braves, who outscored Milwaukee 34-21 in the quarter, were led by Don May's 16 points, and center Bob Kauffman chipped in with 10.

Coach Costello got on his team in the locker room at halftime.

> *"I just told them this was a serious business. Our game is professional basketball and our job is to win. There's no way we're going to win if we keep playing like this."*[1]

After the game, Jon McGlocklin was asked if one would consider the coach's halftime speech a tongue lashing and he responded,

> *"You hit it on the head."*[2]

Early in the third quarter with the game tied at 64, the Bucks outscored the Braves 25-4, taking an 89-68 lead. Bob Dandridge scored 13 points during that run, and Robertson had four assists. The Bucks outscored Buffalo 37-19 in the third quarter and took a 94-78 lead into the fourth quarter.

What was different about the Bucks' play? Costello noted,

> *"We started moving in the second half. Lew was hitting the open man on the weak side, not trying to go against three guys to get at the basket. Allen gave us a good lift about that time too."*[3]

Costello also gave credit to the Bucks' defense, in particular Bobby Dandridge.

> *"He did a darn good job on Don May. He (May) couldn't get the ball in the second half, and as a result we picked off quite a few passes and turned them into baskets."*[4]

Braves' center, Bob Kauffman, agreed with Costello.

> *"I was trying to tell the other guys not to sag off their men to help me. Lew is such a great passer that we wanted to cut off his assists, which we accomplished pretty well in the first half, but then he made some fantastic passes, and all of a sudden we're out of it."*[5]

Buffalo Coach Dolph Schayes was not impressed with his team's play.

> *"We were putrid. This was our poorest game of the year. We had good shots and they wouldn't go in, and then we started throwing the ball away. Then we got within 14 points (113-99) and had a glimmer*

*of hope, and we lost the ball eight times without
getting a shot. After that, they got 18 points to our
two."⁶*

That 18-2 run contributed to the Bucks' outscoring
Buffalo 37-23 in the fourth quarter, *en route* to a 131-101
victory.

Alcindor led the Bucks with 27 points, 13 rebounds
and eight assists, Dandridge was right behind with 23
points, connecting on 11 of 14 shots from the field, and
Robertson had 22 points, along with 11 assists. Guard
Mike Davis led Buffalo with 23, and Don May and Bob
Kauffman each added 18.

GAME 32—BUCKS DROWN LAKERS:
BUCKS 113, LAKERS 88

The NBA schedule-maker wasn't kind to the Bucks. They
had to prepare for their fourth game in four days with the
next contest against the formidable Los Angeles Lakers.
Coach Costello gave his opinion on the schedule.

*"The trouble with professional basketball is you
don't get enough time to practice. You can't prepare
for every game like a college team can. If we had off
tomorrow and played L.A. Tuesday, we could put in
six or seven plays that work and really drill them."⁷*

Despite the tough schedule, the Bucks came through in
front of another sellout crowd at the Milwaukee Arena, and
a national television audience, defeating the Lakers
113-88, on December 21.

It was a close game in the first quarter, which ended
with the Bucks leading, 27-22. The Lakers took the lead
briefly early in the second quarter, but with the score tied
at 33, the Bucks took the lead for good after consecutive

baskets by Lucius Allen, Alcindor, and McGlocklin. The Bucks led 50-42 at the half, and the scoring battle between the two centers, Alcindor and Chamberlain, was tied at 14.

The Bucks came out hot early in the third quarter, getting three quick baskets in the first 1:12 and taking a 56-42 lead. There was an anxious moment for Lakers' fans early in the quarter when Lakers forward Harold ("Happy") Hairston injured his right knee after a collision with Alcindor. He had to be helped off the floor. Fortunately, the injury wasn't serious, and he returned to the game later.

Alcindor scored 14 points in the third quarter, helping the Bucks to a 77-63 lead going into the fourth quarter. There was no letdown in the fourth quarter with the Bucks outscoring the Lakers 36-25 for an impressive 113-88 win.

After the game, Lakers' coach Joe Mullaney compared his team's effort to their last meeting in Los Angeles on November 20.

> *"Even though we played atrociously tonight, we could have put a burst on and caught them. The last time they contributed more to our making mistakes. Tonight we contributed more to our mistakes. I thought it was our fault that we played badly. It's not that their defense was bad, but it was our fault."*[8]

The Lakers only shot 36.6 percent from the field, hitting just 34 out of 93 shots, while the Bucks shot a strong 52.2 percent.

Wilt Chamberlain couldn't say enough about the Bucks.

> *"Lew played well. He is playing better than ever. I can't figure it out. The two worst games we've*

played all season were against the Bucks. I don't want to take anything away from them, but we don't do good against them. There are teams that are better than others in this league, and you play harder against them. Milwaukee is one of them."[9]

Jerry West agreed.

"I don't know if it's them or what, but even in the two exhibition games we didn't play well against them. Those and the two league games are almost identical."[10]

Alcindor compared Chamberlain's defensive strategy to their previous meeting.

"Wilt didn't play me the same way that he did in L.A. In that game he would come out on me and then drop back. This time, I faced him and simply concentrated more on my shooting in the second half."[11]

Alcindor led the Bucks with 37 points, along with 16 rebounds, and Robertson added 19. Chamberlain had 25 points and 14 rebounds, Hairston was right behind with 21, and West had 19.

GAME 33—BUCKS REPEL WARRIORS:
BUCKS 131, WARRIORS 111

After playing four games in four days, the Bucks got a well-deserved four days off to celebrate the Christmas holidays. They returned to the hardwood floor of the Milwaukee Arena on Saturday evening, December 26, before another sellout crowd. They defeated the San Francisco Warriors, 131-111.

The well-rested Bucks burst out of the locker room on fire. They jumped out to an early 14-point lead and led at the end of the first quarter, 39-26. They built the lead up to 20 points during the second quarter only to have the Warriors narrow the score to 70-57 at halftime.

Early in the third quarter, the Warriors cut the advantage to 78-73, but the Bucks made a major run, scoring eight straight baskets, three of them by Greg Smith, taking a 104-83 lead into the fourth quarter. Costello played his bench extensively in the fourth quarter and the Bucks rolled to a 133-111 win.

The Bucks' defense had an amazing defensive feat—they held high-scoring forward Jerry Lucas scoreless for the first time in his career. There was discussion in the locker room about what kind of defense to use against Lucas. Greg Smith commented:

> *"Oscar Robertson mentioned something to me before we went onto the floor. He said to play right up on his right arm so he had to go to his left."*[12]

Robertson had been a teammate of Lucas with the Royals and knew that.

> *"Luke likes his right hook; he hardly ever uses his left hand. Half of defense is keeping a man from getting the ball, and that's what Greg did to him."*[13]

After the game, Lucas said:

> *"It was one of those freak nights. I just couldn't get my hands on the ball. If I stayed outside, the ball came off the board too close. If I went to the board, it would bounce way out. Every place I went was the wrong place."*[14]

Lucas also gave credit to Greg Smith for holding him scoreless for the first time in his career.

"Other people have tried to stick to my right the way Smith did, but none of them ever did it as well."[15]

Smith did such a great job denying Lucas the ball that he only got four shots in 29 minutes and spent most of the second half on the bench.

Coach Costello was pleased with the Bucks' performance, saying it was...

"...one of our best games of the season. We played good, sound basketball—on offense and on defense. We had to be playing defense—we shut Lucas out."[16]

Costello went into more depth:

"Greg was really hustling, and things like that give us a spark. I think just as big a spark was the way Oscar was advancing the ball. When he's running, we're at our best. We ran good last night, like you should, filling the lanes, good ball handling, excellent passing."[17]

Warriors' center Nate Thurmond spoke highly about Alcindor.

"He's without doubt the premier center in basketball today. I notice improvement in his play every time I see him. He's getting better position for that hook of his, and there's no way you can stop it."[18]

Alcindor had 34 points and grabbed 15 rebounds, Robertson chipped in with 22 points, and McGlocklin had 20 points. Nate Thurmond had a good game, scoring 25 along with 10 rebounds. Joe Ellis was close behind with 21, and sharp-shooting guard Ron Williams added 19. The Warriors were also hurt by the limited services of Jeff Mullins, who wore a plastic protective over his face because of a broken cheekbone and was also dealing with a pre-game attack of gastritis. He still played 27 minutes, scoring 12 points.

GAME 34—BUCKS ROUT ROYALS:
BUCKS 137, ROYALS 114

After a day off, the Bucks played on Monday, December 28, the first of five games scheduled for Madison's Dane County Coliseum, against the Cincinnati Royals. The Bucks got revenge for an earlier loss to the Royals, burying them, 137-114.

Hot shooting was the name of the game for the Bucks. In the first quarter, they connected on 16 of 23 field goal attempts, a 69 percent figure, and led 41-32 at the end of the quarter. There was no letup as they shot 61 percent in the second quarter, hitting 14 out of 23, and led 74-58 at halftime.

Costello was happy with the Bucks' performance.

> *"I liked our first half, which was pretty darn good. Dandridge never gave Green (Johnny) a chance to get any life. We changed matchups because last time he (Dandridge) and Greg were switched around on assignments. I don't know what Van Arsdale's problem was, but Greg did all right on him."*[19]

Greg Smith agreed with Costello's analysis.

> *"I don't think it was what any guy did. We played a good half and got a big jump on them. After that it was a running game, a lot of turnovers."*[20]

The Bucks led 106-86 going into the fourth quarter.

With 8:57 left in the game and the Bucks ahead, 115-91, a melee occurred. Lucius Allen punched Nate Archibald, and Archibald never returned to the game. After the game, Allen talked about what provoked the incident.

"They had been grabbing on my arm all night long. I just had to protect myself. Archibald got me in the stomach with an elbow, and it had been building up the whole game, so I lost my composure and hit him with my fist. I'm sorry about it now, but at the time it seemed like the only thing to do. It just happened to be Nate that I hit. I didn't want to hurt anybody, but I just had to let it out."[21]

Archibald needed two stitches near his ear from Royals Trainer Joe ("Doc") Keefe to close the cut.

Royals coach Bob Cousy commented on the incident.

"It was a sucker punch. I found that players have a way of dealing with guys who do that. I think guys who like to do that get reputations and the players take care of them."[22]

When Allen was told of Cousy's comments, he responded,

"Maybe they do take care of guys like that, but I'm not that type of player. I was provoked, and I feel bad about it."[23]

Another unusual incident happened later in the fourth quarter. With the Bucks ahead, 117-92, Flynn Robinson was going to the free throw line in a bonus situation. Game officials Jerry Loeber and Mike DiTomasso forgot to give him the bonus shot. The Bucks got the rebound, and Alcindor scored a basket. The Royals protested, and it was upheld.

Much to the dismay of the crowd, Alcindor's basket was taken away, and Robinson was given the free throw. These two incidents got the Royals going. They scored nine straight points, making the score 117-101. The Bucks got moving again and cruised to a 137-114 win.

After the game, Coach Cousy said,

> *"We played badly, but that was primarily because Milwaukee played well. Usually we're a pretty unselfish team, but tonight we started to play like one. We started to take the quick shot, started dribbling and we didn't move without the ball. When we don't move, we're not a good team."*[24]

In the other locker room, Costello said,

> *"I thought it was a sloppy game. The first half was played well, but when two teams are running so much, it becomes a real scatter game."*[25]

The Bucks had balanced scoring. Alcindor led with 29 points and 15 rebounds, Smith matched his career high with 26 along with 13 rebounds, Dandridge had 23, and Robertson 22. Flynn Robinson led the Royals with 22, and three players had 14: Van Arsdale, Archibald, and Charlie Paulk.

GAME 35—MILWAUKEE SLAYS CLEVELAND:
BUCKS 119, CAVALIERS 97

The largest turnout of the season, 7,652 fans, packed the Cleveland Arena on Tuesday, December 28, to watch, hopefully, their Cavaliers win another game. Two nights earlier they had defeated the Philadelphia 76ers, 114-101, for their first victory against an established NBA team, and with their win over Buffalo before the 76ers game,

Cleveland had a two-game winning streak. Cavaliers coach Bill Fitch was excited about the opportunity to have a three-game winning streak.

> *"It's great to have a streak like this going, but I'd feel better if we didn't have to play Milwaukee."*[26]

Fitch was right on his analysis as the Bucks burst the Cavaliers' dream with an impressive 119-97 win.

The Cavaliers stayed close for the first quarter and were behind 29-23 going into the second quarter. The Bucks' defense held the Cavs to only 19 points in the second quarter and had a 59-42 lead at halftime. The rout continued in the second half, and the Bucks led, 92-63, after three quarters.

Early in the fourth quarter, with the score 100-65, Costello started using his bench extensively. He only played one or two of his starters at the same time, and Alcindor sat out the last ten minutes. Cleveland made a comeback, outscoring the Bucks during one stretch 20-5, but still came out on the short end of a 119-97 game.

Coach Fitch was very impressed with the Bucks.

> *"With Lew Alcindor in the middle, they can kill you both ways. All they have to do on offense is get the ball to him, and they can gamble on defense because he's in there. They're just too much. He's the reason Milwaukee is such a great defensive club. They're smart enough to play aggressively with him in there because even if you get by your man, you've got to lick City Hall when you get to the basket. They can make a lot of mistakes and still cover for each other."*[27]

Fitch went on to compare the Bucks and the Knicks:

"People talk about the big guy scoring, but he hurts you on defense quite a bit. Their guys up front have a little more room to gamble. I'd see Lucius Allen or somebody overplay one of our guys, but when we got a shot, there was Lew in the way. Milwaukee is smart enough to play aggressive defense because the big guy is there. The Bucks and the Knicks play very sound defense, better than anybody for the same reason. They're both strong in the middle. That's why the Knicks have success against the Bucks, though, because Willis Reed hits from outside and can make Lew come out."[28]

The Bucks continued their hot shooting, hitting on 48 of 87 shots for 55.4 percent. Costello was pleased with his team's performance.

"We had three good quarters. Our defense was terrific, Greg Smith got some good steals and fast breaks, and McGlocklin did a good job."[29]

The Bucks were led in scoring by Dandridge and Alcindor, who each had 23 points, Greg Smith had 20 points, and McGlocklin added 18 points. John Johnson led Cleveland with 22 points.

GAME 36—PHILLY FLATTENS BUCKS: 76ERS 119, BUCKS 107

So Cleveland beat Philadelphia, the Bucks routed Cleveland, and when the Bucks played the 76ers, it should have been an easy victory, right? Wrong! The Bucks lost to Philadelphia, 119-107.

As if the schedule weren't enough to deal with—three games in three days in three different cities—the Bucks had to deal with travel issues. They woke up at 6:30 A.M. to get ready to catch their flight from Cleveland to

Philadelphia. Their plane experienced mechanical trouble, and they sat in the plane for an hour and a half before taking off.

On December 30, 14,835 fans packed the Spectrum, the largest crowd there since a game against the Celtics in March of 1969, to watch the Bucks- Sixers game. Coach Jack Ramsay was pleased with the turnout:

> *"It's nice to have the noise. It makes you feel good. This is what they mean by home court advantage. It's no home court edge if only 3,000 are around. Players get a big lift on a night like this. Our guys responded with what's probably their best game of the season. So much of this game is desire, or call it emotion. When you play Milwaukee or New York, you want to bust your tail out there. Our guys did that tonight."*[30]

The Bucks fell behind, 9-0, and it took them over three minutes to get their first basket on a Jon McGlocklin jumper. They came back in the game very quickly. Trailing 15-6, they outscored Philadelphia 15-1, and they had a 29-24 lead at the end of the first quarter. Early in the second quarter, the Bucks built their lead to 35-26, but the 76ers had a big surge, and they led, 65-55, at halftime.

The second quarter also featured a near fight between Alcindor and reserve forward Bailey Howell. Howell was not pleased with an elbow he took from Alcindor, and he swung at Lew and missed. Luckily, peace was restored before Alcindor could respond, and things didn't get out of hand.

There must have been a rousing halftime speech in the Bucks' locker room. They tied the game at 70, and with five minutes gone in the third quarter, they held a 78-72 lead. The see-saw game continued as Philadelphia out-scored the Bucks, 15-7, and took an 87-85 lead into the fourth quarter.

The Bucks tied the score at 87, but Dennis Awtrey's three-point play gave the Sixers the lead. The foul was on Alcindor, his fifth, and he went to the bench for more than four and a half minutes.

Ramsay was very pleased with Awtrey's performance:

"He played the ball well. He gambled and denied Alcindor position. Some lobs went over him for easy layups, but he deflected a lot of passes too. We went through them and got the good shots. Even when Lew came back in we got better as a team. It was a big game for us."[31]

Sharp-shooting guard Jon McGlocklin. (Lulloff collection)

Alcindor returned to the game with 5:27 left with the Sixers ahead, 105-99, but Billy Cunningham and Hal Greer got hot and took a 112-100 lead with 3:40 left in the game. In the next two and a half minutes, all the Bucks got was a basket from Greg Smith, and with 1:09 left, they trailed 118-102. Costello played his bench the rest of the game, which ended with the Bucks losing, 119-107.

Costello didn't have much good to say about his team's performance.

"We hardly played at all. We gave them too many good shots. Their guards (Hal Greer and Archie Clark) got wide open. If they'd been really hitting we'd have been beaten by more than 30 points."[32]

Costello did not take playing Philadelphia as an easy game.

"We knew they'd be tough. They're always tough for us. They're a good ball club. We just didn't play well defensively, that's all. We were very, very bad."[33]

Despite his foul trouble, Alcindor led the Bucks with 30 points, Robertson had 23, and Greg Smith tossed in 20. Billy Cunningham paced the Sixers with 35, which included 17 of 17 from the charity stripe. Greer and Clark scored 19 each, and Awtrey added 17 points and 17 rebounds.

GAME 37—BUCKS CRUSH CAVALIERS:
BUCKS 118, CAVALIERS 73

The Bucks' first game of 1971 took place on January 2 before a sellout crowd at the Milwaukee Arena against the Cleveland Cavaliers. The only good thing going for Cleveland was the wit of their coach Bill Fitch as the Bucks won big, 118-73.

Things got out of hand early as the Bucks took a 26-16 lead after the first quarter and built it up to 54-39 at the half. Their defense and fast break were a big part of the third quarter as they outscored the Cavs, 29-14, and took an 83-53 lead into the fourth quarter.

It was garbage time for the remainder of the game as the starting lineups were on the bench for both teams for almost the entire quarter. Lucius Allen and Bob Boozer had good games, and the Bucks ran away with it.

Cavaliers' coach Bill Fitch had plans for his team when they returned home.

> "We were so bad that we're going to find a gym in Cleveland tomorrow, or maybe my backyard, and see if we can do something together. There must be somebody charitable enough who saw this game on television back home to take us in. If not, I need my driveway shoveled anyway."[34]

Despite the loss, Fitch was optimistic:

> "At least when you hit rock bottom, there's only one way to go, and this was rock bottom. After a while you get 'lose-itis' and things just get worse. This has to be the worst we've played."[35]

It was a special night for the Cavaliers' John Johnson, though. The game was his night. Johnson graduated from Milwaukee Messmer High School, where he was All-State, and went to the University of Iowa, where he was All-Big Ten. He was the first player selected by the Cavaliers in the draft and was making a transition in the pros playing guard, after playing forward in college. Johnson, who had a good game earlier in the week against the Bucks, had trouble in this game.

"It was all in my mind. I told myself not to rush my shots, but I started missing and I got discouraged, plus I had a pretty good game against Milwaukee in Cleveland the other night and I don't think Costello liked that very much. I imagine he was out to stop me, because Oscar Robertson was on me pretty good. I'm very proud that they had this night for me, but I'm sorry I couldn't give them anything to cheer about. I like to come home, but not to play the Bucks. They just won't let up."[36]

Alcindor only played 31 minutes, but he led the Bucks with 27 points and 10 rebounds. Bob Boozer had 17 points and 14 rebounds, and Lucius Allen added 16. The Cavaliers, who shot an ice-cold 33.7 percent from the field, were led by Dave Sorenson's 17 points.

GAME 38—TURNING ON THE JETS:
BUCKS 124, SUPERSONICS 110

On Monday, January 4, the smallest turnout in almost a year, 8,835 fans at the Milwaukee Arena, watched the Bucks defeated the Seattle Supersonics, 124-110. Spencer Haywood played in the game for Seattle, which resulted in the Bucks filing a protest.

Spencer Haywood played on the gold-medal-winning U.S. Olympic basketball team in 1968 and was an All-American the following year at the University of Detroit. He decided to go professional and signed a contract with the American Basketball Association's Denver Rockets. He later left the Rockets and signed a contract with Seattle. The problem was by NBA rules, Haywood was ineligible to play until his college class graduated, which would occur at the end of the 1971 season.

In Haywood's first two games in the NBA, he played against Chicago and Portland. Both teams protested, claiming he was ineligible. If Haywood suited up for the Bucks game, they would likely follow suit.

In addition to the Haywood situation, the Sonics had another issue: getting to Milwaukee to play the game. They departed Seattle on Sunday but couldn't land in Milwaukee because of a snowstorm. They landed in Cleveland, waited for five hours, and took an eight-hour bus ride to Milwaukee. They made it at 5:30 A.M., 14 and a half hours later than planned.

The game was tied at 28 at the end of the first quarter, but the Bucks had a great second quarter. Early in the second quarter, with the game tied at 33, Dandridge scored seven points and Alcindor four, helping the Bucks to a 48-39 lead, which they expanded to 62-49 at halftime.

At the beginning of the second half, Haywood got his first playing time in the NBA. After the game, Sonics coach Lenny Wilkens explained why he decided to play him:

> *"Let's face it, we had won four in a row until tonight. Do you sit somebody down when he's been doing a good job for you and you're winning? No, I was waiting for the right spot to use him, and I decided that the start of the second half was the spot. I wasn't surprised at how good he looked, and I think he'll get better. Anyone who lays off that long is bound to be rusty."*[37]

Bucks' coach Larry Costello commented:

> *"I was surprised. I didn't think they would play him. I think if the game had been close they wouldn't have. They wouldn't have wanted to take a chance of losing on a protest."*[38]

Costello could see a reason to play Haywood.

"If you're going to dress a guy, you might as well play him. Why pay him if you're not going to play him? After all, dressing him amounts to the same thing as playing him. You don't make a practice of having ineligible players sitting around in uniform."[39]

Haywood's play on the court didn't help get the Sonics back in the game. He played the entire second half, making five of 13 shots, scored 14 points, and grabbed nine rebounds. He missed a dunk, hit a rebound basket over Alcindor, and got called for goaltending when he blocked a shot by Alcindor. The Sonics were down by as many as 20 in the third quarter and took the 124-110 loss.

After the game, Haywood talked about playing in the NBA:

"You better believe I was tired. All I've had was two days of practice with this team. I've been going to court all the time. I know I haven't proven myself yet, but I know I can. I love the competition in this league. They'll push me harder in the NBA than they did in the ABA, and I'll become a better player because of it."[40]

Costello's assessment of Haywood was:

"He looked rusty to me, but he has a lot of talent. I'd say if the league made him be up for the draft when his class is graduated he would be the top pick without a doubt. He can jump and do a lot of things."[41]

The NBA's leading scorer, Alcindor, led the Bucks with 38 points and 15 rebounds, Dandridge had 26 points, Robertson 19 points, and McGlocklin 15 points. Former Marquette University star Don Kojis led the Sonics with 24 points, and Lenny Wilkens had 19 points.

The Bucks played the game under protest. Bucks assistant Coach Tom Nissalke informed Wilkens before the game.

The legal battle over Haywood's status went all the way to the United States Supreme Court. In March of 1971, the Court upheld a lower court's ruling that banning Haywood from the NBA would cause him financial hardship and he could continue his career.

GAME 39—BUCKS TAME BULLS:
BUCKS 119, BULLS 106

On Wednesday, January 6, on a chilly evening in Madison, 6,093 fans came to Dane County Coliseum to watch the Bucks play the Bulls. They weren't disappointed as the Bucks came through with a 119-106 win.

The Bulls had a great start. The first quarter ended with Alcindor called for his third foul, and when Bob Love converted both free throws, the Bulls led, 32-29. Alcindor sat out the entire second quarter, but the Bucks' bench came through in a big way. Lucius Allen, Bob Boozer, and Dick Cunningham sparked the Bucks. They went on an 18-6 run, going ahead 47-38, and led, 57-49, at halftime.

Costello was very proud of the job the bench did in Alcindor's absence:

"Our reserves, particularly Allen, gave us a big lift. They were running. Boozer did a good job defensively on their big forwards. He's got size and can match up with them. Allen gave us the spark in the second quarter. He makes us move better than any

guard we've got now. One thing you can't beat is
speed. If you don't have it, you're struggling."[42]

Bulls' coach Dick Motta talked about his team's performance:

"If there was ever a night for us to beat the Bucks,
this was it. We had them playing our kind of game
in the first quarter instead of letting them run like
they like to do, and when Lew got into foul trouble,
we really had hopes. Maybe we got too confident
when Lew went out, but whatever the reason,
Cunningham attacked us all by himself. He gave
them a change of pace, he hit the boards, and he
set good screens. I like Cunningham. He's an
excellent backup man, and he always plays well
against us. He did the same thing to us the last
time we played the Bucks. (in Milwaukee on
December 3) *This was the worst rebounding we've*
ever had against Milwaukee. The second quarter
was an eternity."[43]

After the game, Costello was asked if the Bucks' slow start
could be because they were looking ahead to tomorrow's
game against the Knicks.

"I wasn't thinking about New York at all, and I
don't think the guys were either. Oh, I've been
thinking about the Knicks since the last loss
to them, but Chicago was my immediate
problem."[44]

There was no letdown in the third quarter. The Bucks shot
65 percent, hitting 13 of 20 shots, and outscored the Bulls
in the first 9:58 of the quarter to take their biggest lead at
88-63. The Bulls made a comeback in the fourth quarter.
Bob Love sparked the Bulls, at one-point scoring seven
straight points, and they trailed, 111-100 with 2:39

remaining. Alcindor and Allen scored consecutive baskets to give the Bucks more breathing room, and they went on to a 119-107 victory.

Alcindor led the Bucks with 24 points along with nine rebounds, Robertson was right behind with 23 points and ten assists, and McGlocklin added 14 points. The bench contributed with Boozer adding 15 points, nine rebounds, and five blocked shots, while Allen had 10 points and six assists. Bob Love led the Bulls with 29 points, Chet Walker had 17 points, Sloan added 16 points, and Tom Boerwinkle had 12 points and 13 rebounds.

GAME 40—BUCKS KNOCK KNICKS:
BUCKS 116, KNICKS 106

On January 7, before a sellout crowd at the Milwaukee Arena, the Bucks beat their nemesis team, the New York Knicks, 116-106.

This game meant a lot to the Bucks. Jon McGlocklin commented:

> *"We were pointing toward this one. It's just the way you feel, a kind of confidence and enthusiasm. It was obvious in the locker room before the game. The guys were more serious. There was a lot of positive thinking. We felt ready and the final score bore it out."*[45]

In a close game with the Bucks ahead, 21-16, Alcindor picked up his second and third fouls just seconds apart and went to the bench. Oscar Robertson scored 11 points in the quarter, and the Bucks took a 28-22 lead to the second quarter. With 4:30 left in the second quarter with the Bucks ahead, 43-38, Alcindor came off the bench, and his two baskets helped the Bucks to a 51-48 lead at halftime.

Ten of the Bucks' first 13 points of the third quarter were scored by Alcindor, and the Bucks maintained their lead. With 3:30 left in the quarter and the Bucks winning, 70-65, Alcindor picked up his fifth foul and went back to the bench. Robertson stepped up and filled the void. He hit a 12-footer, an 18-footer, stole the ball, got an assist on a McGlocklin basket, and hit a 15-foot jumper. This helped the Bucks to an 80-72 lead going into the fourth quarter.

The Bucks withstood a number of Knicks challenges to their lead in the fourth quarter. They were winning, 97-89, with 6:22 remaining, but baskets by Reed and Frazier trimmed the lead to 97-93. Robertson hit two free throws, but Dave Stallworth answered back with a jumper. With 5:11 on the clock, Smith and Alcindor scored baskets and Boozer had a free throw. Cazzie Russell scored for the Knicks, but Smith and Dandridge scored baskets, putting the Bucks up 108-97.

The Knicks made another comeback. With 2:05 left and trailing 110-98, they scored six straight points on a Dave DeBusschere jumper, a basket by Frazier, and a Barnett free throw. Dandridge was assessed a technical foul, and Frazier's free throw made it 110-104 with 1:10 on the clock.

With 53 seconds left, Alcindor went to the foul line for three to make two and missed all three. Fortunately, Lucius Allen got the rebound and hit a 10-footer. The Knicks answered with 28 seconds left on a Dick Barnett basket. The Bucks put the game away on a layup by Dandridge with 21 seconds left, and Robertson hit a pair of free throws, giving the Bucks the 116-106 win.

After the game, there was agreement about Robertson's great game. Knicks guard Dick Barnett said:

> *"You can boil the game down to two words—Oscar Robertson. He did a lot of things out there and all of them hurt us. He shot more than he did the last times we played against them. He hit the open man, he made the Bucks offense go. When Alcindor got into foul trouble, Oscar just took over the show and ran it until the end of the game. He looked as though he was charged up tonight."*[46]

Willis Reed also spoke highly of Robertson:

> *"The Big O did it all tonight. He played like the guy I used to see when I was a rookie in this league seven years ago. He can still run a ball club and he can still shoot that ball. Some people have been saying that he's fat and out of shape, but he didn't look that way to me."*[47]

There was also high praise for Robertson in the Bucks' locker room. Alcindor talked about the Big O.

> *"He took over the game when I was gone and gave the Bucks a big help. He played an excellent game.*[48]

Larry Costello agreed with Alcindor's analysis.

> *"He was fantastic offensively. I was never so happy to see him take charge. I want him to do that even when Lew is in there. He's too good a shooter not to be doing what he can do best."*[49]

What were Robertson's own thoughts about this big game?

> *"I didn't feel any particular pressure myself. It was just another game to me. When Lew went out, I had to play more like I did at Cincinnati. We had to set*

*more picks, and Dick (Cunningham) can do it. He's
big, he's broad, he's a natural for the job. My best
game? I don't know. Points mean a lot, but they
don't mean everything."*[50]

There was a lot of agreement about what a big win it was
for the Bucks. Larry Costello said,

*"It means a lot in many ways. Psychologically, it
helps. If we would have lost, it wouldn't have
meant we couldn't beat the Knicks again, but it
sure helps to win."*[51]

Guard Jon McGlocklin thought,

*"It was a must game as far as our own pride was
concerned."*[52]

Back-up center Dick Cunningham, who played a key role
filling in for foul-plagued Alcindor, commented:

*"That win was a big part of our season. We had to
have this one. If this doesn't give us a lift, nothing
will."*[53]

Robertson had a huge game, scoring 35 points, along with
13 assists and nine rebounds. Even though his playing
time was limited to 25 minutes, Alcindor had 24 points
and seven rebounds, Dandridge added 17 points and ten
rebounds, and McGlocklin scored 13. Walt Frazier led the
Knicks with 23, and right behind was DeBusschere with
22. Willis Reed, who had spent time in a New York hospital
recovering from the flu and abdominal pains, had 19
points and seven rebounds. Reed commented:

*"I just didn't have the extra effort tonight. Against
Alcindor you need the extra effort. I was trying
though."*[54]

Right next door to the Milwaukee Arena, at the Milwaukee Auditorium, fans who were unable to get tickets for the game had the opportunity to watch a closed circuit, color telecast of the game. Tickets were $5 for adults and $3 for students and children. Cameras in the Arena transmitted the action on the court, and Bucks' announcer Eddie Doucette's radio call was used for the audio. The Bucks were thinking of showing some playoff games utilizing this setup. Attendance was around 2,500, and most were disappointed with the picture quality. This ended up being the only occasion where the Bucks tried this approach.

Bucks	FG-FGA	FT-FTA	Rebs.	Pts	Knicks	FG-FGA	FT-FTA	Rebs.	Pts.
Alcindor	11-22	2-6	13	24	Barnett	7-12	1-1	2	15
Allen	4-7	0-0	3	8	Bradley	3-9	1-1	1	7
Boozer	3-7	1-2	6	7	DeBusschere	9-13	4-5	11	22
Cunningham	1-7	0-0	5	2	Frazier	9-18	5-6	1	23
Dandridge	6-18	5-7	10	17	Jackson	2-3	1-1	4	5
McGlocklin	6-9	1-1	1	13	Reed	9-19	1-3	7	19
Robertson	11-19	13-15	9	35	Riordan	0-1	0-0	0	0
Smith	5-10	0-0	11	10	Russell	1-5	2-2	2	4
					Stallworth	5-8	1-2	6	11

Game 40 Box Score

GAME 41—BUCKS POUND PISTONS:
BUCKS 118, PISTONS 100

The Bucks enjoyed a day off after their big win over the Knicks and were back in action in front of a sellout crowd at the Milwaukee Arena Saturday, January 9, against the team closest to them in the division standings, the Detroit Pistons. After a slow start, the Bucks came through with a decisive 118-100 win.

The game started as a blowout as the Bucks built up an 11-point lead at 20-9. The Pistons made a comeback, tying the score and trailing 30-28 at the end of the first quarter. The Bucks outscored the Pistons 25-12 in the beginning of the second quarter, but Detroit made another comeback and trailed 62-56 at halftime.

Costello analyzed the first half after the game:

> *"We started real well, running right away from them, then we lost our aggressiveness. They capitalized on our turnovers and they kept getting back into the game when they shouldn't have."*[55]

The Bucks broke the game open in the third quarter and took a 90-73 lead into the fourth quarter. One of the big reasons for the Bucks' surge was Bob Dandridge. He only had two points in the first half but had a good second half. Costello commented on his play:

> *"He* [Dandridge] *had a bad first half, but he came back and rebounded very well for us. He was a great player in the second half."*[56]

In the fourth quarter, Dandridge and Lucius Allen helped the Bucks take a 22-point lead, only to have the Pistons mount yet another comeback, making the score 107-95. The Bucks put the game away, outscoring Detroit 11-5 en route to a 118-100 victory.

Pistons' coach Bill van Breda Kolff was unhappy with his team's play.

> *"We didn't get that far playing like this. You can't play poor games against a good team, and we played a poor game."*[57]

Costello was pleased with the win.

> *"It was a big game for us. It puts us seven games up in the loss column and that's the important one*

because those are the ones you can't go back and play again. It's like winning two games any time you beat somebody in your division, and to beat Detroit again, the second-place team."[58]

Alcindor led the Bucks with 27 points, 14 rebounds, and 10 assists, Robertson had 24 points, and Lucius Allen had a season-high 20. Dandridge, despite the bad first half, ended up with 14. The Pistons were led by Dave Bing with 25, and Bob Lanier had 17 points and 11 rebounds.

This game marked the end of the first half of the regular season, with the Bucks at 34-7. Responding to a question about the Bucks' performance, Costello answered:

"I never really had any figures in mind. Sure, I thought about it. I thought about 41-0, but naturally I'm pleased. You've got to utilize the talent you have or you're not going to win in this league. You don't win games on paper. It figures to get tougher as we go along, though. The other teams are in better shape than they were, and if we don't need some games near the end, it will be hard to get them up night after night."[59]

Endnotes to Chapter 9

1) Bob Wolf, " Costello's Lecture Arouses Bucks," *Milwaukee Journal*, December 21, 1970, pt. 2, p. 12.

2) *Ibid.*

3) Rel Bochat, "Bucks Get the Message, And Buffalo Gets Blitzed," *Milwaukee Sentinel*, December 21, 1970, pt. 2, p. 1.

4) *Ibid.*

5) *Ibid.*

6) Bob Wolf, December 21, 1970.

7) Bob Hill, "Bucks Wake Up After Slow Start," *Wisconsin State Journal*, December 21, 1970, pt. 2, p. 1.

8) Bob Hill, "Alcindor's Elbows Win in the Battle of Giants," *Wisconsin State Journal*, March 22, 1970, pt. 3, p. 1.

9) Rel Bochat, "Bucks Trim Lakers," *Milwaukee Sentinel*, December 22, 1970, pt. 2, p. 1.

10) *Ibid.*

11) "Lakers Bow to Bucks as Lew Gets 37 Points," *Los Angeles Times*, December 22, 1970, pt. 3, p. 2.

12) Bob Wolf, "Bucks Stymie Lucas and Win," *Milwaukee Journal*, December 27, 1970, pt. 3, p. 1.

13) *Ibid.*

14) *Ibid.*

15) John Devaney, *Alcindor and the Big O* (New York: Lancer Books, 1971), 142.

16) Glenn Miller, "Bucks Have a Holiday," *Wisconsin State Journal*, December 27, 1970, pt. 3, p. 1.

17) Rel Bochat, "Bucks Sharp, Set For Cincy Tonight," *Milwaukee Sentinel*, December 28, 1970, pt. 2, p.1.

18) Wolf. December 27.

19) Rel Bochat, "Bucks Batter Royals In Rough Duel, 137-114," *Milwaukee Sentinel*, December 29, 1970, pt. 2, p. 1

20) *Ibid.*

21) Bob Wolf, "Bucks Win, Show Punch," *Milwaukee Journal*, December 29, 1970, pt. 2, p. 10.

22) Bob Hill, "Lucius Sneaks One In," *Wisconsin State Journal*, December 29, 1970, pt. 2, p. 1.

23) Wolf. December 29, p. 10.

24) Hill. December 29, p. 2.

25) *Ibid.*

26) Bob Wolf, "Bucks Burst Cleveland's Bubble," *Milwaukee Journal*, December 30, 1970, pt. 1, p. 19.

27) *Ibid.*

28) Rel Bochat, "Bucks in Title Form, Gun Down Cavaliers," *Milwaukee Sentinel*, December 30, 1970, pt. 2, p. 1.

29) *Ibid.*

30) Rel Bochat, "14,835 76er Fans Sit In on Bucks' Execution, 119-107," *Milwaukee Sentinel*, December 31, 1970, pt. 2, p. 1.

31) *Ibid.*

32) Rel Bochat, "Costello Raps 'Do Nothing' Play," *Milwaukee Sentinel*, January 1, 1971, pt. 2, p. 1

33) Bob Wolf, "Bucks Victim as 76ers Rebound From Upset," *Milwaukee Journal*, December 31, 1970, pt. 1, p. 17

34) Bob Wolf, "Bucks' Romp Fails to Dull Wit of Fitch," *Milwaukee Journal*, January 3, 1971, pt. 2, p. 1.

35) *Ibid.*

36) *Ibid.*

37) Bob Wolf, "Bucks Win, and Protest," *Milwaukee Journal*, January 5, 1971, pt. 2, p. 11.

38) Bob Hill, "Bucks Win, Still Protest," *Wisconsin State Journal*, January 5, 1971, pt. 3, p. 1.

39) Wolf. January 5.

40) Rel Bochat, "Welcome to the NBA, Haywood!" *Milwaukee Sentinel*, January 5, 1971, pt. 2, p. 1.

41) *Ibid.*

42) Tom Butler, "Bucks Breeze Past Bulls," *Wisconsin State Journal*, January 7, 1971, pt. 2, p. 1.

43) Bob Wolf, "Cunningham Sparks Bucks," *Milwaukee Journal*, January 7, 1971, pt. 2, p. 15.

44) Rel Bochat, "Bucks Put 119-106 Bite On Bulls," *Milwaukee Sentinel*, January 7, 1971, pt. 2, p. 1.

45) Jim Slocum, "Knicks Give 'O' Oscar Award," *Milwaukee Sentinel*, January 8, 1971, pt. 2, p. 1.

46) *Ibid.*

47) Thomas Rogers, "Robertson Stars With 35 Points," *New York Times*, January 8, 1971, p. 23.

48) Slocum, p. 4.

49) *Ibid.*

50) Bob Wolf, Big O Big Enough to Tip Knicks," *Milwaukee Journal*, January 8, 1971, pt. 2, p. 15.

51) Bob Hill, "Bucks' Big O Fouls Up the Knicks," *Wisconsin State Journal*, January 8, 1971, pt. 2, p. 2.

52) Wolf. January 8, p. 15.

53) Oscar Robertson, *The Big O: My Life, My Times, My Game* (Emmaus, PA: Rodale Inc., 2003), p. 261.

54) Rogers, p. 23.

55) Glenn Miller, "Bucks Are Halfway Home," *Wisconsin State Journal*, January 10, 1971, pt. 3, p. 1.

56) *Ibid.*

57) Bob Wolf, "Bucks Win, Set Record Pace," *Milwaukee Journal*, January 10, 1971, pt. 2, p. 2.

58) Miller. p. 1.

59) Wolf. p. 2.

CHAPTER 10

THE SECOND SEASON
HALF BEGINS

GAME 42—BASKET-BREAKING BLOWOUT:
BUCKS 151, BULLETS 99

Forty-one games were in the books, and 41 remained as the Bucks rolled into the second half of the 1970-71 regular season with a 34-7 record. The Bucks' record was being followed by many to see if they could surpass the NBA's best regular-season mark of 68-13, accomplished by the 1966-67 Philadelphia 76ers. The question of an asterisk being applied if the Bucks broke the record was brought up. The Bucks were scheduled to play 82 games, while the 76ers played 81.

The Bucks opened the second half of the season on a cold Sunday evening on January 10, 1971, at home, in front of another sellout crowd versus the Baltimore Bullets. The Bucks undoubtedly remembered their 30-point loss, 127-97, at Baltimore on December 9, and came out with a vengeance. They ran up a 38-19 lead after one period and never looked back, humiliating the visitors, 151-99. Obviously, Costello was extremely pleased:

> *"It's the first time we've really exploded offensively. It was a magnificent performance, with great defense as well. Everybody played a great game."*[1]

When asked if the Bucks remembered the earlier 30-point humiliation, Costello replied,

> *"Of course we remembered that one. They (the Bullets) will remember this one too. Nobody likes to get beat by margins like that. We're pros, and these guys have pride. We just put everything together tonight."*[2]

At halftime, the Bucks led, 70-38, and extended the margin to 43,108-65, going into the fourth quarter. After the game, Dick Cunningham commented:

> *"The amazing thing about it was that it was actually garbage time from the second quarter on. We were so far ahead and yet we kept playing as well as ever. Lew was so fast, he kept going past Unseld like Wes was standing still. If we played like this every night, we'd be 82-0."*[3]

There was even more excitement ahead. With ten minutes left in the game and the score 116-70, Bullets' forward Gus Johnson intercepted a Bucks pass at midcourt. He took off just inside the free throw line and went in for a dunk. It would be more than a dunk. The force of Johnson's right arm had yanked the basket from its foundation, put a gaping hole in the backboard, and shattered the glass, which sprinkled all over the floor, causing a 30-minute delay until replacement with a new basket took place.

Johnson recalled the shattering moment.

> *"As soon as I hit it tonight, I knew the board was gone. I tried to run away and closed my eyes, and I hoped Lucius Allen got out of the way too. I wound up with a headful of glass, but I was more worried about my arm. There's a big knot on it near the wrist."*[4]

Maintenance person's thoughts: "When was the last time I did this?" (Author's collection)

The entire crowd was thrilled, let out a roar, and the players were excited also. Alcindor jumped on his bench chair and waved his arm above his head. After the game, Alcindor said,

> *"It was a thrill. I've always been a fan of his. He gives that special kind of effort. I saw him do it one time on TV when I was in high school."*[5]

Costello summed up the Bucks' performance:

> *"We were magnificent tonight. Our offense hadn't reached its potential until tonight. We've been playing good defense, but this time we put it all together."*[6]

When Costello was asked why Alcindor was playing in the closing minutes, he answered,

> *"I wanted to see how he would work together with our other big guy, Dick Cunningham, playing forward. It worked out pretty good, I'd say."*[6]

Dandridge led the Bucks with 34 points, and Alcindor had 30 along with 17 rebounds; Gus Johnson had 17 to lead the Bullets, and Kevin Loughery and Wes Unseld scored 15 points.

Bucks	FG-FGA	FT-FTA	Rebs.	Pts	Bullets	FG-FGA	FT-FTA	Rebs.	Pts.
Alcindor	13-19	4-5	17	30	Carter	6-13	1-1	3	13
Allen	2-5	2-2	0	6	Gus Johnson	7-18	3-4	7	17
Boozer	4-11	4-5	14	12	Geo Johnson	1-5	0-0	4	2
Cunningham	7-11	0-0	1	14	Loughery	7-14	1-1	2	15
Dandridge	14-20	6-7	8	34	Marin	4-19	2-3	8	10
Freeman	2-4	0-0	1	4	Miles	1-6	1-1	1	3
McGlocklin	7-10	1-1	2	15	Monroe	4-12	1-1	0	9
Robertson	7-14	5-5	4	19	Murrey	0-2	0-3	0	0
Smith	2-6	0-0	8	4	Tresvant	4-6	1-2	6	9
Zopf	5-9	3-4	2	13	Tucker	3-4	0-0	1	6
					Unseld	7-15	1-2	7	15
					Zeller	0-4	0-1	2	0

Game 42 Box Score

GAME 43—BUCKS DRUB ROYALS:
BUCKS 135, ROYALS 116

After a four-day break for the NBA All-Star Game, the Bucks got back to the Milwaukee Arena on Friday, January 15, and in front of another sellout crowd of 10,746, they defeated the Cincinnati Royals, 135-116, for their seventh consecutive win.

Even though the Bucks had a few days off, they still had issues. Oscar Robertson's groin injury was aggravated in the All-Star Game, and he didn't do any running in Thursday's workout.

Bucks' coach Larry Costello worried,

"We may not play Oscar unless we need him. This thing has been going on and on, and we've got to find a solution. We'll see how he is at game time."[8]

If Robertson were unable to start, Lucius Allen would take his place in the lineup. Lew Alcindor also missed Thursday's practice because of another migraine headache but was expected to be ready.

One of the game's most interesting moments happened midway in the first quarter. Alcindor went to the basket for a dunk and was, in the opinion of many people, fouled by Royals center Sam Lacey. However, no foul was called, and a series of technical fouls were given out by referee Jack Madden. The first one was on Alcindor, then coach Costello, and finally one on Robertson. Royals guard Norm Van Lier made two of the three foul shots, giving the Royals a 20-18 lead. The game stayed close for most of the first half with the Bucks leading, 34-30, at the end of the first quarter, expanding it to 66-57 at halftime.

The Bucks came out strong for the second half, scoring the first 11 points for a 77-57 lead. One of the keys to the spurt was Bob Dandridge, who scored five of those 11 points. The lead ballooned to 97-67 before the Bucks let up a little. The Royals trimmed the deficit to 14 points, 115-101, with a little over six minutes left in the game and stayed close, trailing 123-110 with 3:45 left. The Bucks ended the game outscoring the Royals 12-6 for a 135-116 victory.

Oscar Robertson did start and played 28 minutes, connecting on five of six shots from the field, scoring 14 points with five assists. Costello explained about Robertson's Achilles tendon and groin issues.

> *"The doctor told me today that Oscar can't injure the tendon, so he has to play with it. He's favoring it because he has some pain and tenderness, but rest for a game or two isn't the answer. It just stiffens up on him. Maybe a rest over the summer will fix it, but there's nothing we can do about it now. And he has to practice to keep his weight down."*[9]

The Royals were led in scoring by Sam Lacey's 27 points and 18 rebounds. Former Buck Charlie Paulk had 19 points, and ageless wonder Johnny Green chipped in with 17. Alcindor had a big game for the Bucks, scoring 35 points, going 14 out of 17 from the field along with 16 rebounds in 35 minutes of play. Dandridge had 29, and Jon McGlocklin added 16, connecting on 8 of 13 field goal attempts.

After the game, Royals coach Bob Cousy had high praise for Alcindor.

> *"They can talk theory all they want, but if Lew comes to play, we can just go home. He just toyed with us. Let's face it. He can score against us whenever he feels like it. There's no way we can beat these guys when he's playing."*[10]

GAME 44—BUCKS TROUNCE BULLS:
BUCKS 110, BULLS 90

Despite an all-day snowstorm, 14,013 fans, the largest crowd of the season at Chicago Stadium, watched the

Bucks defeat the Bulls, 110-90, for their eighth straight victory, raising their record to 37-7.

The contest was unique in another way; it was officiated by one referee, veteran Mendy Rudolph. Jerry Loeber, the absent referee, lived in New York City like Rudolph, so Loeber probably misunderstood his schedule.

The Bucks led, 29-26, after the first quarter, but three minutes into the second quarter, Alcindor picked up his third foul and sat out the rest of the period. Due to his limited playing time, he only had three points and four rebounds at halftime. The Bulls didn't take advantage of Alcindor being on the bench. Dick Cunningham did a decent job off the bench, and the game was tied at halftime.

With 7:23 remaining in the third quarter and the score tied at 59, the Bucks took control with Alcindor and Robertson leading the way. Lucius Allen talked about the Bucks' duo:

> *"We have two controlling players and we feel it's supposed to happen."*[11]

After the 59-59 tie, they took an 81-72 lead at the end of the third quarter. Alcindor explained his surge by saying,

> *"I was definitely rested and ready to play."*[12]

Bulls' center Tom Boerwinkle was impressed with Alcindor's play.

> *"Lew is a great athlete and he came out in the second half determined to put some points on the board. If you can play him to a standoff, you're lucky."*[13]

Bulls' coach Dick Motta agreed.

> *"I don't think I've ever seen a guy like Alcindor. We just shot our wad and they trampled us. We played about as well as we can play. It was like sending a boy to do a man's job."*[14]

Even though Alcindor sat on the bench for some time in the first half, he still led the Bucks with 25 points, 18 rebounds, and eight assists. Robertson and McGlocklin chipped in with 21 points each. The Bulls were paced by former Buck Bob Love, who led all scorers with 27, and guard Jerry Sloan added 23.

Before the 110-90 rout ended, there was some aggressive play by Sloan. Lucius Allen and Sloan collided, and Allen was not happy.

> *"Sloan just jumped out there and knocked me down. I almost blew up but I caught myself. He's the only guy in the league who does that kind of stuff."*[15]

Former Bull Bob Boozer was also involved in an incident with Sloan.

> *"He grabbed me around my waist, so I threw a light elbow into him. He gets away with murder."*[16]

Coach Motta defended Sloan.

> *"There are 50 incidents a game like that. You hear a lot of lip service, but nobody ever attacks Sloan. Boozer just likes to talk."*[17]

GAME 45—BUCKS TURN BACK CELTICS:
BUCKS 120, CELTICS 113

The strenuous schedule continued for the Bucks as they played their third game in three days against the Boston Celtics in front of another sellout crowd at the Milwaukee Arena on Sunday evening, January 17. The Bucks were lethargic, but they came away with a 120-113 win.

The Bucks likely went into the game overconfident after they learned about the depleted Celtics lineup. Boston had played the night before in Detroit. John Havlicek suffered a thigh muscle injury and would be unable to play against the Bucks. To make matters worse, Celtics guard JoJo White was back in Boston serving an assignment with his Marine Corps Reserve unit.

The Bucks came out flat. Costello was asked if it was a result of Havlicek and White being out. He responded,

"Yes, it's always a problem. There had to be a letdown. I knew before the game that White wouldn't be here. And then we found out Havlicek wouldn't be in uniform. But they're all pros, and I don't care what five they play, you'd better be ready."[18]

Boston led, 60-56, at halftime, due to the Bucks' ice-cold shooting. They shot only 40 percent from the field. It could've been worse, but Alcindor's 18 first-half points kept the Bucks close. Coach Costello agreed.

"He saved us in the first half. We were four points down as it was, and we would've been buried if it hadn't been for him."[19]

No complacency was evident in the third quarter as the Bucks took a six-point lead early in the second half.

Boston came back to tie the score five times in the quarter, but the Bucks led 86-83 going into the fourth quarter.

Early in the fourth quarter, with the Bucks ahead 88-85, they scored 13 straight, taking a 101-85 lead. One of the big plays during the streak was a steal by Alcindor, who dribbled three-quarters of the court for an easy layup.

Game over? No way—as Boston came back, outscoring the Bucks 19-5, closing it to 106-104 with 3:10 left in the game.

With about two and a half minutes left in the game, Alcindor got fouled by Don Chaney. After a discussion by the referees, Alcindor was given three to make two from the foul line. Celtics coach Tommy Heinsohn blew up and received a technical foul, his second of the game, which resulted in his ejection. John Havlicek took over as coach for the remainder of the game. Heinsohn was still angry after the game about Jake O'Donnell's call.

"We played our tails off and that guy took the game away from us."[20]

With 1:42 left on the clock and the Bucks ahead, 111-108, an Alcindor hook shot, a Bob Dandridge steal and layup, and two free throws by Greg Smith gave the Bucks a 117-108 lead. They held on for a 120-113 victory.

Don Nelson paced the Celtics with 29 points, Don Chaney added 21, and Dave Cowens had 19 points and 19 rebounds in a losing effort. Alcindor had 44 points along with 20 rebounds, Bob Dandridge chipped in with 29, and Jon McGlocklin had 23 for the Bucks.

After the game Alcindor talked about the Celtics double, even triple-teaming him every time he got the ball.

"Once I started hitting the guys outside with passes, they started falling off me. That's the best way to get guys off your back, although it only works when the outside men are hitting."[21]

GAME 46—BUCKS DISPATCH BULLETS:
BUCKS 120, BULLETS 116

The Bucks and Bullets had met ten days earlier at the Milwaukee Arena, and now they were set for a rematch at the Baltimore Civic Center. Coach Costello previewed the game:

"I know they haven't forgotten. They'll come back to prove they're better than a team that gets beat by 52 points. That's the way we felt going into that game after getting beat by them by 30 points (127-97) a couple of weeks before. Nobody likes to get beat like that, not if you're a competitor. I look for a real physical game, a tough one. They'll be waiting for us to walk out there."[22]

On Wednesday, January 20, 12,289 fans watched the Bucks win a much closer game than their last two meetings with the Bullets, 120-116, for their 10th consecutive victory. Alcindor had a big game, scoring 39 points, connecting on 17 of 28 shots, grabbing 20 rebounds, and blocking five shots.

After the game, Bullets' coach Gene Shue gave credit to Bob Dandridge. Shue said,

"Let's face it, Alcindor is going to do that every time out. The thing that beat us was letting Dandridge score too many points. We let him get too many easy shots. Dandridge is a good hustling player and an opportunist. He always seems to be at the right place at the right time. But if I had figured

before the game that he would beat us—well, I wouldn't have. The rest of the game went the way we planned, but we didn't stop Dandridge."23

Dandridge had 28 points on 13 of 19 shooting along with five assists, Robertson added 17 points, and Bob Boozer 13. The Bullets had balanced scoring, Earl Monroe with 24, Gus Johnson with 23, and Kevin Loughery with 20.

The game was tied after one quarter at 26, and the Bullets led at halftime, 59-57. Gus Johnson got hot and helped the Bullets to a 70-60 lead midway through the third quarter. Lucius Allen contributed off the bench, and Alcindor, Dandridge, and Boozer brought the Bucks back. Boozer's jumper at the end of the third quarter tied the score at 89.

The game stayed close throughout the fourth quarter. With the game tied at 93, Boozer nailed a three-point play, and Allen added a basket, giving the Bucks a 98-93 lead. Kevin Loughery had a big fourth quarter, scoring 11 of his 20 points, and in one stretch scored seven straight points.

Baltimore cut the Bucks lead to 104-103, but the Bucks went ahead, 109-103. Robertson helped fuel the spurt with a three-point play and a basket. The Bullets cut the Bucks' lead to two points on four occasions. With the score 116-114, Dandridge hit a key turnaround ten-foot jumper, giving the Bucks a 118-114 advantage. Alcindor blocked an Unseld layup with 45 seconds left, and the Bucks held on for a 120-116 win.

Costello liked the Bucks' performance:

"We came back after being down by 10. They pressured us, but we maintained our poise. In fact, the key was our defense getting more aggressive than it has been. We doubled up on them, made some steals and created baskets. They [Bullets] got

a little wild, scattery, and were forced into rushing their shots."[24]

Alcindor talked about the Bullets' defense on him.

"Unseld really plays a physical game against me, and he has to because of his size, but Johnson's even more physical. He could get a job as a hockey puck, that's how strong he is."[25]

Robertson commented on what a physical game it was.

"I don't ever remember being on the floor so much. I was really beat up out there. Miles (Eddie) played me real tough. It looked like the Bullets wanted this one real bad."[26]

The victory also gave the Bucks a psychological advantage. Costello pointed out that...

"...in case we should meet Baltimore in the playoffs, we know we can beat them in Baltimore, and our 4-1 edge in the season series gives us a mental advantage against them."[27]

GAME 47—ATLANTA CLIPS BUCKS:
HAWKS 117, BUCKS 110

After an off day, the Bucks returned home on Friday, January 22 to face the Atlanta Hawks before another sellout crowd of 10,746.

The Hawks were struggling a little this season. During the off-season, they had lost a key player, forward Joe Caldwell, who jumped to the Carolina Cougars of the ABA. An important addition was rookie Pete Maravich out of LSU. Costello assessed the new-look Hawks:

"They've got a lot of talent on that club. It's still there on paper, and it's a matter of putting it back

together. Some people blame Maravich for their troubles, but if they played as hard as he does, they might be all right. Size, mobility, rebounding and shooting, it's all there.[28]

The Hawks might have read Costello's evaluation of their team as they put it all together, upsetting the Bucks, 117-110, ending the Bucks' ten-game winning streak. Amazingly the Hawks pulled off the victory without the services of star guard Lou Hudson, who was out of the lineup because of the death of his father in Greensboro, North Carolina.

Hawks' coach Richie Guerin had some ideas how to beat the Bucks. They opened the game with a full-court press and it kept them close, trailing only 32-28 at the end of the first quarter. Guerin explained about using the press:

"We wanted to take them away from their set offense. We didn't want them to get set up for Lew Alcindor around the basket. It only succeeds when you win."[29]

The Bucks extended their lead to 58-52 at halftime, but Costello was unhappy with their performance. He benched Alcindor because he wasn't rebounding, and he wasn't pleased with Robertson's 0-4 from the field in the first half.

Costello elaborated:

"He's got to shoot more to help us. You can't go a half without shooting and just pick it up. Are you telling me that Hazzard or Maravich could shut him off? Are they good defensive players? There are tougher guys. He just didn't shoot."[30]

Maravich also had a bad first half, going one of seven from the field and two free throws.

Another strategy Guerin used was double and even triple-teaming Alcindor, challenging the Bucks to hit outside shots, which they didn't. The ice-cold shooting of the Bucks and great play by the Hawks enabled Atlanta to outscore the Bucks 36-19 in the third quarter, giving them an 88-77 lead at the end of the quarter.

The Bucks stormed back in the fourth quarter and took a 108-105 lead, but it was all Atlanta, in particular Pete Maravich, for the remainder of the game. Pistol Pete hit a 15-foot shot, then a shot from 20 feet, and he scored on a layup after intercepting a Robertson inbounds pass, making the score 111-108 with 1:16 left. The big play in the Maravich scoring spree was stealing the inbounds pass. Maravich said,

> *"I watched Oscar throw the ball in three times with a sort of a lob pass. At the time-out period just before that I made up my mind to try it. I put my head down to make him think I wasn't watching, and when he threw the ball toward Jon McGlocklin, I jumped up and picked it off. It was a gamble, but it paid off."*[31]

Bill Bridges hit a layup with 38 seconds left. The Bucks' only basket was a Boozer jump shot with 28 seconds left, and the Bucks lost, 117-100.

The Bucks were led in scoring by Dandridge with 22 and McGlocklin with 21. The double and triple teaming of Alcindor paid off as he scored only 16. Bellamy led the Hawks with 25 despite his bad first half. Maravich ended up with 22, and Bridges chipped in with 20.

Guerin was pleased with his team's play, saying that it was one of the best team games they played all year. He also gave high praise to guard Walt Hazzard, who despite having the flu, played 38 minutes. His illness was so severe, though, that he vomited in the locker room right after the game.

In the Bucks locker room, Costello was not happy:

> *"You can't play one quarter and expect to win. I just wish these teams would come in with their full rosters. Boston played without Havlicek and White and we barely won that game, and now we lose to these guys without Hudson. It wasn't overconfidence, really, just a matter of motivation— or lack of it."*[32]

GAME 48—BUCKS CRUSH PORTLAND:
BUCKS 142, TRAILBLAZERS 117

Both teams had very little rest before a 1:30 P.M. game at the Milwaukee Arena played on Saturday, January 22. The Bucks played the night before, losing to the Hawks, and the Trailblazers also had played the night before in Detroit. The Bucks started a new winning streak, routing Portland, 142-117.

Portland coach Rolland Todd justified his team's lethargic play:

> *"We had to get up at 5:45 to catch a plane for Milwaukee, and that's 4:45 Milwaukee time. It would be tough enough to play Milwaukee under ideal conditions, but we got awfully tired, and when that happens it's tough to maintain your concentration. You take shortcuts, and every time you do, you get burned."*[33]

The Bucks were also tired. Alcindor yawned a few times during the pre-game warm up and he explained,

> *"We had that game yesterday night, you know."*[34]

The way the Bucks shot the basketball, it would have been unlikely for a well-rested NBA All-Star team to beat them. They made 64 field goals, shooting an incredible 62.9 percent. Alcindor hit on 20 of 23 attempts from the field.

The game was close after the first quarter with the Bucks ahead, 35-32. They built on the lead in the second quarter and took a 72-59 lead into the locker room at halftime. The leading scorer for the Bucks in the first half was Alcindor with 28 points.

If you thought the Bucks were hot in the first half, they shot even better in the third quarter, connecting on 18 of 25 field goal attempts, and they led, 113-85, going into the fourth quarter.

Coach Todd talked about the Bucks' performance:

"I thought they shot extremely well. If Alcindor's putting the ball in the hoop nobody's going to stop him. The game got a little out of hand. It's tough enough to maintain mental conditioning when you're tired. When you're down by 20, it's impossible."[35]

The Bucks had a 30-point lead early in the fourth quarter, and Portland narrowed it to 19 with about seven minutes left. The fans were chanting, *"We want Lew,"* so Costello brought him in and he scored seven more points before going to the bench with four and a half minutes remaining.

After the game, Alcindor was asked if he considered his 44-point performance in the 142-117 rout of Portland as one of his outstanding performances and he answered,

"Not especially."[36]

Oscar Robertson scored 23, hitting on 10 of his 12 shots, Dandridge had 19, and McGlocklin 18. Portland center Dale Schlueter led Portland with 20, guard Shaler Halimon had 19, and Rookie of the Year candidate Geoff Petrie had 16.

GAME 49—BUCKS FLY OVER HAWKS:
BUCKS 142, HAWKS 120

The Hawks had used the strategy of a full court press, with double, even triple-teaming Alcindor to achieve a victory two days ago in Milwaukee. Why not use it again in their rematch against the Bucks in a home game at the Alexander Memorial Coliseum on the Georgia Tech campus on Sunday afternoon, January 24? They did so but without much success as the Bucks got revenge in a big way, blasting Atlanta, 142-120.

At the conclusion of a high-scoring first quarter, the Bucks led, 42-35. The big reason Atlanta stayed close was the hot shooting of Pete Maravich, who scored 16 points in the quarter. He cooled off in the second quarter with five points, but Lou Hudson scored 10, and the Hawks took the lead at 54-52.

There was a worrisome moment for the Bucks during the second quarter when Alcindor fell to the floor and bruised his knee. He sat out the rest of the quarter but returned with it heavily wrapped for the third quarter. Bob Boozer and Lucius Allen came off the bench and sparked the Bucks, and they took a 67-63 lead into halftime. Costello had high praise for Boozer:

> *"He does a good job against big forwards and gives us more flexibility up front. When he's in there, they have to put their bigger forward on him, and that*

leaves Dandridge with a smaller man to go against."37

The Bucks sank their first nine shots of the third quarter, led by McGlocklin and Robertson, who each scored nine points. The Bucks connected on 16 of their 21 shots in the third quarter for 76.2 percent and led 107-90 going into the fourth quarter. They outscored Atlanta 32-29 in the fourth quarter, avenging their home court loss of two days earlier, 142-120.

In contrast to the previous game, the Bucks broke the Hawks' full court press immediately, and they hit their outside shots, forcing Atlanta to abandon their overplaying of Alcindor. Coach Richie Guerin noticed:

*"They were fired up. On top of that, they shot the hell out of the ball. We didn't play that badly; we scored 120 points, and it wasn't as though our defense was that bad either. You usually don't win in this game with outside shooting, but this was an exception. They were super, that's all."*38

Costello was impressed with the Bucks' performance:

*"Man, we were doing things good today. We filled the lanes and had some fine passing. We didn't waste time dribbling, and we hit the open man consistently. We got a lot of layups. Dandridge was very active. His quickness helps him running off Lew's picks and leaving his man behind. Atlanta pressured us just as they did last Friday, but we shook loose, and when you're hitting like we were, it kills 'em. We had the same good shots against Atlanta the last time but they weren't dropping through. When they don't, you look lousy. When they do, you can't help but look terrific."*39

Bucks' forward
Bob Boozer.
(Lulloff collection)

Dandridge led the Bucks with 33 points, hitting 15 out of 20 from the field. Robertson had 29, Alcindor had 24, and Bob Boozer did a great job off the bench, hitting 8 of 10 shots, scoring 18. The Hawks' leading scorer was Maravich with 30, Walt Hazzard added 29, and Lou Hudson had 27.

GAME 50—ANOTHER KNICKS VICTORY: KNICKS 107, BUCKS 98

After three games in three days, the Bucks took a day off, and traveled to New York for their next game against their nemesis, the Knicks. On January 26, in front of another sellout crowd of 19,500 in Madison Square Garden, the Knicks continued their success against the Bucks, winning 107-98.

The game was very competitive, tied at 27 after the first quarter, and the Bucks took a 46-45 lead at halftime. Both teams shot poorly in the first half, the Bucks 37.5 percent, and the Knicks 36 percent. With two minutes left in the third quarter, neither team had more than a five-point lead. There were 17 lead changes, and the score was tied on 13 occasions. The Knicks finished off the third quarter with a spurt, giving them a 77-70 lead.

The Knicks came out hot in the fourth quarter, and helped by DeBusschere's outside shooting, took a 95-84 lead with five minutes left. The Bucks, behind consecutive three-point plays by Robertson and Boozer and a Robertson basket, scored 10 straight points, narrowing the lead to 95-94 with 2:38 on the clock. The Knicks increased their lead to three when Willis Reed rebounded a missed free throw by Walt Frazier and scored, but the Bucks countered with a basket, making the score 97-96 with 2:08 remaining.

The remainder of the game belonged to the Knicks. Dick Barnett hit a fall-away jumper with 1:47 to go, and after Dandridge missed a jumper, Barnett scored again, making it 101-96 with 1:12 left. McGlocklin's inbounds pass bounced off Greg Smith's foot, the Knicks got possession, and Bill Bradley's jump shot made the score 103-96 with 52 seconds left. If the Bucks had any chance, it disappeared when Dandridge lost a pass, and Bradley added two free throws. McGlocklin's basket provided the only points for the Bucks in the last 2:06 of the game, and they went down to defeat, 107-98.

DeBusschere reflected after the game:

> *"Winning three out of four from them gives us a little confidence, and it has to hurt them. Psychologically, they have to feel as though we've got their number. They've got to press when they play us again. Let's face it. We're the only team they don't manhandle, for that matter."*[40]

Costello talked about the last two minutes of the game.

> *"I can think of about five things we did wrong near the end that might have put it down to the wire. We're only one point down and still in it up to then. Our defense was good, especially in the first half, but our offense just wasn't there all night. We didn't get anything from our forwards. It's happened before against this team. We don't get enough movement and let their defense get set."*[41]

Coach Red Holzman gave his thoughts about the game.

> *"I know Costello feels like I do. They are a great team and can beat us on any night. We made some big steals, and we got some big buckets from Walt Frazier and Willis Reed on offensive rebounds. We don't do too well on offensive rebounding too often. We didn't change anything the second half. It was just what came up — guys moving and creating opportunities and we started hitting. That's the name of the game."*[42]

Oscar Robertson offered no excuses.

> *"They beat us good in every department. We didn't run any patterns. We didn't play our game."*[43]

In the Knicks locker room, Dave Stallworth leaned out of the shower and yelled,

"The Bucks are down the trough again!"[44]

Alcindor led the Bucks with 29 points and added 25 rebounds, but on the down side he shot 11 of 32 from the field. Robertson had 20 and McGlocklin 15. Willis Reed was the leading scorer for the Knicks with 35 points and 15 rebounds. Frazier had 22, DeBusschere scored 18, connecting on 8 out of 13 with 14 rebounds, and Bill Bradley also had 18.

GAME 51—BUCKS PREVAIL OVER CELTICS: BUCKS 132, CELTICS 129

The Bucks were looking to start a new winning streak after the loss to the Knicks, and they did so on January 27, defeating the Celtics in an exciting, fast-paced game, 132-129 at the Boston Garden.

Before Alcindor scored his first basket, he was poked in the eye by Celtics center Dave Cowens. Later in the game, Alcindor got into a tussle with 6-foor-9, 235-pound reserve center Garfield Smith.

Costello observed,

"It was almost like a boxing match, and no foul was called. I don't know how Lew keeps his composure. Guys bump him constantly and hang all over him, but he goes about the business of playing basketball. He never fights himself. He's got a great temperament for this game."[45]

The game against Boston was similar in many ways to the game the evening before against New York. The game was tied at 25 at the end of the first quarter, and the Bucks led, 63-58, at the half. The Bucks were hot early in the third quarter, taking an 86-75 lead, only to see Boston narrow the advantage to 96-89 at the end of the quarter.

The Celtics were hot early in the fourth quarter and had what looked like a secure 127-122 lead with a little over a minute and a half left. The Bucks came storming back. Robertson scored on a layup with 1:33 left, and after John Havlicek missed a shot, Alcindor tipped in a missed shot by Robertson, making the score 127-126.

McGlocklin had a key steal from Jo Jo White and went in for an uncontested layup, giving the Bucks a 128-127 lead with 53 seconds left. Boston took back the lead with 40 seconds remaining when Havlicek tipped in a missed shot by Henry Finkel. Alcindor came through again, scoring after he rebounded a missed shot by Dandridge, giving the Bucks a 130-129 lead.

With 16 seconds left, Boston called time-out to discuss their strategy. What should the Bucks do? With a one-point lead, should they let the Celtics take the last shot, or should they intentionally foul? Maybe Boston would miss the free throws, but they'd have the ball back to win the game.

Havlicek talked about what happened after the game.

> *"I took the pass from Nelson (Don) and heard Costello yelling for them to take a foul. Alcindor tried to foul me and missed, but he messed up my rhythm and forced me to go toward midcourt. I saw that I didn't have a shot, so I looked to the right and went up to pass. I committed myself, and there was Oscar, and I threw the ball right to him. I'm not even sure what man we had in the area. I think it was White, but I didn't come close enough to tell who it was. This has to be the most stupid mistake*

*I've ever made. We can lose them a million ways,
but this was the worst. We had it right in our pocket
and I turned around and gave it to them."*[46]

Robertson ran out the clock while Boston coach Tommy
Heinsohn shouted to commit a foul. Steve Kuberski fouled
Bob Boozer with no time remaining, and he hit both free
throws with a majority of the players already heading to
their locker rooms.

Alcindor, who played the entire 48 minutes, liked
playing against the Celtics.

*"I like playing against a running club like the Celts.
There's less chance for them to double and triple
team me, and one-on-one defense is great for me."*[47]

The Bucks were led by Alcindor's 53 points, hitting on 22
of 31 from the field, he also grabbed 14 rebounds, and had
seven assists. McGlocklin had 21, Dandridge added 19,
and Robertson chipped in with 17. JoJo White led the
Celtics with 30, Steve Kuberski had 27 points, connecting
on 11 of 13 shots, and Havlicek had 26 with 10 assists.

GAME 52—GREER GREAT BUT PHILLY FALLS:
BUCKS 142, 76ERS 118

On Friday, January 29, the 76ers' first regular season
sellout since 1969, 15,244 fans braved snow showers and
went to the Spectrum in hope of seeing their heroes defeat
the Bucks like they did a month ago. The Bucks
disappointed them, posting a 142-118 victory. Those in
attendance did witness a historic event as hometown
favorite Hal Greer scored his 20,000th point, the sixth
player at that time in NBA history to accomplish this feat.

After a close first quarter that ended with the Bucks ahead, 32-28, the Bucks opened up the lead to 10 points in the second quarter, but the 76ers came back and trailed, 63-60, at halftime.

Early in the third quarter, Sixers rookie Dennis Awtrey and Alcindor got into a tussle. Alcindor said,

> *"Awtrey was pushing me around and I started to shove him, so he got belligerent. I told him if he wanted to fight, let's fight and get it over. Then Oscar got involved, but nothing came of it."*[48]

Midway through the quarter, with the Bucks ahead, 75-74, they scored 16 straight points, blowing the game open. Everyone got in the act. Dandridge hit a pair of free throws, Alcindor hit a hook shot, and McGlocklin sank two free throws. Philadelphia called time out, but it didn't stop the Bucks. Dandridge had a steal and layup, Greg Smith had a layup, Robertson hit a pair of free throws, another layup by Dandridge, and Smith scored on a stuff shot off a great pass from Dandridge. The lead ballooned to 101-83 when Lucius Allen hit a 40-footer at the end of the third quarter.

With four minutes left in the game and the Bucks ahead, 125-104, Greer scored his 20,000th point on a driving layup. The game was halted, Greer was given the game ball, and he posed for pictures with Irv Kosloff, the 76ers owner. A 79-point second half propelled the Bucks to a 142-118 win, raising their record to 43-9.

After the game, Costello visited the 76ers' locker room to congratulate his former teammate from his time with the 76ers and their predecessors, the Syracuse Nationals, on scoring his 20,000th point.

When Greer was asked how he felt, he responded,

"It's beautiful, it's great."[49]

Costello talked about the Bucks' effort:

> *"In the first half we were a little wild. We talked it
> over at halftime and were determined we wouldn't
> play their game. We drove their guards into the
> corners, from where they don't particularly like to
> shoot. We applied the pressure and it opened up
> with steals. When we didn't get a steal, we worked
> for good shots and we were hitting pretty good."*[50]

Alcindor led the Bucks with 31 points, connecting on 12 of
16 from the field. McGlocklin had 23, and Dandridge and
Robertson each had 21. Greer and Archie Clark shared the
scoring honors for Philadelphia with 21 each, and Billy
Cunningham added 18.

GAME 53—BUCKS GRIND PISTONS:
BUCKS 131, PISTONS 104

The Bucks' next game was a "home" game scheduled for
the Dane County Coliseum in Madison, Wisconsin, on
Sunday, January 31. This was the Bucks' third game of
five scheduled there for the regular season. Coach Costello
reflected on playing games there.

> *"The Coliseum is not like a home floor; it's like a
> neutral floor. We don't have our own surround-
> ings—floor, backboards, baskets, crowd, ceiling,
> but don't get me wrong. We are glad to come over to
> Madison to expose our game and our team. We
> hope we can generate the same excitement there
> that we get from our Milwaukee fans. We need your
> support."*[51]

The Pistons were plagued with numerous injuries. A
broken ankle had put forward Steve Mix out for the

season. Bob Quick was out indefinitely with a broken knee cap, and guard Jimmy Walker was doubtful with a shoulder injury. The Pistons were still a formidable team with Dave Bing at guard and Bob Lanier and Otto Moore in the front court.

Coming into the evening's game, the Bucks had a nine-game lead in the Midwest Division over the second-place Pistons, and they padded that lead with a 131-104 victory.

Coach Costello commented after the game:

> "It was like winning two games in one. They're the team we have to beat right now to win our division."[52]

Sloppy play by the Bucks led to the Pistons taking a 31-29 lead at the end of the first quarter. Lucius Allen sparked the Bucks early in the second quarter. At one point they scored 10 straight points to take a 47-38 lead. Allen hit a buzzer-beater to end the half, giving the Bucks a 61-49 advantage.

It was all Milwaukee in the third quarter. Sparked by Dandridge and McGlocklin, the Bucks opened an 87-65 lead, which the Pistons narrowed to 93-80 going into the fourth quarter.

Pistons coach Bill van Breda Kolff came into the game leading the NBA in technical fouls with 31, way ahead of the tie shared at second place by Billy Cunningham and Jerry Sloan with 12, and he added to his lead with two more. He picked up his first one early in the fourth quarter with the Pistons down, 95-84.

Detroit cut the lead to 106-96 with seven and a half minutes left in the game when van Breda Kolff got his second and was ejected. It was the sixth time that season that van Breda Kolff had been ejected from a game. Terry

Dischinger and Howie Komives assumed the coaching responsibilities whenever van Breda Kolff got ejected.

On the way to the dressing room, van Breda Kolff stopped to talk to Alcindor. Alcindor said,

> *"He was trying to get some sympathy about how he was being victimized. He was telling me Madden picks on him."*[53]

The Bucks outscored the Pistons 25-8 to end the game, capping off the 131-104 victory, ending the month of January with a 15-2 record, the best mark in franchise history.

Alcindor led the Bucks with 28 points along with 10 rebounds. Sharp shooter Jon McGlocklin connected on 11 out of 14 from the field and ended up with 24, and Bob Dandridge had 23 points and 15 rebounds. There was also solid play off the bench. Bob Boozer scored 18 points, and Lucius Allen scored 15 points, with six of seven from the field. Dave Bing had 26 points to lead the Pistons, followed by Dischinger with 24, and Otto Moore had 18 points and 15 rebounds.

After the game, Costello commented on the Bucks' effort:

> *"We played hard when we had to. We built up a good lead, and then when they cut it down, we started playing again and wrapped it up. Lucius Allen gave us a good lift in the first half, and Bobby Dandridge was rebounding well in heavy traffic, especially in the second half."*[54]

Endnotes to Chapter 10

1) Rel Bochat, "Bucks Break Up Bullets, 151-99," *Milwaukee Sentinel*, January 11, 1971, pt. 2, p. 1.

2) *Ibid.*

3) Bob Wolf, "Glass Isn't Bullet Proof, but Bucks Are," *Milwaukee Journal*, January 11, 1971, pt. 2, p. 10.

4) *Ibid.*

5) *Ibid.*

6) Alan Rothstein, "Bucks Stun Bullets in 151-99 Rout," *Baltimore Sun*, January 11, 1971, C1.

7) *Ibid.*

8) Bob Wolf, "Robertson May Not Play," *Milwaukee Journal*, January 15, 1971, pt. 2, p. 15.

9) Rel Bochat, "Bucks Breeze to 7th Win in Row," *Milwaukee Sentinel*, January 16, 1971, pt. 2, p. 1.

10) Bob Wolf, "Alcindor Makes Difference as Bucks Outclass Royals," *Milwaukee Journal*, January 16, 1971, pt. 2, p. 16.

11) Bob Logan, "Bucks Beat Bulls," *Chicago Tribune*, January 17, 1971, sec. 2, pg. 1.

12) Bob Wolf, "Bucks Blast Bulls, 110-90," *Milwaukee Journal*, pt. 2, p. 1.

13) *Ibid.*

14) *Ibid.*

15) *Ibid.*

16) *Ibid.*

17) Logan. p. 6.

18) Rel Bochat, "Bucks Find Out It Takes Sweat to Win," *Milwaukee Sentinel*, January 18, 1971, pt. 2, p. 1.

19) Bob Wolf, "Crippled Celtics No Patsies for Bucks," *Milwaukee Journal*, January 18, 1971, pt. 2, p. 10.

20) *Ibid.*

21) *Ibid.*

22) Rel Bochat, "Bucks Will Visit Vengeful Bullets," *Milwaukee Sentinel*, January 20, 1971, pt. 2, p. 1.

23) Bob Wolf, "Dandridge Stopper; Bucks String to 10," *Milwaukee Journal*, January 21, 1971, pt. 2, p. 17.

24) Rel Bochat, "Hot 'Pistol' Here Tonight," *Milwaukee Sentinel*, January 22, 1971, pt. 2, p.1.

25) Alan Rothstein, "Bucks Beat Bullets By 120-116," *Baltimore Sun,* January 21, 1971, C4.

26) *Ibid.*

27) Bochat, pp. 1-2.

28) Bob Wolf, "Bucks Risk Streak Against Maravich," *Milwaukee Journal*, January 22, 1971, pt. 2, p. 14.

29) Bob Wolf, "Crowd Inspires Maravich, Bucks' Streak Ends at 10," *Milwaukee Journal*, January 23, 1971, pt. 1 p. 18.

30) Rel Bochat, "Pistol Pete Guns Down Bucks," *Milwaukee Sentinel*, January 23, 1971, pt. 2, p. 1.

31) Bob Wolf, January 23, 1971. p. 18.

32) *Ibid.*

33) Bob Wolf, "Lew's Hot Hand Burns Foe," *Milwaukee Journal*, January 24, 1971, pt. 2, p. 1

34) *Ibid.*

35) Bob Hill, "Trail Blazers Lose, 144-117, in Early Game," *Wisconsin State Journal*, January 24, 1971, Sec. 3, p. 1.

36) Wolf. January 24. pt. 2, p. 1.

37) Bob Wolf, "Hawk Strategy Is Same, but Bucks' Reaction Isn't," *Milwaukee Journal*, January 25, 1971, pt. 2, p.11.

38) *Ibid.*

39) Rel Bochat, "Hot Bucks 'Cook' Hawks, 142-120," *Milwaukee Sentinel*, February 13, 1971, pt. 2, p. 4.

40) Bob Wolf, "Are Bucks Victims of Buck Fever?" *Sporting News*, January 27, 1971, p. 8.

41) Rel Bochat, "Knicks Throttle Bucks Again," *Milwaukee Sentinel*, January 27, 1971, pt. 2, p. 4.

42) *Ibid.*

43) Bob Wolf, "Bucks' Offense Stutters; Knicks Gloat Over Victory," *Milwaukee Journal*, January 27, 1971, pt. 2, p. 14.

44) *Ibid.*

45) Rel Bochat, "King Lew Learning Ropes," *Milwaukee Sentinel*, January 29, 1971, pt. 2, p. 2.

46) Bob Wolf, "Bucks Big Heroes: Lew and Havlicek," *Milwaukee Journal*, January 28, 1971, pt. 2, p. 17.

47) Rel Bochat, "Big Lew's 53 Lift Bucks Past Celts," *Milwaukee Sentinel*, January 28, 1971, pt. 2, p. 3.

48) Bob Wolf, "Bucks win; 76ers' Greer reached plateau," *Milwaukee Journal*, January 30, 1971, pt. 1, p. 15.

49) *Ibid.*

50) Rel Bochat, "Bucks Hit on 16 in Row To Bomb 76ers, 142-118," *Milwaukee Sentinel*, January 30, 1971, pt. 2, p.1.

51) Glenn Miller, "Bucks Happy to Win 3," *Wisconsin State Journal*, January 31, 1971, Sec. 3, p.1.

52) Bob Wolf, "Bucks Hand Pistons Back of Hand; Coach Gets Thumb," *Milwaukee Journal*, February 1, 1971, pt. 2, p. 10.

53) *Ibid.*

54) Rel Bochat, "Bucks Pummel Pistons, 131-104," *Milwaukee Sentinel*, February 1, 1971, pt. 2, p. 1.

Bucks' forward McCoy McLemore. (Lulloff collection)

CHAPTER 11

A TRIP OUT WEST

McLemore Trade

A MAJOR NEED FOR THE BUCKS was having a strong rebounding forward. They hoped they'd answered that issue with a trade made with the Cleveland Cavaliers on February 1, nine hours before the NBA trading deadline. The Bucks sent their No. 1 draft choice from last season, forward Gary Freeman out of Oregon State, along with a second-round choice in the upcoming draft, and an undisclosed amount of money to obtain McCoy McLemore.

Bucks' coach Larry Costello talked about the trade.

> *"I'm extremely pleased that we acquired McLemore. We need a big experienced forward for the playoffs. We should get a consistency of performance from McLemore that we couldn't expect from a first year man like Freeman. It was a tough decision to give up a No. 1 draft choice, but we had to assess our needs as of the moment. We feel we have helped ourselves with this trade."*[1]

Bucks' president Ray Patterson seconded Costello's analysis.

> *"We are pointing toward the playoffs and we need an experienced forward to help Lew Alcindor on the backboards and guard against possible injury. Fitch gives him credit for holding his team together and felt that he owed him this chance to go to*

a contending club. Freeman hasn't had much opportunity to play and he figures to get that chance at Cleveland."[2]

When Cavaliers coach Bill Fitch was asked how difficult it was to trade one of their better players, he replied.

"Easy. We made the trade for what Freeman can do for the Cavaliers next season. Remember, we also got the Bucks' second pick in this year's draft, plus money."[3]

During a phone interview, McLemore discussed the transaction.

"I haven't talked to Coach Costello yet, but I think my role will be to give them defense and rebounding, especially in the playoffs. Milwaukee has two fine scorers at forward in Bob Dandridge and Greg Smith, but both are on the short side compared to a guy like DeBusschere."[4]

Indeed, one of the reasons for the Bucks 1-3 record against the Knicks was the strong rebounding of the Knicks. Hopefully, McLemore would narrow the gap in New York's rebounding advantage.

Game 54—Trailblazers Top Bucks: Trailblazers 123, Bucks 111

The first game of a west coast trip for the Bucks didn't go as planned. On Tuesday, February 2, in front of 9,040 fans at the Veterans Memorial Coliseum, Portland upset the Bucks, 123-111. It was the first time this season that the Bucks lost to an expansion team.

Costello reflected after the game:

> *"They just played a good game and we played a*
> *lousy one. I warned the guys before we came in*
> *here what they were up against. Portland beat New*
> *York here, Portland beat Boston here, Portland beat*
> *Baltimore here. There's no letting up in this league.*
> *We only played one quarter tonight. You've got to*
> *play four quarters in this league every night."*[5]

There were three ties early in the first quarter, the last one at 12-12, but Gary Gregor and Rick Adelman paced Portland to a 34-29 lead at the end of the first quarter.

Ice-cold 42 percent shooting from the Bucks in the first half and sizzling 54 percent shooting from Portland, gave them a 59-40 lead late in the second quarter. Led by Gregor, who had 18 points in the first half, and Jim Barnett's 13, the Trailblazers led at halftime, 65-48.

The Bucks made eight of their first 12 shots in the third quarter and narrowed the Portland lead to 79-71 with just over four minutes to play in the quarter. The Bucks tied the game at 85, but guard Geoff Petrie had a three-point play giving Portland an 88-85 lead going into the final quarter.

Portland coach Rolland Todd was pleased with his team's play.

> *"I know what climbing the hill can do to a team.*
> *We've tried to do that a lot—fall behind and then*
> *rally. You get there, or you get close, and then you*
> *fall back from exhaustion. I told my guys when we*
> *had the big lead I didn't care if we got out of the*
> *third quarter no more than even. I figured if we*
> *could play them close it would finally get to them."*[6]

With ten minutes left in the game, the Bucks took the lead, 91-90, on Alcindor's follow-up of a missed shot. The game continued to stay close with the teams tied for the last time at 106. Portland dominated play for the rest of the game, outscoring the Bucks 17-5 to end the game with a 123-111 win. The big contributors to the surge were the hot shooting of Gregor, Barnett, and Rick Adelman, who had three big steals for Portland, the first of which gave the Trailblazers a 108-106 lead, and they never looked back.

Todd couldn't say enough about the victory.

"Adelman played a great game. A lot of his success is anticipation. Gary Gregor did a great job for us at forward too. Usually that's where we get killed, but Milwaukee doesn't have the big rebounding forwards, and so we could concentrate on trying to block Alcindor out of there."[7]

Costello agreed.

"Adelman stole everything but our pants. He was really hustling, and credit to him. They're the kind of team that gives us trouble with their speed and quickness. We didn't move the ball well. Oscar Robertson is the one who has to do that for us, and we weren't moving most of the time tonight."[8]

Portland's pressure defense forced the Bucks into 28 turnovers, one of their highest totals for the season.

The Bucks were led in scoring by Alcindor with 38 points, and McGlocklin had 23 points, hitting 11 out of 15 from the field. Portland was led by Barnett with 27 points. Gregor and forward Stan McKenzie each had 22 points, and Adelman and Petrie each scored 15 points.

Game 55—Bucks Defuse Rockets:
Bucks 108, Rockets 101

There was no rest for the Bucks as they traveled to San Diego to play the next day, Wednesday, February 3, for a game against the Rockets. The Bucks came into the game with three of their starters with ailments. Oscar Robertson had sore knees and ankles, Jon McGlocklin's ribs were bothering him, and Greg Smith had a case of the flu. Only 6,483 attended in the 14,000 seat International Sports Arena, and they watched the Bucks come away with a 108-101 win.

In addition to the nagging ailments of the team, the Bucks had a difficult trip to San Diego. When they arrived at the Portland airport for their departure flight, they found out that the plane that was supposed to take them to San Diego was grounded in Vancouver, British Columbia due to a snowstorm. An alternate flight was arranged that would go to Phoenix, and then they would catch a flight to San Diego. As a result of these altered travel arrangements, the team got very little rest, arrived much later, and managed to get in just a short work-out before the game.

San Diego opened the game taking a 5-0 lead, which they expanded to 22-11 with four minutes left in the first quarter. Costello inserted rookie Billy Zopf into the line up and he gave the Bucks a spark. He only scored two points, but his quickness helped set up the offense, and his aggressive defense narrowed the score to 32-26 at the end of the first quarter.

The Bucks came out hot in the second quarter, and a 15-3 run gave them a 41-35 lead. Elvin Hayes sparked a Rockets comeback tying the score at 45, and little Calvin

Murphy hit two baskets giving San Diego a 49-45 lead. The rest of the quarter belonged to the Bucks. Boozer and McGlocklin each had two baskets, helping the Bucks score 13 in a row to take a 58-49 lead at halftime.

The final five seconds of the first half took a lot of time. There was a scoreboard malfunction, and the repairs took so much time that the start of the second half was delayed until it was operable.

Dandridge hit three baskets early in the third quarter, opening the lead up to 70-57 midway through the third quarter. Hot shooting by Robertson, McGlocklin, and McCoy McLemore's first basket as a Buck gave then an 81-64 going lead into the fourth quarter.

Elvin Hayes got hot early in the fourth quarter and the Rockets narrowed the lead to 86-75. Alcindor came back in the game, Hayes scored again, but a pair of free throws by Dandridge and McLemore made the score 90-77. The closest the Rockets came was the final score, 108-101.

Elvin Hayes had a big game for San Diego, scoring 41 points along with 19 rebounds. Stu Lantz was the only other Rocket in double figures with 19 points. Alcindor led the Bucks' balanced attack with 25 points and 12 rebounds. Close behind were McGlocklin with 21 points and Robertson with 19 points.

Rockets coach Alex Hannum talked about the contest after the game:

> *"We didn't let Lew Alcindor overpower us inside tonight, but we couldn't stop their fast break and that was what probably beat us. We like to run against them; tonight they ran well against us."*[9]

Game 56—Hollywood Performance by Lakers:
Lakers 116, Bucks 93

On Friday, February 5, in front of a sellout crowd of 17,505 at the Forum in Los Angeles, the two division leaders in the NBA's Western Conference squared off. The Lakers came away with a decisive 116-93 victory over the Bucks, the first time they had beaten them all season.

The Bucks grabbed an early 4-0 lead, but the score was tied on 12 occasions in the first quarter, which ended in a tie at 26. Early in the second quarter, the Lakers opened a seven-point lead, and things looked bleak when Alcindor went to the bench with six and a half minutes remaining and stayed there for the remainder of the half. The Bucks, aided by two baskets by Boozer, a Cunningham stuff, and some free throws by Robertson, tied the score three times, the last at 45. A Robertson free throw and a buzzer beater jumper by Dandridge gave the Bucks a 48-45 lead at the half.

The game stayed close for most of the third quarter, but tied at 61, the Lakers blew it open. Jerry West and Gail Goodrich helped the Lakers on a 12-0 run, opening a 73-61 lead, which they increased to 81-66 going into the fourth quarter. The Lakers had a huge quarter, outscoring the Bucks by a 36-18 margin.

Costello played the bench extensively in the fourth quarter. The closest the Bucks cut the deficit to was ten points, as the Lakers routed the Bucks, 116-93. A big factor for the win was the shooting percentages. The Bucks shot only 38.6 percent, while the Lakers connected on 50.5 percent. The Bucks were also beaten on the boards, 59-46.

The Bucks only had three players score in double figures. Despite playing only 34 minutes, Alcindor scored 27 points, and Robertson had 16. The balance-scoring Lakers were led by Hairston with 24 points and 19 rebounds. Goodrich and West each added 23 points, and Chamberlain had 14 points along with 14 rebounds.

Costello was very upset with the Bucks' play and talked to them before letting the press in the locker room. He told the reporters.

> *"Desire is what's missing. We had a little talk about that. We haven't played well on this trip. We've got a few injuries, but we should play better than this. How can anyone not have the desire? Here we in the Forum tonight, the most beautiful basketball place in the league. We have a sellout crowd. It's got to be a dream of every one of the guys to play basketball in a situation like that. So how can we play like we did? We didn't play defense, and we didn't move on offense either. We've played this way on the coast all three games. We'll have to snap out of it."*[10]

It was a different atmosphere in the Lakers' locker room. Coach Joe Mullaney talked about defense.

> *"Wilt did a tremendous job. He forced Lew out farther than he normally shoots—although it still looked like he was taking short shots—and beat him to his position. The biggest single factor in the game was Wilt's defense."*[11]

Chamberlain gave credit to his coach:

> *"Give this one to Joe. We practiced certain things and then went out and did them."*[12]

Chamberlain also had great respect for Alcindor.

"I've never seen a man his size who is as quick as he is. If anyone else comes into the league as quick as he is I'm on my way out. When he gets the ball, he's devastating. He's just tough to stop and regardless of his size, he has a wealth of talent. I'd like to watch him rather than play against him. One time I was looking for the ball on the floor, and the next thing I knew, he [Alcindor] dunked it."[13]

Alcindor talked about defensive strategies used by NBA centers against him.

"He played real well on defense tonight. He's not the most physical center in the league tonight. Willis Reed of New York and Wes Unseld of Baltimore play me much harder. It's more like playing soccer or hockey. With them, it's a very personal thing. They play me one on one. Wilt looks to the total defense and tries to jam up the middle and help out. They gave him some help tonight, too, and that's the way it should be on defense."[14]

Keith Erickson, who started off slowly but ended up with 13 points, was elated about the win.

"It's about time we took a game from them. We thought we could beat them but you have to go out and prove it. As for the poor shooting, I had some good shots in the first half but I guess I got a little excited, and I got some good shots in the second half too."[15]

GAME 57—MILWAUKEE MASSACRES WARRIORS:
BUCKS 111, WARRIORS 85

After the Bucks' big loss against the Lakers, they flew to Oakland for a game on Saturday, February 6, against the San Francisco Warriors. In the Oakland Coliseum, before

13,298 fans, the first capacity crowd there since the 1969 NBA playoffs, the Bucks finally played a good game, the last one of the road trip, defeating the Warriors, 111-85.

Lucius Allen, the Bucks' top reserve guard, was still plagued with a bad back. He had already missed the games against San Diego and Los Angeles, and on Saturday he flew back to Milwaukee for treatment. Costello said,

> *"He's been having spasms, and there's no use*
> *trying to play him again until he's right. Maybe*
> *he can get the proper rest and treatment in*
> *Milwaukee."*[16]

The game started poorly for the Bucks as they fell behind 6-0, but Jon McGlocklin led the Bucks with 10 first-quarter points, and the Bucks led, 33-18, at the end of the first quarter. Late in the second quarter, Oscar Robertson's layup, his 23,044th point of his career, put him, at the time, as the second-leading scorer in NBA history behind Wilt Chamberlain. Robertson surpassed Elgin Baylor.

The Bucks shot a torrid 62.2 percent from the field in the first half, McGlocklin leading the way connecting on 10 of 11 field goal attempts. After the game, Costello commented,

> *"We were moving the ball so well that Jon had time.*
> *Give him time, and he'll put the ball in."*[17]

The Bucks opened up a 20-point lead during the second quarter and led 62-44 at halftime.

There was no letdown in the second half. The Bucks led, 88-66, going into the fourth quarter, and with the advantage 96-71 with 8:20 left in the game, Alcindor went to the bench for the remainder of the game. The Bucks went on to a convincing victory, 111-85.

Dandridge and McGlocklin shared scoring honors for the Bucks with 20 points, Robertson right behind with 19 points, and Alcindor with 17 points with 11 rebounds. Jerry Lucas led the Warriors with 17 points and 17 rebounds.

Costello was happy with the Bucks' effort:

> *"We had movement and we played defense. We could beat Los Angeles with that kind of play and we could beat New York. You don't get anywhere in this game playing conservatively. You've got to be aggressive, take some chances. We stole a few passes and blocked some shots and got the ball right up the floor. We were running for some layups, and you're going to shoot better then."*[18]

Endnotes to Chapter 11

1) Rel Bochat, "McLemore Goes to Bucks for Freeman," *Milwaukee Sentinel*, February 2, 1971, pt. 2, p. 1.

2) "Bucks Get McLemore," *Milwaukee Journal*, February 2, 1971, pt. 2, p. 11.

3) Phil Elderkin, "NBA East," *Sporting News*, February 20, 1971. p.14.

4) Rel Bochat.

5) Chuck Johnson, "Oregon Trail Is Bumpy for Bucks," *Milwaukee Journal*, February 3, 1971, pt. 2, p. 13.

6) *Ibid.*

7) *Ibid.*

8) *Ibid.*

9) Chuck Johnson, "Bucks Ailing and Ragged, but beat Reeling Rockets," *Milwaukee Journal*, February 4, 1971, pt. 2, p. 16.

10) Chuck Johnson, "Costello Lectures his Bucks," *Milwaukee Journal*, February 6, 1971, pt. 2, p. 15.

11) Mal Florence, "Lakers Finally Do It—Beat Bucks," *Los Angeles Times*, February 6, 1971, pt. 3, p. 1.

12) *Ibid.*

13) *Ibid.*

14) Chuck Johnson, February 6.

15) Florence. February 6.

16) Staff Correspondence "Allen of Bucks Leaves for Home," *Milwaukee Journal*, February 7, 1971, pt. 3, p. 2.

17) "Bucks Return to Play Suns," *Milwaukee Journal*, February 8, 1971, pt. 2, p. 10.

18) *Ibid.*

CHAPTER 12
RUNNING IT UP

GAME 58—SUNS ECLIPSED BY BUCKS:
BUCKS 118, SUNS 94

It had been a long time—since January 23 to be exact—since the Bucks had played in the friendly confines of the Milwaukee Arena. They returned in front of yet another sellout crowd on Monday, February 8, and routed the Phoenix Suns, 118-94.

There were three ties in the first quarter and the Suns took a 27-26 lead late in the quarter, but the Bucks outscored them 10-4, taking a 36-31 lead after the first quarter. The Bucks opened a 14-point lead in the second quarter and took a 63-54 lead at halftime.

Phoenix cut the Bucks' lead to 66-60 early in the third quarter, but the Bucks scored eight straight points for a 14-point lead and built it to 19, taking a 92-73 advantage into the fourth quarter.

Alcindor scored point number 100 for the Bucks, giving them a 100-78 lead. His last point of the game came on a tip-in with 5:35 left giving them their biggest lead of the game, 108-80. He sat on the bench for the rest of the game, which ended, 118-94.

Costello was proud of the Bucks' performance:

"Our defense was the answer tonight. Maybe we weren't that sharp on offense, but our pressure forced them into errors and gave us opportunities to

run. Lew worked the boards hard, and he went out to pressure their big guys. That Counts (Mel) has to be played or he'll shoot holes in you. Lew has to rebound for us against a big team like this. We kept their big men away from the boards and made Phoenix play our way."[1]

Costello was also impressed with the Bucks' offense:

"We ran pretty well tonight. They are bigger than we are and we have to do that. This is what we always want to do, run, run, run. That's what we've tried to do from the start of the season, and we did it well tonight."[2]

Rookie Jeff Webb, a West Milwaukee native and Kansas State alumnus had a good game off the bench, scoring eight points in 15 minutes. He will see increased playing time because of injuries. Costello reported,

"Lucius Allen will be in the hospital (Lutheran) for eight to ten days in traction for his back trouble, and we've got to check out what depth we have at guard. McCoy McLemore at forward is still adjusting to our style of play, but he did a good job."[3]

Webb's college coach, Suns' coach Cotton Fitzsimmons, talked about Webb's performance.

"I was proud of him. If he keeps improving, I may try to get him."[4]

Phoenix guard Dick Van Arsdale was amazed by Alcindor's play.

"I saw the big guy do some things tonight that were unbelievable. Can you imagine anybody his size leading a fast break?"[5]

Teammate Connie Hawkins agreed.

"Lew is fantastic. You play in front of him and they throw the ball over the top to him. You play behind him and he throws a hook shot over your head. You double-team him and he hits the open man. After that, forget it. He's improved about 100 percent in the last year."[6]

Alcindor had a huge game for the Bucks scoring 39 points, hitting on 15 of 24 shots, was nine of 10 from the free throw line and had 23 rebounds. Robertson had 20 points along with 12 assists and Dandridge had 16 points. Connie Hawkins paced Phoenix with 23 points and 10 rebounds and Neal Walk scored 17 points.

GAME 59—CLOSE CALL IN DETROIT: BUCKS 107, PISTONS 106

Nice home stand! After one game at the Milwaukee Arena, the Bucks flew to Detroit the very next day, February 9, for an evening game against the Pistons. A record crowd of 11,468 at Cobo Arena saw an exciting 107-106 Bucks win. The victory raised the Bucks' season record to 48-11 and gave them an 11-game lead over second-place Detroit.

Pistons guards Jimmy Walker and Dave Bing kept Detroit in the game. After the first quarter, the teams were tied at 27. The Bucks led 59-55 at halftime and 87-81 at the end of the third quarter.

The fourth quarter was very exciting. The Pistons outscored the Bucks 10-4, tying the game at 91 with nine minutes remaining on a basket by Bing. The Bucks reclaimed the lead on two baskets by Robertson, only to have Detroit take a 96-95 lead with 5:10 left courtesy of a Walker basket.

It was Oscar Robertson time. With the Bucks trailing 99-97, his two free throws tied the game, and his hook shot from 10 feet gave the Bucks a 103-101 lead. The Pistons scored, tying the game at 103, and took a 105-103 lead. Alcindor tied the game at 105 with a 10-foot hook shot. Dave Bing missed a shot, Otto Moore rebounded, and missed a shot from the corner.

After the game, Coach van Breda Kolff talked about the play.

> *"Otto could have passed the ball out and we could have used up the whole 24 seconds that were left, but he acted on instinct and put the ball up, even though he was falling away at the time."*[7]

What made things worse for the Pistons was that Alcindor rebounded the missed shot and passed to Robertson. Robertson, who saw Greg Smith open, threw him a perfect pass from one free-throw lane to the other. Smith scored on a layup, giving the Bucks a 107-105 lead with 22 seconds remaining.

Robertson talked about the play after the game.

> *"I was surprised they didn't get back. When I saw Greg down there by himself, I just pitched it."*[8]

Coach Costello was right on top of the play.

> *"After Lew got the rebound, I wanted to call time-out and set up the tie-breaking basket. I was all set to signal for it when I saw Greg break loose."*[9]

The game wasn't over. With eight seconds left, Terry Dischinger was fouled, giving the Pistons an opportunity to tie the game. He made the first but missed the second. Robertson grabbed the rebound and passed the ball to

Alcindor, who held the ball above his head as the game ended, 107-106.

After the game, an exuberant Coach Costello had a lot to say:

> *"Oscar played a hell of a game. He put in a lot of time, considering his bad knees. He's been the key in the last three games because he gets us running. We got careless down the stretch and made some costly turnovers. You can't do that and survive in this league. I thought everybody played well for us, and Detroit played real tough. Oscar got the big rebound and gave it to Lew. Those guys (Pistons) were running around like crazy, but who's gonna take it away from him?"*[10]

Van Breda Kolff was proud of his team's performance.

> *"I can't ask for any more than the guys gave us tonight. It's something just to stay close to Milwaukee. Either Oscar moves off a pick and goes one on one, or Lew takes out his hammer and nails and builds his little cabana around the basket. That's an awful lot to beat."*[11]

Alcindor led the Bucks with 16 rebounds and 38 points, connecting on 13 of 22 from the field and all 12 of his free throw attempts. Robertson had 25 points, 10 rebounds, and 14 assists. Walker and Bing each had 28 points to lead the Pistons, while Otto Moore had 18 points and Dischinger 17 points.

Robertson summed up things pretty well.

> *"No doubt it was one of the toughest game we've had this season. Detroit played well all the way."*[12]

GAME 60—BUCKS SLAM-DUNK LAKERS:
BUCKS 122, LAKERS 88

Revenge was key for the Bucks' next game. Six days ago, the Lakers had humiliated the Bucks at The Forum, 116-93, but now on Thursday, February 12, in front of another sellout crowd at the Milwaukee Arena, the Bucks routed them, 122-88.

The Bucks were looking forward to the rematch. Oscar Robertson commented on that,

> "It will be different than last Friday. We'll be playing before our fans, and some of our guys who were ailing last week are in a lot better shape now."[13]

The game was competitive in the first quarter. Chamberlain and Goodrich were hot, and the Lakers led 22-16 late in the first quarter. The Bucks cut it to 28-27 going into the second quarter.

With two minutes gone in the second quarter and the Bucks ahead 37-35, the blowout began. The Bucks scored 10 straight points, six of them by Alcindor, and took a 47-35 lead. Alcindor went to the bench with 2:42 left, but the Bucks expanded the lead to 59-43 at the half.

In the third quarter, the Bucks got their fast break going. They had five layups in the first eight minutes of the quarter, taking a 95-63 lead into the fourth quarter.

Costello put in four reserves to start the final quarter, and they played great. The largest lead was 115-78, and the Bucks closed it out with a 122-88 victory.

After the game, Costello talked about the difference in this game compared to, their previous meeting with the Lakers:

"It was a complete contrast to last week's game. We had life and they didn't. When they got down, they went to the subs like we did when we were out there. They could have had a good jump on us if they'd been hitting early in the game. They had a lot of good shots but kept missing."[14]

In the visitors' locker room, Coach Joe Mullaney talked about the game.

"Our shooting broke down really bad. Part of it was missing reasonably good shots and then their good second effort on the boards. It was always just one shot for us, not occasionally, always."[15]

Lakers' forward "Happy" Hairston assessed the Lakers' performance.

"The basket just closed on us. We might have been pushing them, but don't forget, Milwaukee isn't an ordinary team, they're a great basketball team."[16]

Alcindor was very pleased with the Bucks' win.

"We needed this one for our own self-confidence. I think they went to Wilt a couple more times than usual, I guess because I had four fouls, but it really didn't do much good because they had to catch up so much."[17]

Jerry West, who had one of his worst games ever, making one of seven shots and scored only six points, agreed with Alcindor.

"Every shot I had was a very good one. Of course, I didn't get very many. We had been moving the ball well, but tonight we stayed with one thing too much. We get stagnant when we're not moving, and we're not the most intelligent team as far as passing is concerned."[18]

Chamberlain talked about Alcindor's performance.

"Lew did a hell of a lot of things besides put the ball in the basket. His tremendous quickness is what sets him apart from every other big man."[19]

The Bucks out-rebounded the Lakers 73-42, and out-shot them from the field, 47.6 percent to an ice-cold 32.4 percent. Alcindor led the Bucks with 31 points and 21 rebounds, even though he sat out the last 14 minutes of the game. Dandridge had 20 points and Robertson added 19. The Lakers only had two players in double figures, Chamberlain with 25 and Goodrich with 16.

Bucks	FG-FGA	FT-FTA	Rebs.	Pts	Lakers	FG-FGA	FT-FTA	Rebs.	Pts.
Alcindor	13-30	5-6	21	31	Chamberlain	10-19	5-6	11	25
Boozer	5-10	3-3	6	13	Erickson	4-12	0-0	5	8
Cunningham	2-6	0-0	9	4	Goodrich	7-14	2-2	3	16
Dandridge	8-11	4-4	9	20	Hairston	1-8	3-4	2	5
McGlocklin	7-14	3-3	3	17	Hetzel	2-7	2-2	5	6
McLemore	3-7	0-0	3	6	McCarter	0-6	2-3	3	2
Robertson	7-11	5-6	9	19	McMillian	2-11	1-1	5	5
Smith	3-7	0-0	9	6	Riley	3-7	3-4	2	9
Webb	2-4	1-2	2	5	Roberson	3-11	0-0	5	6
Zopf	0-5	1-1	2	1	West	1-7	4-4	1	6

Game 60 Box Score

GAME 61—BULL BASHING:
BUCKS 103, BULLS 96

After their big win against the Lakers, the Bucks had a day off. Costello was happy they had a break in the schedule.

"We're resting today while Chicago is playing the Lakers, so that should benefit us. Chicago always gives us a real physical game. Tom Boerwinkle—(7 foot-0", 270 pounds) will lean on Lew and get a rest from Jim Fox. Their forwards [Bob Love and Chet Walker] are tough and good shooters, and Jerry Sloan is a man in motion. Chicago has good team-

*work. They sacrifice as individuals. You don't get
into a running game with them because they play it
more cautiously than other teams. They don't make
many turnovers, and that's why most games
they're in are close."*[20]

On Saturday afternoon February 13, despite trailing the
majority of the game, the Bucks won their fifth straight
game and also their fifth in a row against the Bulls in front
of another sellout crowd at the Milwaukee Arena, 103-96.

The Bulls came out hot and stormed to an early 23-10
lead. The Bucks came back and outscored the Bulls 14-4
and trailed, 27-24, at the end of the first quarter. The
teams played pretty even in the second quarter, and the
half ended with Bulls ahead, 48-45.

With 3:40 left in the third quarter and the Bucks
behind by 14 points, 75-61, they woke up. Alcindor paced
the Bucks as they outscored the Bulls 14-4 to end the
third quarter and trailed, 79-75, going into the fourth
quarter.

Costello gave Alcindor time on the bench to rest and
brought him back into the game with 7:55 left. With the
Bulls winning 89-82, and 5:43 on the clock, the Bucks
started their comeback. Jon McGlocklin got hot from the
outside and tied the score at 91 with 3:11 left. McGlocklin
hit yet another shot with 2:30 on the clock, giving the
Bucks a 93-91 lead. McGlocklin talked about the play the
Bucks were using after the game.

*"They were both off the same play. The ball went
into Lew in the pivot on the strong side. A couple of
our guys went past Lew and he turned and looked
for me on the weak side. I had an open shot both
times."*[21]

Jerry Sloan cut the lead to 93-92 with a free throw, but the rest of the game belonged to the Bucks. Alcindor's pair of free throws, layups by Robertson and McGlocklin off turnovers, and free throws by Robertson helped the Bucks to a 103-96 victory.

The Bulls led for a majority of the game, and Bulls' Coach Dick Motta was very unhappy with his team's play.

> *"We hurt ourselves with about 12 turnovers in the last quarter. The ball didn't mean anything to us. It's strictly a lack of poise, and I don't understand what happened to us. Last year we were winning the close games; this year we're losing them. We've had good leads in four of the five games against Milwaukee and have lost every one."*[22]

There was also displeasure expressed about the Bulls' schedule, having to play three games in 42 hours. Chet Walker wondered,

> *"How do they expect us to win with a schedule like this? It really tolled on us at the end today."*[23]

Jerry Sloan agreed with Walker's opinion.

> *"I try to condition myself to go as long as needed. Our schedule's not the greatest in the world, so what are you going to do? This sort of thing (afternoon games the day after a night game) was supposed to be stopped two years ago. It's been the same way ever since I came to Chicago five years ago, the rich get richer. Milwaukee is winning and they don't have this sort of thing. They were sitting here resting last night, waiting for us."*[24]

Things were different in the Bucks' locker room, with Larry Costello giving his team credit.

"Rebounding and defense won it. We're a slow-starting team, and they (the Bulls) sag so much on Lew that the weak side is wide open. When we started hitting some shots from there, we caught up."[25]

Alcindor led the Bucks with 35 points and ten rebounds. Robertson scored 25 points along with nine assists, and McGlocklin had 15 points. Chet Walker led the Bulls with 32 points going 14 for 14 from the charity stripe, Jerry Sloan scored 23 points and Bob Love added 15.

GAME 62—BUCKS TORCH ATLANTA: ### BUCKS 124, HAWKS 88

They couldn't take a midnight train, but the Bucks took an airplane to Georgia for a game against the Atlanta Hawks on Sunday, February 14. The Hawks, like the Bucks, had a five-game winning streak going, with two of those wins against the New York Knicks. A national television audience and 7,192 attendees at the Georgia Tech Coliseum saw the Bucks destroy the Hawks, 124-88.

Midway through the first quarter, the Bucks had an 18-8 lead, which they expanded to 37-18 going into the second quarter. There was no letdown, and the Bucks took a 61-38 lead into the locker room at halftime. Alcindor had a big first half, scoring 16 points and grabbing 13 rebounds. In contrast, the Hawks' hot-shooting guard, Pete Maravich, was held scoreless in the first quarter and had only three points at the half.

Costello gave credit to the Bucks' defense.

"It opened up everything for us. It didn't give them any good inside shots and it constantly got the ball

for us. They pressed us, but we went right through them for easy baskets.[26]

The Hawks shot a frigid 37.2 percent for the game, as for their guards, Maravich connected on seven of 17, and Lou Hudson hit five of 16. The Bucks shot 53.5 percent from the field. Costello was impressed with Bob Dandridge.

"We anticipated real well on defense. We used great judgment on when to double team and when not to. Dandridge did a hell of a job doubling up on Bellamy."[27]

There was no comeback in the second half as the Hawks went down to their worst loss of the season, 124-88. Hawks Coach Richie Guerin didn't have too much good to say about his team's performance.

"It was a completely bad game for us. It was a combination of the Bucks playing well and our guys having a very poor game. We made a lot of mistakes that we could overcome against other teams, but not against an outfit like the Bucks."[28]

Hawks' guard Walt Hazzard couldn't say enough about the Bucks.

"They're the best team I've ever seen since I've been in the league. Lew Alcindor alone makes the Bucks a great team. Just look what the franchise has done in the two years he's been with them. Besides him, they've got the luxury of having Oscar Robertson to control things, and they've got the same solidarity the Celtics and Knicks had."[29]

Despite sitting out due to the rout, Alcindor still led the Bucks with 23 points along with 19 rebounds. Dandridge was right behind with 22 points, Robertson had 17 points, and McGlocklin added 16 points and 11 assists. Maravich led the Hawks with 15 points, and reserve center Jim Davis had 13 points.

GAME 63—HOT TIME IN BUFFALO:
BUCKS 135, BRAVES 103

After three difficult games against the Lakers, Bulls, and Hawks, the Bucks' next contest was against the expansion Buffalo Braves. When Jon McGlocklin was asked if it's difficult getting up for a team like Buffalo, he responded,

> *"No more than any other game. Oh, there are some teams like the Knicks when you get worked for it up more than ordinarily, but I look at one team pretty much like I do at any others. It's not a matter of getting up for certain games. Sometimes a ball club is tired, may have traveled a lot, or just hits one of those dull spots during a long season. You've got to try to play your good game every time."*[30]

Another factor that distracted the Bucks from focusing on the game was a fire in their hotel. Shortly after the Bucks arrived from Atlanta, a fire started in a mattress in a room on the ninth floor of the Statler Hilton Motel. Smoke filled the 10th and the 11th floor where the Bucks had their rooms. Oscar Robertson, Bob Dandridge, Jon McGlocklin, Dick Cunningham, trainer Arnie Garber, radio announcer Eddie Doucette, and radio producer Chet Coppock had to take a smoke-filled elevator down to the lobby for safety. After an hour wait, all was safe, but some of the players transferred to rooms on lower floors.

On Tuesday, February 16, after a sluggish three quarters of basketball, the Bucks had a huge fourth quarter and in front of 7,242 fans at the Memorial Coliseum, routed the Braves, 135-103, for their seventh straight win.

The Bucks led 35-22 after the first quarter, and they shot the basketball well in the first half, shooting 59 percent from the field. Alcindor had 25 points in the first half, but their defense was poor and they led by just 65-60 at the half. The Braves stayed in the game in the third quarter, tying the score at 81 late in the quarter, and they trailed 96-93 at the end of the third quarter.

The fourth quarter was all Milwaukee as they outscored Buffalo by a whopping 39-10 margin. The 10 points scored by Buffalo tied the record for fewest points scored against the Bucks in a quarter, shared with a game the Bucks played against Detroit the previous season.

Costello commented about the big fourth quarter performance.

> *"There's no question it's tougher to get up for these kind of games. It took us three quarters to get untracked. We were dribbling under pressure, and that's the worst thing you can do. I told our guys to start whipping the ball around and when we did, everything opened up."*[31]

He also praised his team's play off the bench.

> *"All the reserves did a great job in the last quarter too. They played hard and made things happen. Maybe I should have started them."*[32]

Alcindor left the game with 5:44 to play with the Bucks winning, 114-101, but the bench, and a big contribution by Greg Smith, who scored 17 of his 25 points to finish the game, helped the Bucks outscore Buffalo 21-2 to end the game. Buffalo coach Dolph Schayes talked about the Bucks' big surge.

"Our team ran out of gas, and when we made substitutions all hell broke loose. Bob (Kauffman) and Donnie (May) got tired, and I took them out with about six minutes left. All of a sudden we were down by 20 points, so why put them back in? We have a tough game coming up tomorrow night. It's difficult to contain a team like Milwaukee for a full game, however. We allowed too many uncontested layups, and then I don't think they missed on their last 10 shots."[33]

Lew Alcindor led the Bucks with 38 points and 20 rebounds. Greg Smith, who connected on 12 of 17 shots, had 25 points. Robertson and McGlocklin each had 18 points, and despite playing most of the second half with five fouls, Dandridge added 17 points and 11 rebounds.

Guard Don May, who hit 15 out of 23 field goal attempts, led the Braves with 34 points, and center Bob Kauffman, despite having 27, was disappointed with his performance.

"I should have had more. I missed some easy shots. It was partially Lew's defense, but I didn't shoot as fluidly as I should have. As for covering Lew, he's just too much. I started playing in front of him and then I shifted behind him, and he would just wheel around me and go in."[34]

GAME 64—EIGHTH WIN IN A ROW:
BUCKS 119, 76ERS 114

There was no rest for the Bucks as they returned to the hardwood floor of the Dane County Coliseum in Madison, Wisconsin, February 17 for a "home" game against the Philadelphia 76ers. The Bucks came through with a close win, 119-114.

A big announcement about the upcoming games in Madison was made by the Bucks the same day. With the Milwaukee Arena unavailable for the beginning of the NBA playoffs because of a prior commitment to a home show, the games would have to be played in Madison. The Coliseum couldn't give the Bucks a guarantee for all of the possible playoff dates, so the home playoff games for the first round, and possibly the first home game of the second round, would be played at the University of Wisconsin Field House.

The first quarter was very close, with eight ties, and the Bucks led, 31-27, at the end of the quarter. During the second quarter, the Bucks took an 11-point lead twice, only to have the 76ers outscore them 16-3, taking a 57-55 lead to the locker room at halftime. Guard Wally Jones, who had recently rejoined Philadelphia after suffering a fractured kneecap, was a big part of the 76ers' rally.

The game stayed close for the first three minutes of the third quarter, but the Bucks, sparked by Alcindor, Smith, and Dandridge, outscored the Sixers, 13-1, to take a ten-point lead, 77-67, and led, 91-84, going into the fourth quarter.

The Bucks took a 13-point lead in the fourth quarter, but sparked by the hot-shooting of Billy Cunningham, the 76er's took a 108-104 lead with four minutes left. Highlighted by a three-point play by Dandridge, the Bucks scored eight straight points and took a 112-108 lead with 2:39 left. Archie Clark broke the Sixers' scoring drought, but Alcindor scored on a tip-in, making it 114-110 with 2:12 on the clock.

The Bucks dodged a bullet when an apparent basket by Cunningham was disallowed because he had stepped on the baseline. After the Bucks missed, Philadelphia hit a basket, but McGlocklin answered with a jumper, making it 116-112.

Things took a turn for the worse when Alcindor fouled Jim Washington with 0:41 left. Washington hit a pair of free throws, making it a two-point game. On two occasions, the 76ers stole Bucks' passes, but each time, they failed to capitalize when Jones missed a shot, and with 0:19 left, Hal Greer misfired.

After Greer's missed shot, Washington fouled Smith, who made good on one of his two foul shots. With the 76ers down three, Cunningham took a shot with eight seconds left. He missed, and after Smith grabbed the rebound, he fired a perfect pass to McGlocklin, who went in for an uncontested layup, giving the Bucks a 119-114 lead with five seconds left that proved to be the final.

After the game, both coaches complained about the officiating. Philadelphia coach, Jack Ramsay, was upset about the Bucks playing what he thought was a zone defense:

> "Costello was yelling for them to play zone so loud you could hear it up in the stands. If the refs don't see that, they're the only guys in the arena that didn't. They (the Bucks) play it all the time, but they do it to protect Lew when he's in foul trouble or in special situations, and they did it tonight. He (Alcindor) is a goalie in there."[35]

Costello responded to Ramsay's accusations, saying,

> "Did I yell 'zone'? We have a different terminology. Officials recognize this. If sagging and doubling up means zone, every team in the league does it. All you have to do is be within six feet of the man is the

way it is defined to me. Every team in the league does it, and Philly did it to us all through the playoffs last spring.[36]

Costello changed the discussion about the zone defense to a critique of the officials' performance.

"One time Lew must have been fouled about eight times before they called a foul, and the joke of the whole thing was that he wound up fouling out. It's all right to play aggressive defense, but you can't shove and push all the time and get away with it. That was ridiculous."[37]

Alcindor agreed with Costello.

"It was obvious all the time, and yet nothing was being done about it until the end. Then all of a sudden everything became visible. You've got to be a genius to figure those people (referees) out."[38]

Alcindor led the Bucks with 41 points along with 13 rebounds. Smith had 25 points, and Dandridge and Robertson each had 17 points. Despite having two points at halftime, Cunningham led the 76ers with 26 points, Clark had 24 points with ten assists, and Washington added 15 points with 12 rebounds.

GAME 65—LOWERING THE BOOM ON THE SONICS: BUCKS 128, SUPERSONICS 112

It was off to the West Coast for a game against the Seattle Supersonics. On Friday, February 19, in front of a sellout crowd of 12,865 at the Seattle Center Coliseum, the Bucks defeated the Supersonics, 128-112. It was their ninth straight win over them, and the fourth of the season.

In a high-scoring first quarter, Seattle, led by forward Don Kojis and guard Dick Snyder, took a 31-30 lead at the end of the quarter. Early in the second quarter, with the game tied at 36, the Sonics outscored the Bucks 14-5 to take a 50-41 lead. With 3:40 left in the quarter, trailing Seattle 54-47, the Bucks woke up.

Helped by three baskets by McGlocklin, the Bucks scored 15 straight points. Seattle guard Leroy Winfield ended the streak with a pair of free throws, but the Bucks scored the last basket of the quarter and had a 64-56 lead at halftime.

Seattle scored the first four points of the third quarter, but the Bucks, behind four baskets from Alcindor, had a 79-69 lead midway through the quarter. The Sonics made a comeback. Player-coach Lenny Wilkins and Dick Snyder led a surge that brought the Sonics to within one point at 93-92. An Alcindor hook-shot gave the Bucks a 95-92 lead going into the fourth quarter.

Five quick points by Greg Smith helped the Bucks take a 106-96 lead three minutes into the fourth quarter. Costello started playing the bench, and baskets by McCoy McLemore and Alcindor made the score 110-96. The onslaught continued as Robertson, McGlocklin, and Alcindor helped the Bucks take a commanding 120-104 lead. With a little under three minutes left and the Bucks leading 124-106, Alcindor went to the bench. The Bucks won by a final score of 128-112.

Alcindor led the Bucks with 42 points, grabbing a career-high 29 rebounds, blocked seven shots, and had seven assists. Robertson hit 13 out of 18 field goal attempts on his way to 28 points, and Greg Smith added 20. Dick Snyder connected on 15 out of 20 from the field scoring 31 points, and Don Kojis had 26 points along with 11 rebounds.

Kojis was very impressed with Alcindor.

> *"I thought we did a good job on the big guy, and he still got 42 points. He's in a class by himself. Alcindor makes them the best, and their record says they are too, but the playoffs are a different matter. That's a whole new season."*[39]

Wilkens was impressed with the effort of Sonics rookie center Pete Cross.

> *"Cross did very well against Alcindor in the first half, but he's only 6-8 1/2, and when Lew makes up his mind to score, he can do it. We got close again at 86-83, but then Lew would get the big hoop as usual. You either have to play a perfect game against them or catch them on a bad night."*[40]

Alcindor talked about how the game played out.

> *"I was able to stay around the basket all the time. If Cross could hit from the outside, it would have been a different game. Their other guys were hitting their outside shots for a while, but once they started missing and we started running, it changed the whole game."*[41]

GAME 66—BUCKS WALLOP WARRIORS:
BUCKS 104, WARRIORS 96

The Bucks were leaving on a jet plane and flew down to San Francisco for their next game on Saturday, February 20. They continued their quest to clinch the NBA Midwest Division championship and won their tenth game in a row with a 104-96 victory.

Maybe it was because of playing the day before, or the flight from Seattle, but the Bucks came out flat. They didn't score a point in the first three minutes of the game and trailed 8-0. With five and a half minutes remaining in the first quarter, they were behind 14-3.

A big contributor for the Warriors was center Nate Thurmond, who scored six points. The lead grew to 23-8 before the Bucks got going. Jon McGlocklin had four baskets and Robertson one cutting the deficit to 24-18 with two minutes left. The Bucks ended the quarter with a 10-5 run and trailed 29-28 at the end of the first quarter.

McGlocklin scored six points and Alcindor added five as the Bucks outscored the Warriors 17-4, taking a 45-33 lead with seven minutes remaining in the second quarter. Thurmond led a Warriors comeback and helped narrow the Bucks' lead to 53-47. Baskets by McCoy McLemore and Alcindor helped the Bucks take a 59-50 halftime advantage.

Three minutes into the third quarter, the Bucks had stretched their margin to 69-54, but San Francisco made another comeback, narrowing the lead to 71-65 midway through the quarter. A 13-6 run, helped by eight points from Robertson, gave the Bucks an 84-71 lead going into the fourth quarter.

The trend of Warriors' comebacks continued in the fourth quarter. Thurmond was again the main contributor. After Joe Ellis scored a basket after a steal and Thurmond hit an inside bank shot, the score was 97-92. Alcindor scored two baskets and a free throw, giving the Bucks a 102-94 lead, and the final score ended up 104-96.

McGlocklin led the Bucks with 26 points, scoring 21 in the first half and Alcindor had 25 points. The Warriors, who played a great game without their All-Star guard Jeff Mullins, who sprained an ankle in a game the night before, were led by Thurmond with 30 points and guard Ron Williams with 27.

GAME 67—BUCKS ORBIT THE SUNS:
BUCKS 125, SUNS 97

Whoever made out the NBA schedule showed no sympathy to the Bucks. They were playing their third game in as many nights, and the stretch was six games in six cities in eight days. They conquered adversity in a big way in front of 12,371 fans at the Phoenix Memorial Coliseum on Sunday, February 21, defeating the Phoenix Suns, 125-97 for their 11th win in a row.

Coach Larry Costello couldn't say enough about the team's performance:

> *"I'm very, very proud of our players. With all the traveling and the fatigue resulting from it, they still went out and played one of their best games of the year. For a team to play as hard as these guys have been playing under such tough conditions is fantastic. It's a matter of individual pride in each player, and believe me, they've showed me they've got it."*[42]

There were no signs of fatigue early in the game as the Bucks had a 28-19 lead at the end of the first quarter. In the second quarter, with the Bucks ahead 36-30, they outscored Phoenix 19-7 to take a 55-37 lead late in the quarter and led 61-55 at halftime.

Early in the third quarter, led by Dick Van Arsdale, the Suns staged a comeback. They outscored the Bucks 22-14 and trailed 75-67. The Bucks' offense woke up, and a 12-2 spurt helped them take a 90-77 lead going into the fourth quarter. Costello played the bench the last five minutes of the game and, led by Bob Boozer's 14 points and eight rebounds, they outscored the Suns 35-20 in the fourth quarter for a 125-97 win.

Alcindor led the Bucks with 36 points and 21 rebounds, Dandridge had 22 points, Robertson 20 points, and McGlocklin with 18. Van Arsdale led the Suns with 21, and Connie Hawkins was right behind with 19.

The Bucks shot 51 percent from the field and outrebounded Phoenix, 57-47. Costello talked about controlling the backboards.

> *"When Lew rebounds like he has been, we're awfully tough. We've got the speed, and we've got the shooters, and we only need four or five of those fast breaks and pretty soon the game opens up."*[43]

GAME 68—BUCKS CLINCH DIVISION TITLE TIE: BUCKS 118, WARRIORS 107

On Tuesday, February 23, after a day of rest from their recent road trip, the Bucks returned to the Milwaukee Arena for a game against the San Francisco Warriors. In front of a sellout crowd, the Bucks won their 12th straight game, 118-107. The win was also significant because it clinched not only a tie for the Midwest Division title, but also a tie for the NBA's best record, which gave the Bucks the home-court advantage in all playoff series.

Both teams came into the game shorthanded. Warriors' guard Jeff Mullins was recuperating from an ankle injury, and Lucius Allen was still on the sidelines with a sore back. In addition, the Bucks lost the services of Billy Zopf, their second-round draft choice from Duquesne. Zopf was called to active duty with the National Guard and would be reporting in two days for four months of active duty at Fort Leonard Wood, Missouri.

The Bucks trailed the entire first quarter, with the biggest deficit being six points. At the end of the quarter, the Warriors led, 28-27. The Bucks took the lead for good early in the second quarter, 37-36, on a basket by Robertson. They enjoyed a 54-47 lead at the half.

A technical foul on Costello ignited the Bucks, and five points from Greg Smith helped them to a 15-6 run that gave them a 69-53 lead midway through the quarter. The Bucks maintained their lead and were ahead, 84-70, at the end of the quarter. Thurmond and Nick Jones, a rookie guard from Oregon who was in the lineup replacing the injured Mullins, helped rally the Warriors to draw within nine at 88-79 early in the fourth quarter, but the Bucks responded. They rested their starters, played their bench, and ended up with a 118-107 win.

Costello had a lot to say after the game.

> *"They had a hell of a shooting night from the guards and Thurmond. Jones gives 'em speed, but speed doesn't bother us. If they make us run, it's good because that's when we're at our best. Big O got us some big hoops when it was close. He had a lot of opportunities, but he passed off to a wingman. Not many guys would do that. He's such a great shooter, he's the guy who should take 'em. We also got a good chance to look at McCoy McLemore and Jeff Webb and play Greg Smith at guard. Billy Zopf is gone and we don't know when Lucius Allen will be back to help at guard."*[44]

Costello was asked if the 6-0 season series sweep of the Warriors would help give the Bucks a psychological advantage in the playoffs:

> *"If we get to play San Francisco in the first round of the playoffs, beating them six straight could work either way, psychologically, but we'll worry about that when the time comes. Right now the big thing, no, the only thing, is the next game and becoming champions."*[45]

Robertson led the Bucks with 26 points, hitting 12 of 17 from the field. He also had six assists, giving him 263 for the season, a new record for the Bucks in a single season, breaking Guy Rodgers' record set two years ago. Robertson commented,

> *"It's nice, I guess, but I didn't even know about it before the game."*[46]

Alcindor had 25 points along with 16 rebounds, McGlocklin added 18, and Bob Boozer came off the bench and had 16 points and nine rebounds. Nick Jones led the Warriors with 31, Thurmond had 24, guard Ron Williams added 20, and veteran Jerry Lucas had 16 points and 14 rebounds.

GAME 69—BUCKS DISARM ROCKETS: BUCKS 139, ROCKETS 104

On Wednesday, February 24, at the Milwaukee Arena, the Bucks would be playing their fifth game in six days against a hot San Diego Rockets team. The Rockets had won seven of their last eight games, including a 126-109 win against the Knicks at Madison Square Garden the previous evening. The Bucks also had a good streak going, and they extended their winning streak to 13 with a 139-104 win.

The Bucks led, 29-25, at the end of the first quarter and extended it to 62-53 at halftime. In the first five minutes of the third quarter, the Bucks outscored the Rockets 18-8, and that helped them open up a 99-83 lead at the end of the quarter. Alcindor, hampered with an inflamed left knee, played only 31 minutes and sat out the final quarter. An 8-2 run early in the final quarter gave the Bucks a 107-85 advantage. Costello played the bench extensively in the fourth quarter and they did a great job, outscoring San Diego 40-21, winning going away 139-104.

The Bucks were led by Dandridge, who went 14-20 from the field, scoring 33 points. Robertson had 26, and even though he only played 31 minutes, Alcindor had 20 points and 13 rebounds. The Bucks' bench did well. Boozer had 12 points and six rebounds, Dick Cunningham had nine points and nine rebounds, and McLemore added eight points and seven rebounds. Elvin Hayes was the leading scorer for San Diego with 23 points and 14 rebounds. Guard Stu Lantz had 18 and Calvin Murphy chipped in with 15.

Rockets' coach Alex Hannum was impressed with the Bucks.

"I just think they broke us down with the rebounding of their forwards. I know Smith and Dandridge are good athletes, but they shouldn't have that big a night against us. Milwaukee's got this 7-5 center, and we didn't have a chance on the boards."[47]

When Hannum was told that the Bucks' media guide listed Alcindor's height listed at 7-foot-2, he replied,

"He's 7-foot-5."[48]

In the Bucks' locker room, Larry Costello said,

*"The big thing was rebounding. In other games
against them their big front men gave us trouble.
Tonight we had command of the boards and we were
able to run. We did a hell of a job on the boards."*[49]

The Bucks ended the game with a 60-54 advantage in rebounds. They shot 54 percent from the field and did a good job on defense, as the Rockets only shot 36 percent. Costello was very pleased with the Bucks' defense on the Rockets' Calvin Murphy.

*"We did a good job of keeping Cal Murphy from being
effective. He's been scoring well for them lately, but
we doubled up on him more than other teams do."*[50]

The victory assured the Bucks of the best winning percentage in the NBA, worth $20,000, and the best winning percentage in the Western Conference, worth $30,000. They also clinched the Midwest Division title. Alcindor asked ballboy Pat McBride how many games do they need to be sure of having the best record in the league?

When Pat told him the Bucks had already achieved that, Lew responded,

"Really? I guess I'll go out and sign some autographs."[51]

Which he did.

GAME 70—BUCKS RUB OUT ROYALS:
BUCKS 135, ROYALS 111

A letdown after clinching the division title? No way! In their first game after clinching the division at home against the Cincinnati Royals on Friday, February 26, the Bucks won their 14th straight, routing the Royals, 135-111.

The Royals were in a battle for second place with Atlanta in the Central division, which would earn them a spot in the playoffs. The Bucks were set up with home court through every round, but they had to stay on top of their game. Coach Costello said,

> *"We've still got to make sure the regulars get 30 to 35 minutes of playing time each game to maintain sharpness and confidence in everything they try."*[52]

Six minutes into the first quarter, the Royals led, 17-14. The Bucks were red hot and outscored Cincinnati 19-5 in the next four minutes, taking a 33-22 lead. The Bucks hit 17 of their first 27 field goal attempts, a 63 percent pace, and they led, 43-29, at the end of a high-scoring quarter. They extended the lead to 76-57 at halftime.

There was no letdown in the third quarter, and late in the quarter, the Bucks scored 10 straight points, all on fast break baskets, taking a 100-71 lead. The quarter ended with the Bucks comfortably ahead 110-79.

Coach Costello had an interesting observation:

> *"They (Royals) were up at the start. It was a big game for them, as everyone is down the stretch if they want to beat out Atlanta, but once we pulled so far ahead they started shuttling guys in and out, probably saving them for games they have a chance to win. I think our rebounding, more than anything, and tight defense really discouraged them. Defense has been such a big factor for us."*[53]

Alcindor went to the bench with ten minutes left, and the reserves played a majority of the fourth quarter. They played great and the Bucks cruised to a 135-111 win.

The Bucks had balanced scoring. Alcindor, McGlocklin, and Dandridge each had 24 points and Robertson added 18. The bench was led by Boozer's 18, and McLemore added 11. Former Bucks were a big part of the Royals scoring. Charlie Paulk led them with 24, Tom Van Arsdale had 18, and Flynn "The Electric Eye" Robinson added 16.

Costello was very pleased with the Bucks' recent performances.

> *"We're playing the best basketball we've played in three years. We're running the best we have run in three years. When we're running, we're tough."*[54]

Robertson also commented on the recent outstanding play of the Bucks.

> *"I don't know what it is or how big a part I have in it, but Lew [Alcindor] is rebounding better than he ever has, and other guys like Greg Smith are clearing the ball. Lew is really getting it out, and then we go. I'd say it has been just a real good job on the boards that has opened it up for us."*[55]

Royals' coach Bob Cousy offered his evaluation of the Bucks.

> *"We didn't offer much of a criterion for how good Milwaukee is. The big man just dominated us, as he has done almost every time this season. To tell how good the Bucks are, you'd have to see how they do against New York or Baltimore or Los Angeles. You've got to have a center that can negate at least some of the things Alcindor can do, a Reed or a Thurmond."*[56]

GAME 71—BIG WIN IN BEANTOWN: BUCKS 111, CELTICS 99

On Sunday evening, February 28, in front of 10,880 fans at the Boston Garden, the Bucks won their 15th straight game and got their 60th win of the season in a come-from-behind win over the Celtics, 111-99.

It was a tight game through most of the first quarter with 11 ties, but the Celtics had the lead, 33-27, at the end of the quarter. Early in the second quarter, with Alcindor on the bench, John Havlicek and Jo Jo White led a Boston surge, outscoring the Bucks 8-2, giving them a 41-29 lead. The Bucks cut the lead to 59-50 at halftime.

The Bucks scored the first seven points of the third quarter, making the score 59-57, and they later tied the score at 69. Milwaukee took a 73-69 lead on two baskets by Robertson, but the Celtics came back and tied the score at 76. The Bucks went on to score seven straight on an Alcindor tip in, an 18-foot jump shot from Bob Boozer, a Robertson basket from the top of the key, and a free throw by McGlocklin, ending the quarter with the Bucks ahead, 83-76.

With Boston behind 87-83 early in the fourth quarter, Greg Smith and Alcindor scored five straight, giving the Bucks a 92-83 lead, and they never looked back on the way to a 111-99 win.

After the game, Costello talked the improvement in the second half, a half in which they outscored Boston, 61-40.

> *"Our defense turned the game around in the second half. We didn't give them any cheap baskets."*[57]

Greg Smith did a great job on Havlicek, holding him to only six points in the second half.

Celtics' rookie center Dave Cowens had, in the words of Costello,

> *"... made a fantastic effort,"*[58]

leading the Celtics with 36 points and 19 rebounds. Alcindor was also impressed with Cowens.

"I voted for him for Rookie of the Year. He has good basketball sense and he plays the game well. He was going to the boards better tonight than he had in the past."[59]

Havlicek added 21 points and ten rebounds, and Jo Jo White and Don Nelson each scored 14. The Bucks were led by Alcindor's 26 points and a regular-season, career-high 30 rebounds. Robertson had 24, Dandridge 16 and Smith, who hit seven of eight from the field, added 15.

GAME 72—BUCKS SLAM SIXERS:
BUCKS 127, 76ERS 103

The Bucks took a flight out of Boston, returned to Milwaukee, and had a game the next day, March 1, hosting the Philadelphia 76ers. The Bucks didn't let down the sellout crowd as they posted a 127-103 win, their 16th in a row.

The Sixers led, 26-25, at the end of the first quarter and had a 35-31 lead with 9:38 left in the second quarter when Alcindor picked up his third foul, sending him to the bench. The Bucks regrouped, scoring six straight on a driving layup by Robertson, a Dandridge jump shot, and another Robertson basket to tie the score at 37. The Bucks took a brief lead, courtesy of a Dandridge basket and free throw, but the 76ers tied the score at 44.

There was also more than basketball going on during the game. Dick Cunningham, who was doing a great job rebounding and playing defense filling in for Alcindor, took exception to some of the 76ers' tactics and received a technical foul. Two minutes later, he again pushed some opposing players away, and it almost led to a fight between him and Sixers' center Dennis Awtrey.

The only person who received a technical foul was the NBA's leader in that category, Billy Cunningham, whose discussion with the officials did not go as planned. When play resumed, Robertson and McGlocklin helped the Bucks to an 18-7 run, giving them a 62-51 halftime lead.

After the game, Philadelphia coach Jack Ramsay talked about the second quarter.

> *"We might have tried too hard to capitalize on Alcindor's absence, but what really hurt us was letting a couple of bad calls upset us in the second quarter. You're going to get bad calls, and if you let them get the best of you, you're in trouble."*[60]

Guard Archie Clark helped lead a Philadelphia comeback, narrowing the Bucks' lead to 73-71, but Alcindor was back in the game and the Bucks ended the quarter with a 17-6 run, taking a 90-77 lead. The Bucks continued their great all-around play in the fourth quarter, outscoring the 76ers 37-26, and came away with a 127-103 win.

Costello was impressed by the Bucks' recent performances.

> *"We've never put a string of good games like this together before, not even in our other 16-game winning streak, and the big reason has been Oscar. He's been playing fantastic basketball for us. He's shooting more, running our offense, just playing basketball. I've said all along that he should shoot more, and now he is. A great shooter like Oscar should average 20 shots a game."*[61]

Costello also had high praise for the job reserve center Dick Cunningham did when Alcindor was on the bench with foul trouble.

*"He did a heck of a job, some hard rebounding.
Oscar took over offensively and Dick defensively.
The other guys all boarded hard too."*[62]

Coach Jack Ramsay talked about Robertson's game.

*"He was very instrumental. He had 18 at halftime,
didn't he? We should have trapped him, double
teamed him more. He hits the open man pretty well
with his passes, but I'd rather take a chance on
that than give him the shot. He's a great player, no
doubt about it."*[63]

Robertson achieved, a term that hadn't been coined yet, a
triple double, with 29 points, 10 assists, and 12 rebounds.
Despite being on the bench with foul trouble, Alcindor also
scored 29, and grabbed seven rebounds, McGlocklin had
20, and Dandridge, who hit on 8 of 11 shots, had 18.
Archie Clark led the 76ers with 20 points, along with eight
assists and six rebounds, forward Jim Washington scored
18 points and grabbed 11 rebounds, and Dick Cunningham added 15.

GAME 73—BUCKS SINK LAKERS:
BUCKS 112, LAKERS 97

After a day off, the Bucks hosted a depleted Los Angeles
Lakers team on Wednesday, March 3. The Lakers had
suffered a major setback in a game at Buffalo the night
before. During a scramble for a loose ball late in the
second quarter, their All-Star guard, Jerry West, tore
ligaments in his right knee. He would be out of action for
the rest of the season and the playoffs. The Lakers held a
players-only meeting before the game. Perhaps the Bucks
took the Lakers too lightly before posting a 112-97 win,
their 17th straight.

With two minutes remaining in the first quarter, Alcindor went to the bench with the Bucks ahead, 19-16. They expanded the lead to 27-21 going into the second quarter.

Costello noticed about Alcindor that...

> *"...he was discouraged with himself when he came to the bench. He just wasn't having a good game. Heck, everybody is entitled to a bad game sometime."*[64]

Alcindor didn't return until 7:51 remaining in the second quarter with the Bucks ahead, 41-26. The Lakers made a mild comeback narrowing the margin to 53-45 at the half.

Early in the third quarter, with the Bucks winning 59-51, Alcindor picked up his third foul and went to the bench. He returned later, but Costello pulled him with two minutes left in the quarter when he picked up his fourth foul with Bucks clinging to a 73-70 lead. Dick Cunningham gave the Bucks a huge spark, helping the Bucks to an 11-point lead at the end of the quarter. It began with a pair of free throws by Boozer, then Cunningham had a dunk off a great outlet pass by McGlocklin.

After the Lakers missed a shot on their next possession, Cunningham snared the rebound and started a fast break that ended with a Boozer layup. Greg Smith hit a 20-footer to end the quarter, giving the Bucks an 81-70 advantage going into the fourth quarter.

A minute and a half was gone in the fourth quarter when Cunningham picked up his fifth foul, sending him to the bench with Bucks winning 83-74. Alcindor came in for Cunningham and the Bucks maintained their lead. With 5:39 left, Alcindor picked up his fifth foul, so the shuffling of centers continued with Cunningham returning to action. With 2:21 left, and the Bucks ahead 101-89 lead, Cunningham fouled out. Alcindor finished the game, which ended up 112-97.

Costello was not pleased with the Bucks' performance:

"We played our worst game in I don't know how long. It was a lackadaisical performance. What finally won for us was that we got some steals and some fast breaks in the second half. Outside of that, we didn't move much at all."[65]

Lakers' coach Joe Mullaney wasn't too upset with his team's play.

"Wilt played Lew well and he filled the hole, but Gail (Goodrich) was the only guy loose among the others. He shot well. Keith (Erickson) and some others were too intent. Our guys were emotionally up after losing Jerry, wanting to do well, and they tightened up shooting."[66]

He also made a comment about Alcindor.

"I understand Lew may not have been feeling well. He gets those (migraine) headaches and I thought maybe that was why he was off in his play and out of there so much."[67]

Costello was asked if Alcindor was ill.

"He sure played like he was ailing. No, he sat out because he was in foul trouble."[68]

The bottom line about Alcindor was his comments after the game.

"No headache, nothing like that. I just played a terrible game. We were just lucky it happened on a

*night when everybody else was doing well. It's got
to happen sometime, I guess."*[69]

Robertson led the Bucks with 24 points, McGlocklin was
right behind with 22, Dandridge had 17, and Greg Smith,
who went seven for seven from the field, scored 16 points.

Afterwards, Smith talked about the game.

*"It was one of my best games, probably my
steadiest since my rookie year when we beat L.A. I
was hitting from outside early and then was able to
get on the boards and also make some steals."*[70]

Alcindor had season low totals, 15 points and only six
rebounds. Gail Goodrich led the Lakers with 25 points,
connecting on 10 of 17 shots, Chamberlain had 24 points
and 13 rebounds and Happy Hairston added 19 while
grabbing 10 rebounds.

GAME 74—BUCKS SURVIVE BRAVES:
BUCKS 116, BRAVES 113

The Bucks' next game was at home on Thursday, March 4
against the expansion Buffalo Braves. Should have been a
piece of cake, no problem, easy win, the Knicks 18-game
winning streak would be tied. Wrong! The Bucks had their
hands full and won a game that was in doubt until the
final minute, 116-113.

It looked like an easy win early as the Bucks led, 30-
25, at the end of the first quarter, and expanded the
advantage to 63-45 at halftime. Early in the third quarter
they led 70-49. One of the big occurrences in the third
quarter was Bob Boozer getting ejected from the game by
referee Jack Madden because of Boozer expressing a major
difference of opinion in how the game was being officiated.
The Bucks led, 92-76, going into the fourth quarter.

With eight and a half minutes left in the fourth quarter and Buffalo behind 102-82, they made their move. In a two-and-a-half-minute span, led by Bob Kaufmann and Don May, the Braves scored 14 straight points, narrowing the Bucks' lead to 102-96. Robertson ended the Bucks' scoring drought with a basket with six minutes left. The Braves weren't done though. May's basket with 3:40 remaining cut the lead to 105-103. Alcindor, who had to come off the bench, hit a hook shot, but rookie John Hummer answered right back with a basket, making the score, 107-105.

Dandridge hit a free throw and Robertson scored on a hook shot, but Emmette Bryant came back with a jump shot, and the Braves trailed by three. The Bucks scored on a Robertson free throw and a layup by Dandridge, who was on the receiving end of a great behind-the-back pass from McGlocklin.

The Braves cut it to three points on two more occasions. Greg Smith, who sat out most of the second half after aggravating a knee injury in the second quarter, was put back in the game because Boozer wasn't available. Smith scored the big points. He converted three free throws in the last 26 seconds of the game, giving the Bucks a hard fought 116-113 win, their record-tying 18th straight.

Dolph Schayes was very proud of his team.

"Another couple of minutes and we might have pulled it out. We were 20 points down against a great club like Milwaukee, but our guys didn't toss it in. It's easy to just play out the string late in the season when you're not going anywhere. It was a moral victory... but still a loss. Yet I'm proud of

*these guys. I can point to everybody. John Hummer
had played one of his best games he ever has, good
defense against Robertson and he got 16 points,
too. Herm Gilliam gave us a big lift (18) and Donnie
(May) has been doing some great shooting all
season. I continue to be amazed at how a 6-4
player like Don May can get himself open so well.
He's got basketball genes."*[71]

When asked to compare the Bucks and the Knicks,
Schayes observed.

*"They match up defensively. If you can keep
Milwaukee from running you can beat them.
They're both fine clubs."*[72]

Costello called the tying of the record...

*"...a hell of an accomplishment. It came hard, sure it
did. They (Buffalo) ran, kept coming at us. They've
got some fine shooters in May and Kaufmann. Darn
right I was worried when they ran off 14 points in a
row. This is the second time we had a shot at the
record, and the last time the Knicks kept us from
getting it. After tomorrow, I'll really rest these guys.
The hell with the other records, like Philly's 68 wins
in a season. We've got the playoffs coming up and
that's the main thing. We'll take our chances on
how the remaining games go, but there's been a lot
of added pressure trying for this streak record. The
first big thing was winning the division and getting
into the playoffs. The whole season doesn't mean
much if you don't get in the playoffs and have a
shot at the title, does it?"*[73]

Alcindor agreed with Costello.

*"It's kind of an anticlimax after winning the divi-
sion. Once you get that all done, you want to get to
what you have to do. It's a hardship to wait so long*

*for the playoffs to start, but at least the streak has
kept us from getting stale.*"[74]

Robertson expressed his thoughts about the record-
tying victory.

> *"It's just that the record doesn't mean as much as
> winning the division crown, or as much as it would
> have meant if we had gotten it the other time.
> Maybe I feel that it's an anticlimax because I'm
> tired now, but as the years go on, it will mean a lot
> more."*[75]

GAME 75—BUCKS BRAKE PISTONS: BUCKS 108, PISTONS 95

What a rough schedule! Three games in three days as the
Bucks traveled to Detroit for a game on Friday, March 5 at
Cobo Arena against the Detroit Pistons. It proved to be a
historic game as the Bucks defeated the Pistons with a,
108-95, victory for their 19th straight win, establishing a
new NBA record.

In contrast to their previous two games, the Bucks
started quickly, building up a 23-6 lead in the first seven
minutes and led, 31-18, at the end of the first quarter. The
Bucks scored the first five points of the second quarter,
taking a 36-18 lead. The Pistons staged a comeback led by
Dave Bing, who despite suffering a broken cheekbone in a
game Tuesday night, played while wearing a protective,
wrestling-type helmet. The Pistons cut the deficit down to
six points and ended up trailing the Bucks 55-42 at the
half.

The game remained competitive in the third quarter.
The Pistons narrowed the Bucks' lead to three at 79-76
and trailed 83-76 going into the fourth quarter.

Midway through the fourth quarter, with the Bucks ahead 96-89, they got a little more breathing room. McGlocklin hit two long baskets, and Robertson dribbled the length of the floor and scored on a layup. Then with three minutes left, Alcindor blocked a Bob Lanier shot, dribbled to midcourt, and made a great pass to McGlocklin for a layup, making the score 104-93, and the Bucks ended with a 108-95 win.

The Bucks, who converted on 46 of 80 attempts for a sizzling 57.5 percent, were led by Alcindor's 34 points, and 11 rebounds. McGlocklin added 26, hitting on 13 of 16 shots and Robertson had 18 points, 16 assists and 10 rebounds. The Pistons, who only shot 38.7 percent from the field, were led by Dave Bing with 39 and Bill Hewitt had 13. As a team, the Pistons went 23 for 23 from the foul line, including 13 for 13 from Bing.

Understandably, everyone was excited about setting the record. Reserve guard Jeff Webb noticed.

"This is the first time I've heard anybody yell. Believe me, it's something for me just to say I've played on a team like this."[76]

Greg Smith also made note of the loud locker room.

"We're super happy. We're not an emotional bunch, but we're super happy tonight. This is the first time we've been noisy all season. In fact, this is the noisiest we've been in the three years we've been in the league."[77]

Alcindor was glad that the quest for the record was over.

"We tried not to point to it, but once the guys got in position, we went all out. Now that we've set the record, we won't have the pressure on us and we

can concentrate on keeping our health for the playoffs."[78]

Robertson added,

"We're real beat, but the record was there, right on top of us, and an opportunity like this comes once in a lifetime. Actually, though, I was very confident that we were going to do it. When you're not sure of something, the excitement runs higher."[79]

Coach Larry Costello was elated.

"I'm so happy I can't express myself. We've had such great co-operation from everybody. These players are fantastic. This club is only three years in existence, and we did what nobody has ever done."[80]

When Costello was asked about breaking the 76ers, they'd have to win five of their last seven.

"We could do it if we wanted to, but it's not necessarily a goal with us. It will be great if we can do it. But if we went at it real hard and Lew or Oscar say was injured, I'd have to live with that the rest of my life. Winning the title is the thing."[81]

There was more on McGlocklin's mind than just the streak.

"We played good, real good. It felt good all the way. We got off to a fine start, running well, and had great determination. It was obvious from the beginning that everybody wanted this one badly. This one, the streak is in the record book, but there's one big record we want to get in before it's over and you know what that is."[82]

Bucks	FG-FGA	FT-FTA	Rebs.	Pts	Pistons	FG-FGA	FT-FTA	Rebs.	Pts.
Alcindor	14-21	6-8	11	34	Bing	13-30	13-13	6	39
Boozer	0-1	0-0	1	1	Hewitt	6-12	1-1	7	13
Cunningham	0-0	0-0	1	0	Komives	3-10	2-2	1	8
Dandridge	7-14	2-3	9	16	Lanier	5-13	0-0	6	10
McGlocklin	13-16	0-0	6	26	Moore	4-9	1-1	8	9
McLemore	1-3	2-2	4	4	Mueller	0-4	0-0	2	0
Robertson	8-17	2-2	10	18	Quick	3-6	1-1	8	7
Smith	3-7	4-6	1	10	Walker	2-9	5-5	2	9
Webb	0-1	0-0	0	0					

Game 75 Box Score

GAME 76—BUCKS SQUASH SONICS:
BUCKS 104, SUPERSONICS 99

Monday, March 8, 1971 was a big day in the world of sports. The Bucks were playing their final home game in front of another sell-out crowd at the Milwaukee Arena, looking to extend their record NBA winning streak to 20 against the Seattle Supersonics, and right next door at the Milwaukee Auditorium, a sellout crowd watched a closed-circuit telecast of the Muhammad Ali-Joe Frazier heavy-weight championship fight. The Bucks won a close game, 104-99.

Seattle came out strong, taking a 30-25 lead at the end of the first quarter. Great play by Spencer Haywood and former Buck Don Smith helped build the advantage to 49-38, but some baskets by Alcindor helped narrow the deficit to 53-48 at halftime.

It was a strange beginning for the third quarter. At the end of the first half, a technical foul was called on Don Smith. Robertson came out of the locker room during halftime to shoot it, but he couldn't because he wasn't in the game when it was called, so McGlocklin converted the free throw. The Bucks scored the next two times they had the ball, on a hook shot by Alcindor and a basket off a steal by Robertson, tying the game at 55. Midway through

222

the third quarter, the Bucks built the lead to 71-60. Led by Alcindor's ten points and Robertson's nine during the quarter, the score was 82-75 after three quarters.

Although Seattle fell behind by 11 points early in the fourth quarter, they fought back and narrowed the score to 97-93. Robertson hit a basket, but Haywood came right back, making the score 99-95. Greg Smith scored a hoop, and after Sonics' player-coach Lenny Wilkens made a basket with 1:06 remaining, it was a 101-97 game. After a missed shot by Haywood, Robertson hit one of two free throws.

With 0:28 left, Don Smith's 20-foot jumper brought the Sonics within three at 102-99. Using the clock, and waiting patiently for a shot, the Bucks were rewarded when McGlocklin hit a 20-footer with ten seconds left, the final points of the game, in a 104-99 Bucks win, their 20th in a row.

Alcindor led the Bucks with 32 points and 16 rebounds, Robertson added 24, with 11 rebounds and seven assists, and McGlocklin had 15 points. Spencer Haywood had 30 points and 16 rebounds, Don Smith scored 28 while grabbing 18 rebounds, and Wilkens scored 16 with 11 assists.

It was a big win for the Bucks that had playoff implications. Costello elaborated.

> "I think I'd rather play San Francisco or San Diego (which also could clinch the Pacific Division's runner-up spot) than Seattle. The winning streak is immaterial to me. The whole thing is to try to keep them (Seattle) out of second place if we can. The more Spencer Haywood plays, the tougher they're going to be, and they've got more size and depth

than the other two teams we might face. Heck, they've got board power and shooting. I don't care to see them in the playoffs against us. It might have been different before they got the okay on Haywood."[83]

McGlocklin talked about the Bucks' performance.

"We didn't play hungry, but we played better as we went along. I wanted to beat them because I don't want to play them in the playoffs, and besides, I'd rather win than lose. If we can win without knocking ourselves out, so much the better, and that's what we did tonight."[84]

The Sonics received good news earlier in the day. The U.S. Supreme Court ruled that Spencer Haywood could continue to play with Seattle. Haywood talked about the court proceedings.

"I'm still not set. I've got to fly to Los Angeles after tomorrow night's game in New York for a trial on my contract with Denver (ABA). After that it depends on what the NBA might do, but this is the first time I've felt at ease since the thing got started. I've been going through hell."[85]

After the game, many of the players gave brief interviews and departed quickly. Even Haywood's talk with the press corps was interrupted by Alcindor, who was already in street clothes, handing him a ticket to join a few of the players to watch the remaining rounds of the fight next door.

By the way, Joe Frazier won the fight.

Endnotes to Chapter 12

1) Rel Bochat, "Bucks Put Chill On Suns, 118-94," *Milwaukee Sentinel*, February 9, 1971, pt. 2, p. 1.

2) Glenn Miller, "Bucks Chew Up Phoenix, 118-94," *Wisconsin State Journal*, February 9, 1971, pt. 3, p. 1.

3) Bochat. p. 5.

4) Bob Wolf, "Suns Spot Problem: Lew," *Milwaukee Journal*, February 9, 1971, pt. 2, p. 10.

5) *Ibid.*

6) *Ibid.*

7) Bob Wolf, "Oscar Saves Night for Bucks," *Milwaukee Journal*, February 10, 1971, pt. 2, p. 19.

8) *Ibid.*

9) *Ibid.*

10) Rel Bochat, "Lew, Oscar Put Brakes On Pistons," *Milwaukee Sentinel*, February 10, 1971, pt. 2, p. 1.

11) Wolf. February 10, 1971, p. 24.

12) Rel Bochat, "Big O Paid Debt; Bucks Plan Coup for L.A. Tonight," *Milwaukee Sentinel*, February 11, 1971, pt. 2, p. 1.

13) Ibid.

14) Rel Bochat, "Bucks Humble Lakers, 122-88," *Milwaukee Sentinel*, February 12, 1971, pt. 2, p. 1.

15) Bob Hill, "Buck Tremors Rock LA," *Wisconsin State Journal*, February 12, 1971, pt. 2, p. 1.

16) *Ibid.*

17) Bob Wolf, "Bucks Make Lakers Pay," *Milwaukee Journal*, February, 12, 1971, pt. 2, p. 15.

18) *Ibid.*

19) *Ibid.*

20) Rel Bochat, "Bucks Seek 5th Straight Against Bulls Here Today," *Milwaukee Sentinel*, February 13, 1971, pt. 2, p. 1.

21) Bob Wolf, "Sluggish Bucks Beat Bulls," *Milwaukee Journal*, February 14, 1971, pt. 3, p. 1.

22) *Ibid.*

23) Bob Logan, "Bucks Overtake Bulls for 103 to 96 Victory," *Chicago Tribune*, February 14, 1971, pt. 2, p. 1.

24) *Ibid.*

25) *Ibid.*

26) Rel Bochat, "Bucks Put Torch To Atlanta," *Milwaukee Sentinel*, February 15, 1971, pt. 2, p. 1.

27) Bob Wolf, "Hazzard Becomes a Bucks' Believer," *Milwaukee Journal,* February 15, 1971, pt. 2, p. 10.

28) Bochat.

29) Wolf.

30) Rel Bochat, "Fire Routs Bucks From Buffalo Hotel," *Milwaukee Sentinel,* February 16, 1971, pt. 2, p.1.

31) Rel Bochat, "Bucks Tomahawk Braves, 135-103," *Milwaukee Sentinel,* February 17, 1971, pt. 2, p. 1.

32) Bob Wolf, "Bucks Hit Stride Late, Shuffle Off From Buffalo," *Milwaukee Journal,* February 17, 1971, pt. 2, p. 13.

33) Bochat.

34) Wolf.

35) Rel Bochat, "Smith's FT Key to Bucks' 8th in Row," *Milwaukee Sentinel,* February 18, 1971, pt. 2, p. 1.

36) *Ibid.*

37) Bob Wolf, "Treatment of Alcindor Irks Bucks in 119-114 Victory," *Milwaukee Journal,* February 18, 1971, pt. 2, p. 13.

38) *Ibid.*

39) Bob Wolf, "Lew Too Much For Sonics," *Milwaukee Journal,* February 20, 1971, pt. 1, p. 15.

40) *Ibid.*

41) *Ibid.*

42) Bob Wolf, "Bucks' Endurance Trial Finishes With a Flourish," *Milwaukee Journal,* February 22, 1971, pt. 2 p. 10.

43) *Ibid.*

44) Rel Bochat, "12th in Row for Bucks," *Milwaukee Sentinel,* February 24, 1971, pt.2, p. 1.

45) Cleon Walfoort, "Bucks Breeze to Title Tie," *Milwaukee Journal,* February 24, 1971, pt. 2, p. 19.

46) *Ibid.*

47) Nolan Zavoral, "Bucks Retain Composure After Wrapping Up Title," *Milwaukee Journal,* February 25, 1971, pt. 2, p. 12.

48) *Ibid.*

49) Rel Bochat, "Big Payday for Bucks," *Milwaukee Sentinel,* February 25, 1971, pt. 2, p. 1.

50) Rel Bochat, "Costello to Rest Lew in Stretch," *Milwaukee Sentinel,* February 26, 1971, pt. 2, p. 1.

51) Zavoral.

52) Bochat.

53) Rel Bochat, "14th Straight a Breeze for Bucks," *Milwaukee Sentinel,* February 27, 1971, pt. 2, p. 1.

54) Glenn Miller, "Bucks Keep Up Winning Pace," *Wisconsin State Journal*, February 27, 1971, pt. 3, p. 2.

55) Bochat.

56) Chuck Johnson, "Blasé Bucks Batter Poor Royals, 135-111," *Milwaukee Journal*, February 27, 1971, pt. 1, p. 16.

57) Special Correspondence, "Celtics Tough Losers Again," *Milwaukee Journal*, March 1, 1971, pt. 2, p. 9.

58) *Ibid.*

59) *Ibid.*

60) Bob Wolf, "Robertson Up to Old Tricks, and Bucks Are Beneficiaries," *Milwaukee Journal*, March 2, 1971, pt. 2, p. 10.

61) *Ibid.*

62) Rel Bochat, "Big 'O', Bucks Gun Down 76ers," *Milwaukee Sentinel*, March 2, 1971, pt. 2 p.1.

63) *Ibid.*

64) Rel Bochat, "Bucks Roar to No. 17," *Milwaukee Sentinel*, March 4, 1971, pt. 2, p. 1.

65) Bob Wolf, "Bucks Win, Nothing Fancy," *Milwaukee Journal*, March 4, 1971, pt. 2, p. 16.

66) Bochat.

67) Bob Hill, "Bucks, Ho Hum, Rip LA," *Wisconsin State Journal*, March 4, 1971, pt. 2, p. 1.

68) Wolf.

69) Bochat.

70) Rel Bochat, "Streaking Bucks Tie NBA Mark," *Milwaukee Sentinel*, March 5, 1971, pt. 2, p. 1.

71) *Ibid.*

72) *Ibid.*

73) Bob Wolf, "Bucks Hang On. Tie Mark," *Milwaukee Journal*, March 5, 1971, pt. 2, p. 18.

74) *Ibid.*

75) Bob Wolf, "19th Straight No Problem as Bucks Break Record," *Milwaukee Journal*, March 6, 1971, pt. 1, p. 16.

76) *Ibid.*

77) *Ibid.*

78) *Ibid.*

79) Rel Bochat, "Bucks Win Record 19th," *Milwaukee Sentinel*, March 6, 1971, pt. 2, p. 1.

80) *Ibid.*

81) *Ibid.*

82) Rel Bochat, "Bucks Bear Down For 20th in Row," *Milwaukee Sentinel*, March 9, 1971, pt. 2, p. 1.

83) Bob Wolf, "Bucks Win and Do Selves a Favor," *Milwaukee Journal*, March 9, 1971, pt. 2, p. 11.

84) *Ibid*. p 11.

85) *Ibid,* p. 14.

CHAPTER 13

HOME STRETCH

GAME 77—BULLS BEAT BUCKS, STREAK ENDS: BULLS 110, BUCKS 103

Chicago Bulls mascot Bennie the Bull predicted the outcome of the game when he held up a sign before the game that read *The Streak Ends Tonite.* On Tuesday, March 9, before 16,277 fans at Chicago Stadium, a 20-game winning streak that began on February 5 came to an end when the Bulls defeated the Bucks, 110-103, in overtime.

The Bulls took the lead early in the first quarter, but the Bucks came back and took a 27-22 lead at the end of the quarter. A 19-8 run by the Bucks to start the second quarter gave them a 46-30 advantage with 3:30 left in the quarter. The Bulls came back, outscoring the Bucks 11-4, and trailed 50-41 at halftime.

The Bulls made a huge comeback in the third quarter and tied the game at 67. Great play by Bob Love and Tom Boerwinkle helped the Bulls take a 77-71 lead after three quarters.

It was a great, physically demanding fourth quarter. After the game Bulls' center Tom Boerwinkle was asked why he came out with 7:32 left in the quarter. He answered,

"I was exhausted. I had to have a few minutes."[1]

Boerwinkle returned with 3:28 to go, and while he was out, the Bucks had narrowed the deficit to 93-90 and tied the score at 95 on a basket by Robertson with 2:24 left. The next two times the Bulls scored to retake the lead, Robertson answered, tying the score. With the score tied at 99, with seven seconds left, the Bulls called time-out, and Bulls guard Bob Weiss missed a shot, sending the game to overtime.

It was all Chicago in the overtime. Weiss scored the first four points, and after Chet Walker hit a jump shot from the side with 2:11 left, the Bulls had a 105-99 lead and went on to win, 110-103, ending the Bucks' 20-game winning streak.

Alcindor played 46 minutes and led the Bucks in scoring with 39 points, and he also hauled in 17 rebounds. Robertson and McGlocklin each chipped in with 20. The Bulls had balanced scoring: Love had 23, and Jerry Sloan and Boerwinkle each had 21. When asked about his huge 33-rebound performance, Boerwinkle responded,

> *"I just tried to keep Lew off the boards. With Butterbean (Bob Love) and Chet Walker going to the boards as they do, Lew has to take his eyes off me momentarily, and that helps."*[2]

Even in defeat, Costello was proud of the team's effort.

> *"It was a hell of a game, wasn't it? Our guys fought like champions. We made them (the Bulls) work for it. It wasn't a gift. It was a very important game for Chicago, not all that big for us. It's sort of a relief not to have that streak hanging over us. I could sense some of the guys really wanted to keep it going and some of them in there (dressing room) are*

kind of hurt we didn't pull it out. All gave it a hell of an effort, but I did what I figured was best. I kept Lew out three minutes during a tough stretch in the third quarter, and I rested some other guys without worrying what the score was at the moment."[3]

McGlocklin agreed with his coach.

"We played our tails off, and they played as well as they can play and barely beat us. There wasn't any real pressure on us, but 20 was a pretty good stretch."[4]

Bucks' assistant coach Tom Nissalke observed,

"We have to play Dick Cunningham sometimes to keep him sharp in case we need him. If this had been a playoff game, we would have played Lew more, but we finished with our regulars because we figured if we were going to lose, we wanted to lose with the guys who had brought us this far."[5]

Costello looked for positives from the loss.

"Anyway, this may turn out to be the best. We had beaten these guys all five times we played them, and this should make us realize how tough they are, in case we meet them in the playoffs. We just didn't want to give it away, and that's why we played so hard."[6]

GAME 78—KNICKS NAIL BUCKS—AGAIN!
KNICKS 108, BUCKS 103

On the evening of March 13, 1971, in front of another sellout crowd of 19,500 at Madison Square Garden, the Knicks continued their dominance of the Bucks, defeating them 108-103. The loss was the Bucks' fourth in five regular season meetings, and including their playoff games and regular season games of last year, this latest loss gave them a 4-12 record against the Knicks.

In a close first half, the Bucks led, 28-27, after the first quarter and took a 52-48 advantage at halftime. There were nine ties and four lead changes in the third quarter, and two free throws by Dave DeBusschere gave the Knicks an 80-79 lead at the end of the quarter.

The game was tied twice early in the fourth quarter before the Bucks went ahead 89-85. The lead was short-lived. The Knicks scored seven straight, taking a 92-89 lead with 7:54 left. They maintained the lead for the rest of the game, posting a 108-103 win, their 31st home victory of the season, establishing a new team record.

One of the keys to the Knicks' win was the great defensive job DeBusschere did on Bob Dandridge. He held him to only 11 points before Dandridge fouled out in the fourth quarter.

Alcindor had 16 rebounds, and he hit 16 out of 29 shots from the floor, scoring 34 points to lead the Bucks. Robertson was close behind with 28, and Greg Smith had 12 points and 11 boards. DeBusschere had a big game, leading the Knicks with 33 points and 17 rebounds. Willis Reed had 27 along with 12 rebounds, and Walt Frazier had 15.

Bucks' coach Larry Costello singled out a big factor that contributed to their loss.

> "We had 18 turnovers, and they had only nine.
> There was the ball game. I thought we played well
> in the first half, but we lost some of our aggressive-
> ness after that, maybe because of the fouls."[7]

Both coaches gave their thoughts about the psychological benefits of the Knicks winning four of five regular season games. Knicks coach Red Holzman said,

> *"Sure, we played well against them, but they're a great club. Will this mean anything in the playoffs? That's too far away. Just get us far enough to play them in the finals, and we won't worry. Costello has done a magnificent job this season, really magnificent. Just look at the record. They're a great team."*[8]

Costello gave his opinion of any psychological edge.

> *"We played very well against a helluva ballclub. I don't think it will mean anything in the playoffs though if we meet them."*[9]

Costello elaborated further,

> *"There's no such thing as a psychological edge. I don't believe in it. We just didn't get any help from our bench when we needed it, so when our forwards got in foul trouble, we were in trouble."*[10]

One of the big stars of the game for the Knicks, Dave DeBusschere, was pleased with the win.

> *"We've been struggling to clinch first place, and it's been embarrassing. Also we couldn't let Milwaukee get any momentum against us if we meet them in the playoffs."*[11]

Detroit Pistons guard Dave Bing was puzzled about the Knicks' dominance of the Bucks.

> *"I don't know why the Bucks don't beat the Knicks. Nobody can stop Lew Alcindor, Oscar Robertson sets the pace when he wants to, and they've got such a strong lineup that you can't double team anybody."*[12]

GAME 79—SUNS SHADE BUCKS:
SUNS 125, BUCKS 113

On Sunday evening, March 14, a capacity crowd of 9,035 at Madison's Dane County Coliseum saw something that hadn't happened in two years—a third straight loss for the Bucks as the Phoenix Suns defeated them, 125-113. The loss eliminated the Bucks' opportunity to set a new NBA record of 69 wins in a season.

The Bucks took an early 6-0 lead and held a 28-27 advantage at the end of the first quarter. The Suns scored the first nine points of the second quarter, taking a 36-28 lead, and they led 60-51 at the half.

One of the big reasons for the Suns' surge was Alcindor being on the bench. The Bucks had a four-point lead when he went there late in the first quarter. When he returned to action in the second quarter, they trailed by six points.

The Suns opened up a big lead in the third quarter. Connie Hawkins came up with consecutive three-point plays midway in the quarter, helping the Suns take an 80-59 lead. Another negative factor for the Bucks was that Alcindor had five fouls. Robertson helped spark a rally that cut the Suns lead to 80-66, but Phoenix responded, taking a 94-74 lead going into the fourth quarter.

Alcindor returned with 10:23 left in the game with the Bucks behind, 102-79. They managed to cut the lead to 11 points, but the Suns went on to post a 125-113 victory.

Even though he only played 33 minutes, Alcindor led the Bucks with 38 points along with 15 rebounds, Robertson had 20, and McGlocklin added 17. Phoenix was led by Hawkins' 27 points and 16 rebounds, Paul Silas scored 21, and Dick Van Arsdale had 20.

This game meant a lot to Phoenix to try to keep their slim playoff hopes alive, and there were a lot of opinions of the outcome. Costello said,

"Sure, Phoenix had a lot more at stake than we did. It's no reason not to play good ball. Our three most consistent players came up with just about their usual play, but they didn't get much help. They're all getting paid to get the job done. You can't rely on three guys to do it, it has to be a team contribution."[13]

Suns' coach Cotton Fitzsimmons said,

"I think they're tired. I don't think they laid down. Alcindor had 38 points. That's not bad for being on your back." [14]

The players expressed their thoughts after the game. Greg Smith admitted,

"I was a little tired personally. We had a rough game in New York when everybody was going all out to win, and we had a rough game in Chicago."[15]

Jon McGlocklin summed it all up:

"We just didn't come to play. I know I would have liked to have had the record. I just don't think you can turn it on and off whenever you want to. The only way is to play."[16]

The Bucks' forwards had a horrible game. The four forwards combined for 18 points. Bob Dandridge hit one of eight from the field, Greg Smith one of six, Bob Boozer one of six, and McCoy McLemore two of six. Costello commented,

"We've got nothing from these guys the last two nights." [17]

GAME 80—BUCKS BLOT OUT SUNS:
BUCKS 119, SUNS 111

After the Bucks lost to the Suns, Bulls coach Dick Motta raised a question.

> *"I just hope Milwaukee isn't playing games. I understand that they would rather play Phoenix than us in the playoffs."*[18]

Costello responded,

> *"That's a lot of baloney. If anything, our players would rather meet Chicago than Phoenix."*[19]

Suns' general manager Jerry Colangelo would ask NBA Commissioner Walter Kennedy to take action about Motta's comment.

> *"It's unthinkable that a coach in the NBA would make remarks like that. Motta has made a lot of asinine statements, but this one tops them all."*[20]

Motta came back,

> *"All I said was that I hoped Milwaukee didn't let down. I said that might be natural after a 20-game winning streak. I know Larry Costello well enough to appreciate that he's trying to win all the games he can."*[21]

On Friday, March 16, the Bucks proved Motta's theory wrong, defeating the Suns in front of 11,640 fans at Veterans Memorial Coliseum, 119-111, virtually eliminating them from playoff contention.

The Bucks led 31-30 at the end of the first quarter, but Phoenix took a 61-55 lead at halftime. Early in the third quarter, the Bucks cut the lead to one at 62-61, only to have the Suns storm back, reestablishing a six-point lead.

Bob Boozer led a comeback making the score 73-72, but the Suns outscored the Bucks, 15-9, to end the quarter with an 88-81 advantage going into the fourth quarter.

The Bucks opened the fourth quarter scoring 12 straight points, taking a 93-88 lead. The Suns came back, tying the score at 95, and in what proved to be their last lead of the game, a 97-95 advantage on a basket by Connie Hawkins. Greg Smith tied the game, and a McGlocklin jump shot gave the Bucks a 99-97 edge.

The game was still in doubt with two minutes remaining with the Bucks on top, 107-106, when Greg Smith had a three-point play, but Phoenix came back and with 1:24 remaining, the Bucks led, 110-108. Alcindor gave the Bucks some breathing room, scoring four straight points courtesy of a hook shot and a pair of free throws. A basket by Paul Silas with 21 seconds left made the score 114-110, but clutch foul shooting by McGlocklin and Smith gave the Bucks a 119-111 win, raising their season record to 66-14.

Alcindor set a Veterans Memorial Coliseum scoring record with 48 points, and he also had 14 rebounds. McGlocklin, who connected on 10 of 14 field goal attempts, had 23, and Bob Boozer, who replaced Dandridge in the lineup because of his sore back, added 17. Dick Van Arsdale and Connie Hawkins, who started at center because Neal Walk saw limited action due to an injured heel, shared scoring honors for the Suns with 28, and Paul Silas had 18 along with 12 rebounds.

Game 81—Seattle Slews Milwaukee:
Supersonics 122, Bucks 121

On Thursday, March 18, at the Seattle Center Coliseum, the Supersonics hosted the Bucks in a meaningless game. By virtue of San Francisco's win over the Bulls earlier in the evening, the Sonics were eliminated from playoff contention. They played a great game and defeated the Bucks, 122-121.

The Bucks' loss took away any possibility they had to tie the 68-win total established by the 1966-67 Philadelphia 76ers. With one game remaining at San Diego, even a Bucks victory would give them a 67-15 record for the season.

Seattle had a 28-21 lead at the end of the first quarter and opened up an 11-point lead in the second quarter. The Bucks came back and narrowed the deficit to 63-59 at halftime. The game remained competitive with Seattle ahead 94-92 at the end of the third quarter. Early in the fourth quarter, the Bucks tied the game at 98, but the Sonics regained the lead and kept it. The Bucks' chances looked bleak with Seattle on top, 118-111, with only 2:30 remaining. Alcindor led a Bucks rally as they narrowed the score to 120-119.

Sonics' reserve guard Lee Winfield played a huge role in the remainder of the game. Winfield scored a basket that gave the Sonics what looked like a safe 122-119 lead with ten seconds left. McGlocklin answered with a basket with five seconds left, making it a one-point game. The Bucks' fortunes vastly improved when they got the ball back as Winfield's inbounds pass bounced off of Dick Snyder's foot and went out of bounds, giving the Bucks possession. Winfield went from possible goat to hero when he stepped in front of Alcindor and intercepted McGlocklin's inbounds pass, preserving a Sonics win.

It was hard to believe the Bucks lost as they shot a sizzling 60.5 percent from the field compared to the Sonics' 44 percent. They also out-rebounded Seattle, 46-43.

Alcindor led the Bucks with 39 points, hitting 15 of 23 from the field, 9 of 10 free throws, and 13 rebounds. Greg Smith hit all 10 of his shots, scoring 23, along with 11 rebounds, and McGlocklin added 19, converting on nine of 12 attempts. Former Buck Don Smith led the Sonics with 28 points and 16 rebounds, Spencer Haywood had 27 points and 10 rebounds, and Dick Snyder added 25 points along with 11 assists.

GAME 82—ROCKETS BLAST BUCKS: ROCKETS 111, BUCKS 99

On Friday, March 19, at the San Diego Sports Arena, the regular season came to an end as the Bucks lost to the Rockets, 111-99. The Bucks finished the regular season losing five of their last six games.

The game had no importance for either team. The Rockets had been eliminated from playoff contention the night before. The Bucks were resting their regulars, and they came into the game with a depleted roster. Bob Dandridge was out because of a sore back, and his replacement in the line-up, Bob Boozer, had injured his knee in the game against Seattle. Costello rested his regulars extensively. No starter played more than 35 minutes. Robertson played 28, and Alcindor only 24.

There were six ties in the first quarter, but the Rockets finished strong and took a 29-19 lead into the second quarter. While Alcindor and Robertson were on the bench, the Bucks came back, cutting the Rockets' lead to two at 37-35. McGlocklin hit three baskets, giving the Bucks a 41-40 lead. When Alcindor returned, he scored two baskets, but Rockets guard Stu Lantz helped the Rockets take a 54-51 lead at halftime.

McGlocklin opened the third quarter with his sixth basket of the game, but forward John Trapp had a hot hand, scoring five of San Diego's next seven baskets and giving the Rockets a 70-61 lead. McGlocklin and Smith ignited a Bucks' rally, narrowing the lead to 73-69. The Rockets took advantage of Alcindor returning to the bench again and led, 81-71, going into the fourth quarter.

Dick Cunningham contributed a few baskets early in the fourth quarter, but Stu Lantz hit some key baskets, rebuilding the lead to 95-83. Elvin Hayes and forward Don Adams scored clutch baskets down the stretch, and the Rockets coasted to a 111-99 win.

Despite his limited playing time, Alcindor led the Bucks with 22 points, McGlocklin had 20, Smith had 18, and Cunningham had 14. Robertson had a season-low four points. John Trapp had a season high 24, Lantz had 21, Hayes had 20 points and 14 rebounds along with 13 blocked shots, and Adams had 18 points.

The Rockets victory established a new club record of six straight. No one knew at the time, but this would be their last game in San Diego. The team was bought during the off season and moved to Houston.

The Bucks still had a lot to be proud of. They finished with the best record in the NBA at 66-16, set a record for most home wins, most road wins, and the winning streak record of 20. Get ready, Milwaukee, it's time for the playoffs!

Lew Alcindor's back-up, Dick Cunningham, nicknamed "The Cement Mixer" by announcer Eddie Doucette (Lulloff collection)

Endnotes to Chapter 13

1) Bob Logan, "Bulls Snap Bucks Streak!" *Chicago Tribune*, March 10, 1971, pt. 3, p. 1.

2) Bob Wolf, "Streak Broken, Bucks Lose," *Milwaukee Journal*, March 10, 1971, pt. 2, p. 19.

3) Rel Bochat, "Bulls Snap Bucks' String in Overtime," *Milwaukee Sentinel*, March 10, 1971, pt. 2, p. 1.

4) Wolf. March 10.

5) *Ibid.*

6) *Ibid.*

7) Chuck Johnson, "Knicks Tip Bucks With Late Splurge," *Milwaukee Journal*, March 14, 1971, pt. 3, p. 1.

8) *Ibid.*

9) Thomas Rogers, "DeBusschere Star," *New York Times*, March 14, 1971, Sec. 5, p. 1.

10) *Ibid.*

11) *Ibid.*

12) Bob Wolf, "Knicks Are Test for Bucks," *Milwaukee Journal*, March 12, 1971, pt. 2, p. 18.

13) Rel Bochat, "Bucks Lose 3rd in Row," *Milwaukee Sentinel*, March 15, 1971, pt. 2, p. 1.

14) Bob Hill, "Cotton Can Be Kinder," *Wisconsin State Journal*, March 14, 1971, pt. 3, p. 1.

15) *Ibid.*

16) Bob Wolf, "Lethargic Bucks Fall Again," *Milwaukee Journal*, March 15, 1971, pt. 2, p. 9.

17) *Ibid.*

18) Special Correspondence, "Bucks Rally, Blot Suns," *Milwaukee Journal*, March 17, 1971, pt. 2, p. 16.

19) *Ibid.*

20) *Ibid.*

21) *Ibid.*

CHAPTER 14

THE PLAYOFFS TIP OFF

GAME 1—PLAYOFF PREMIER:
BUCKS 107, WARRIORS 96

On Saturday, March 27, the Bucks began their quest for the NBA championship. In front of 11,216 fans at the Oakland Coliseum, 2,000 fewer than capacity, the Bucks defeated the San Francisco Warriors, 107-96, taking a 1-0 lead in the best-of-seven series.

The Bucks led 34-24 at the end of the first quarter and expanded their lead to 50-33 midway in the second quarter. Despite playing with a sore heel, Warriors player-coach Al Attles came off the bench and helped spark a 13-2 Warriors' rally, narrowing the lead to 52-46 with 3:08 left in the quarter. Jeff Mullins hit a 20-footer at the end of the half, and the Bucks led, 58-52. Robertson had a great first half, scoring 16.

After the game, Costello talked about the Bucks' first-half performance:

> *"We played very good ball at the start. Our defense put on a lot of pressure and made them take the shots we wanted them to take. They were tough shots, but unfortunately, they were dropping in. We got a nice lead (50-33), but they picked up on us when we stopped running, for no particular reason. With a lead like we had, there's a tendency to relax, but you can't afford to do that because it's hard to get going again."*[1]

Early in the third quarter, the Bucks opened a nine-point lead, but Ron (Fritz) Williams and Jeff Mullins paced a comeback, cutting the deficit to two points on three occasions at 67-65, 69-67, and 77-75. A layup by Robertson gave the Bucks an 81-76 advantage going into the fourth quarter.

The Bucks began the final quarter with Alcindor on the bench with four fouls. The Bucks adjusted and scored five baskets in the first two minutes of the quarter, and this helped them open up a 95-81 lead. The big contributors were Robertson and Allen, who scored 16 of the Bucks' first 18 points to open the quarter.

Costello was very pleased with the contributions of the Bucks' bench.

> "The main thing is our reserves didn't hurt us. In fact, they kept it going and we built up a lead with them while Lew had to sit out a while because of foul trouble. Allen got us some important points (during the fourth quarter surge), and he didn't turn the ball over, and he did a good job on Williams. Dick Cunningham was in there when we opened it up, and he did a good job on Nate Thurmond. We didn't want to risk Lew getting another foul then, but if we'd lost the lead, he'd have been right back in. As it was, he got a rest and the reserves picked it up. That's what they're supposed to do, are paid to do. Help the starters get rest without hurting us." [2]

The bench maintained the lead as the Bucks went on to win, 107-96.

Even though they lost, Attles was proud of his team's performance.

> "When Oscar decides to take charge, you're in trouble. This may be as well as we played this year. I know some people expected us to get beat by 20 or 30.

*Naturally, I'm disappointed, but we did a good job.
We played probably our best game against the
Bucks—we shut off the forwards (Smith and
Dandridge) who'd hurt us before. We missed some
good shots when we were within two points, and
then we hit that cold spell in the fourth quarter."[3]*

Costello had high praise for Robertson.

*"Oscar was fantastic. I was worried about his
stamina because of the flu attack he had last week,
but what a job he did."[4]*

Warriors guard Jeff Mullins agreed with Costello.

*"I think we would have made it if Oscar hadn't
played so well. He was just too much for us."[5]*

Robertson finished with 31 points, connecting on 14 of 23
attempts from the field. Costello said,

*"We've always wanted him to shoot more. He
averaged only about 15 shots a game during the
season, 15 shots and 19 points."[6]*

Alcindor had 25 points, 10 rebounds, and Dandridge
chipped in with 19 points. Mullins led the Warriors with
30 points, and Thurmond added 19 points along with 15
rebounds.

Costello was impressed with the Warriors' performance.

*"Frisco used every combination possible. Clyde Lee
up front, Al Attles at guard. They were exploratory.
I don't know what else they'll try, but they played
hard, and so did we. That's what it takes."[7]*

Costello also talked about the importance of the victory
having to start the series on the road because of unavaila-
bility of a home venue.

"This was a real big one. Now we're even better off than if we had started with two games at home. We're looking forward to getting back to our own wild fans."[8]

Game 2—A Fine Performance in the Fieldhouse: Bucks 104, Warriors 90

With the Milwaukee Arena booked for the Home Show, Game Two was played on Monday, March 29, in front of a sellout crowd of 12,868 at the University of Wisconsin Fieldhouse in Madison. Larry Costello was excited.

"We're looking forward to Madison and all those screaming Buck fans. It's even more of a home court advantage to play in the UW Fieldhouse than in the (Dane County) Coliseum. People are closer to the floor and the atmosphere is a lot noisier."[9]

The Bucks didn't let their fans down and took a 2-0 lead in their playoff series with a 104-90, come-from-behind win over the San Francisco Warriors.

Both teams shot poorly, but the Bucks led 25-20 at the end of the first quarter. After picking up two quick fouls, his second and third of the game, Alcindor went to the bench with the Bucks ahead 35-30, with 6:19 left in the half. Dick Cunningham played the rest of the half, and the poor shooting continued, with the Warriors on top, 44-43, at halftime.

The Bucks called a time-out with 6:38 left in the third quarter on the short end of a 52-51 score. Alcindor got things going with a hook shot that gave them a 53-52 lead. Greg Smith scored three straight baskets, two of them off missed shots, and had a steal that started a fast break. Along with baskets by McGlocklin, Dandridge, and Allen, the Bucks outscored the Warriors 19-8 and led 72-60 going into the fourth quarter. Alcindor sat out the last two-and-a-half minutes of the quarter because of foul trouble.

After the game Coach Attles talked about Greg Smith's role.

> *"Greg Smith. He hurt us. He comes in to the boards and gets some big baskets and rebounds. If it happened just once or twice, okay, but the guy who is on Smith has to realize that that's his game. He knows what he's doing. The man on him has to stay with him, keep him out. We didn't adjust to him, play him head to head."*[10]

Warriors' guard Jeff Mullins talked about Smith's defense.

> *"He kept clogging up the lane, playing a zone. Every time I went for the basket or drove the baseline, he was there. I had to pull up and take shots I didn't want to take, and on top of that I got called for charging twice, which made matters much worse. These tactics gave us the perimeter shot, but Bob Portman was the only one who could hit it. Our shooting was terrible."*[11]

Smith talked about his style of play.

> *"That's my game, driving to the boards for the layups and for the rebounds. It hurts sometimes when they don't show much respect for my shooting, but this is the thing I do best. There are not too many forwards who play the type of game I do. If the other team makes mistakes, I take all the advantage I can."*[12]

Costello had high praise for Smith.

> *"What Smith does is all desire and hard work. He's not a great natural player."*[13]

Alcindor returned for the fourth quarter and the Bucks kept pouring it on. Before Costello could get him out of the game after his fifth foul, Alcindor managed to get one more stuff in, and with five minutes left, the Bucks had an 18-point lead that would swell to 22. Dick Cunningham scored the last five points for the Bucks, and the Warriors scored the last eight points of the game in a 104-90 Bucks win.

Alcindor led the Bucks, who shot a horrible 40.2 percent from the field, with 26 points and 18 rebounds, Dandridge had 21 points and 10 rebounds, Robertson 15, and Smith added 11 along with 17 rebounds. The Warriors, who shot 34 percent from the field, were led by Thurmond's 18 points and 11 rebounds. Bob Portman had 17, and after a 30-point performance in game one, Mullins was held to 12, hitting on only four of 15 from the field.

Costello gave a lot credit to his defense:

> *"It kept us in there when our offense wasn't going too well. We didn't hit shots when he we had them and it makes your offense look terrible, but they still got only 44 points and we were down only one at halftime. Then in the third quarter we got some breakaways, and that has a demoralizing effect on the opposition. They didn't get back, and they see our guy all alone down there putting in the easy basket. That broke 'em up."*[14]

Costello was also proud of the team effort.

> *"At one time or another everybody picked us up. Greg and Dandridge helped us in the second half— Dandridge probably more offensively than Smith and Greg more defensively than Dandridge."*[15]

Attles talked after the game about his team's play.

"Our mistakes, quite a few of them caused by the Bucks, were the main thing. We weren't hitting in the third quarter, but I can't say anything about that because the Bucks weren't hitting in the first half either, but they were beating us on the boards and Greg was up there. The Bucks are a great team that capitalizes on your mistakes. Everything we've tried against them hasn't worked. We had a three-guard offense for a while, and it gave us some movement, but overall our guys can't stand around against that good Buck defense."[16]

When Attles was asked about any changes for the next game, he replied,

"None that I can speak of. I am going to be doing some thinking about it tonight. The question is if we can even compete with them. They just beat us. It's as simple as that."[17]

Costello was looking forward to Game Three.

"They're a tough team. They've got a big center, big forwards, and an all-star guard in Mullins. We've just got to come back here tomorrow night and beat them. We can't let down. If we win tomorrow, we'll really put the pressure on them."[18]

GAME 3—WARRIORS HELD AT BAY:
BUCKS 114, WARRIORS 102

It wasn't easy, but on Tuesday, March 30, in front of another sellout crowd at the University of Wisconsin Fieldhouse, the Bucks defeated the San Francisco Warriors, 114-102, giving them a 3-0 advantage in their best-of-seven playoff series. The game stayed close until the Bucks outscored the Warriors 14-3 to end the game.

In the first quarter, Warriors guard Ron Williams kept slapping at the ball while Robertson was dribbling. Robertson responded by backing into Williams and was called for an offensive foul. His difference of opinion about the call resulted in a technical foul. After the game, Robertson talked about the call.

"I didn't foul the guy, he pushed me."[19]

Robertson also gave his opinion of NBA officiating.

"I wasn't mad at the technical. I was mad at the call. The refs are so inconsistent it's unbelievable. And you know something, with some refs it's a personal thing against players."[20]

Williams gave his version of the incident, which, of course, was different.

"He hooked me, and they caught it. He does it all the time. He also gives you a little shove once in a while to get the ball."[21]

The Bucks led 24-22 at the end of the first quarter. Late in the second quarter they increased their lead to nine, and they ended the half with a pair of dunk shots by Alcindor and Smith, going up 55-42. They did this without Robertson, who in addition to the technical, sat out the last 19 minutes of the first half with three fouls.

Costello defended his decision to keep Robertson on the bench.

"He got into foul trouble, but Lucius Allen came in and did a good job."[22]

Jon McGlocklin also helped open up the lead, and he talked about his role while Robertson was out.

"I try to handle the ball more when Oscar isn't in there. It's very important for us to run when he's out too. We have to be aware of controlling the game and setting up the good shot."[23]

Midway through the third quarter, the Bucks opened a 15-point lead, 67-52, and led 86-78 at the end of the third quarter. The Warriors made it a game in the fourth quarter and cut the lead to 94-93 with seven minutes remaining. The Warriors trailed 100-99 when Nate Thurmond hit a turnaround jump shot from the corner. Greg Smith answered with a basket, which was followed by a bizarre play.

With 3:30 left in the fourth quarter, Ron Williams, who was playing with five fouls, intentionally fouled Robertson. Williams justified the foul saying,

"I had to take the foul. I knew I had five, but I was afraid Jeff Mullins had five, too (he actually had three) and he's the guy we go to in the clutch. Besides, the board said we only had one team foul and we really had two. If we had known that, we probably wouldn't have taken one at all."[24]

The incident got the Bucks going. After Robertson made one free throw, Dandridge sank a pair of foul shots, and Alcindor hit a hook shot, giving the Bucks some breathing room. Thurmond scored, but the Bucks finished the game with four baskets, the last two of them breakaway stuffs by Smith, giving them a 114-102 win.

The Bucks were led in scoring by Alcindor, who had 33 points along with 12 rebounds. Dandridge scored 23 points with ten rebounds, and Greg Smith added 17 points and 11 rebounds. Jerry Lucas paced the Warriors with 25 points and 20 rebounds, and Nate Thurmond was close behind, scoring 23 and also grabbing eight rebounds.

After the game, Bucks' coach Larry Costello had high praise for the Warriors.

> *"It was probably the best game they've played against us all season. Our defense was good and we made them take the shots we wanted them to, from 15 to 20 feet out, but they made the long bombs, some fantastic shooting. They're no slouches, and they proved it out there tonight. After we got a good lead in the first half, we lost some of our sharpness. We couldn't get the ball off the boards and run as we like to in the second half. I don't think we were aggressive enough for a while. Then Greg Smith and the others picked it up. Greg had some good steals that helped us go."*[25]

In the visitors' locker room, Coach Attles gave his thoughts.

> *"It's always a different guy who beats us. The first night it was Oscar Robertson, the second night it was Greg Smith, and the third night it was Lew Alcindor. We go along all right for a while and start making mistakes. Take the third game, for instance. We haven't played a better game all year, but we turned the ball over four or five times in the last three or four minutes, and you just never make mistakes against these guys and get away with it."*[26]

Some of the Warriors' players agreed with their coach. Jerry Lucas said,

> *"We've played our best three games of the year and lost. We just can't get over the hump."*[27]

Nate Thurmond added,

"We play them good for 37 minutes or 40 minutes or three quarters, then blow it."[28]

Even with a 3-0 lead in the series, Costello said the series was not over.

"They've got the talent on that club. You can't take them lightly, even at this stage. We haven't got this won yet."[29]

The Warriors were not giving up either, with Attles saying,

"I never give up against anyone. It's not the money but the pride. It's not over until the fourth game is finished."[30]

When Costello was asked about returning to Madison for a game on Sunday, he replied,

"I hope not. You've got to take four to move to the next round, and that's what we want as soon as we can get 'em." [31]

GAME 4—WARRIORS WIN ON LONG JUMP SHOT: WARRIORS 106, BUCKS 104

You can put the brooms back in the closet, Bucks fans, there will be no sweep! On Thursday, April 1, in front of 7,615 fans at the Oakland Arena, the Warriors staved off elimination with a 106-104 win, cutting the Bucks' lead in the series to 3-1. They did it in dramatic fashion as guard Joe Ellis hit a 38-foot jump shot for the game winner. It was the first time in 10 meetings during the season that the Warriors had beaten the Bucks.

Both teams played poorly in the first quarter, and the Bucks led 24-19 going into the second quarter. After the game, Costello talked about what he saw in his team.

"We could have had them buried in the first quarter, but you could see right from the start that we took it too lightly. Sometimes there's a natural tendency to have a letdown in a situation like this, but that's no excuse for the way we played."[32]

McGlocklin agreed with Costello's analysis.

"Both teams started poorly and we could have blown the game open right there. Then we let them get a lead, and we couldn't get over the hump."[33]

Al Attles opened the second quarter with a layup, Jerry Lucas followed with a three-point play, and another layup by Lucas gave San Francisco the lead. The running game was non-existent for the Bucks, and the Warriors seized the opportunity with hot shooting and good rebounding. With the Warriors ahead 37-34, paced by three baskets by Lucas, they grabbed a 45-35 lead. Late in the quarter, the Bucks answered with two stuffs and a pair of free throws from Alcindor, but the half ended with Lucas' eighth basket of the half, and the Warriors led, 53-44.

A Costello halftime talk got the Bucks' running game going, and baskets by Robertson, Smith, and Dandridge cut the deficit to 57-55. Mullins and Williams came back with baskets, opening up the lead. The Bucks cut the advantage to 72-68, but the Warriors, helped by baskets by Ellis, Clyde Lee, and Bob Portman, took a 78-69 lead at the end of the third quarter.

On two occasions in the fourth quarter the Bucks narrowed the deficit to four points, but they trailed, 101-93, with four minutes remaining. The Bucks scored four straight on a basket by Alcindor and a pair of free throws by Bob Boozer, cutting the lead in half. After Mullins hit a pair of free throws, Robertson took charge. He scored on a

Lew Alcindor guarding
Nate Thurmond.
(Lulloff collection)

baseline shot with 1:10 remaining. He then beat Mullins for a loose ball and started a two-on-one fast break that culminated with a three-point play by Boozer, narrowing the lead to 103-102.

Joe Ellis missed a long jumper, the Bucks got the rebound, and Robertson hit a basket on a 12-foot, right-side, baseline jumper with four seconds left, giving the Bucks a 104-103 advantage. During a Warriors time-out, a play was designed for Mullins, but because of tight defense, Williams inbounded the ball to Ellis. He unleashed a 38-foot shot that went in, giving the Warriors a 105-104 lead. After the shot went in, there were two seconds left on the clock. The Bucks immediately called a time-out, but they didn't have any left. A technical foul was called, and the Warriors converted the free throw. Any chance of the Bucks winning was lost when Robertson's inbounds pass was intercepted by Attles.

Both teams shot poorly from the field, the Bucks 40.7 percent and the Warriors 41.6 percent. Jerry Lucas led the Warriors with 32 points, Mullins had 20, and Thurmond 17. Alcindor had 32 points to lead the Bucks and Bob Dandridge added 17 before fouling out.

After the game, Ellis talked about his game-winning basket.

> *"I had to let it go, but it was a little farther than I wanted. It was a lucky shot. You don't win the playoffs until you win that fourth game."*[34]

He added,

> *"Anytime you hit a shot like that, I'd have to say it was luck. There's no way you could say it was a skill shot. I said a few prayers when the ball was in the air. It felt good when I let it go, but you never can tell about that. It might have been 10 feet short."*[35]

Costello gave a detailed evaluation of the Bucks' performance.

> *"What hurt us more than anything was not getting much off the offensive boards. We'd get one shot and that was it except for a few times Lew got a couple and when Dandridge came in for his own shot, but we didn't get what we ought to. We've got to come out and play 48 minutes. We beat them so often that we think we can turn it on whenever we want to. The papers out there said the Warriors*

*didn't stand a chance, and I think our guys got to
believe that. We had a poor start in the first half
because we weren't running.*

*The second half we got some cutters and Dandridge
was coming around, but we didn't have enough of
it. I don't think we've been running enough. We
were getting the fast breaks pretty often during the
regular season and that brings the percentage way
up. We can't stand around because it's too easy to
defense. We've got to have movement. San Francisco has played real aggressive defense."[36]*

There was some optimism that Costello noticed.

*"I think this game will wake us up. When I was
playing for Philadelphia, we led Boston 3-1 in the
playoff series and got beat."[37]*

The loss caused the Bucks to do a little more travel.
Costello said,

*"It would have been nice to wrap it up last night
and relax a few days before the next round. But
now we have to take that bus ride to Madison and
do it. We certainly don't want to go to San Francisco
again."[38]*

GAME 5—FRISCO NIXED IN FIELDHOUSE FINALE:
BUCKS 136, WARRIORS 86

San Francisco coach Al Attles summed up what happened
when Game Five was played at the Wisconsin Fieldhouse
in Madison on Sunday, April 4.

*"We kept waiting for the hammer to fall, and it
finally did. It hadn't happened before in the series,*

*but we knew all along that they were capable of it.
They're the best team in basketball."*[39]

*Jon McGlocklin was very confident. "We were very
relaxed in the locker room before the game, but I
just felt we'd blow them out. I felt confident that
everybody was ticked off about the other night and
ready to play."*[40]

A sellout crowd of 12,868 watched the hammer come down
as the Bucks concluded their best-of-seven series with a
136-86 rout of the San Francisco Warriors.

After a basket by Lucas, the Warriors took a 4-2 lead.
The Bucks scored the next nine points, three of them on
fast-break baskets, and took an 11-4 lead. Robertson was
doing a great job running the team's offense. He had eight
assists in the first quarter, tying a record held by Bob
Cousy and Hot Rod Hundley. (The current record is 11 by
John Stockton.) Late in the first quarter with the Bucks on
top 28-18, led by Bob Boozer, they scored ten straight
points, taking a 38-18 lead into the second quarter.

Costello, obviously, was pleased with the Bucks' performance, and he also had a theory.

*"We set the tempo early in the game. We ran, we
passed, we rebounded. There wasn't much they
could do. Maybe the key was our team breakfast.
I've never done it in three years. I got everybody up
at 9:30 and we all ate together. I wanted to make
certain everyone was well fed."*[41]

Robertson gave his thoughts on the Bucks coming out hot.

*"We kept the ball humming, we moved a lot. We
talked it over after the loss out there and were
convinced that if we played defense and kept*

*moving on offense, we'd be all right. It's old hat
playing the same team 10 or 11 times a season, but
the way we took them wasn't especially surprising.
It's a long season and nothing really surprises
you."*[42]

There was no letdown in the second quarter, and the
Bucks led 69-35 at the half.

What do you tell your team at halftime when they're
getting routed? Attles answered,

*"What can I say? They came right out and took the
game away from us. I don't know if we had an
unconscious letdown after we won the game the
other night. Whether we figured we'd take them
easy now, or not. They kept shooting hot, 58 per
cent at halftime and we were cold. I figured it might
change, but it didn't."*[43]

Jeff Mullins wasn't looking forward to the second half.

*"You know Oscar and Lew are going to score, and
you try to keep the others from hurting you. We
didn't. At halftime, I just wanted to get the last 24
minutes over with."*[44]

The massacre continued in the second half. The first
time the Warriors scored consecutive baskets in the game
happened midway in the third quarter. The score was 105-
57 going into the fourth quarter. A basket by McGlocklin
pushed the lead to 50. It increased to 60 on two occasions
in the fourth quarter.

With 5:42 left in the game, with the Bucks winning
128-68, a fight broke out. After Levi Fontaine was elbowed
while Dick Cunningham was setting a pick, he gave
Cunningham a blow to the chest, and Cunningham
retaliated.

"I didn't care about it, but when they tossed both of us out of the game and he was acting up I thought, 'I'll get my money's worth for the fine.'" [45]

After Cunningham and Fontaine were ejected, rather than put Alcindor back in the game, Costello used Bob Boozer and the Warriors scored 11 straight points, helping cut the lead to the 136-86 final score

The Bucks, who shot 55.8 percent from the field, were led by McGlocklin, who connected on 14 of 21 field goal attempts, scoring 28. Alcindor had 23 along with 17 rebounds, and Robertson scored 12 points and had 15 assists. The Warriors shot 36 percent and had only four players scoring in double figures, Williams with 13 and Thurmond, Portman, and Clyde Lee with 11 each.

Great defense by the Bucks played a big part in the poor shooting by the Warriors. Jeff Mullins, who was having a great series, was held to four points, and after scoring 57 in the previous two games, Lucas was held to nine points. Lucas talked about the Bucks' defensive performance.

"Smith played me close and forced me inside. I'd get around him and get good shots, but I'd keep running into Lew. He blocked four of my shots in the first half alone." [46]

The victory earned the Bucks some time off. They still didn't know who they would face in the next round, the Bulls or the Lakers. Their series was deadlocked at three, with Game Seven scheduled for Los Angeles on Tuesday. The Bucks would open up the series back home in the Milwaukee Arena on Friday.

Bucks	FG-FGA	FT-FTA	Rebs.	Pts	Warriors	FG-FGA	FT-FTA	Rebs.	Pts.
Alcindor	9-15	5-8	17	23	Attles	2-2	3-5	0	7
Allen	6-9	1-1	5	13	Ellis	2-8	0-0	1	4
Boozer	6-11	2-3	3	14	Fontaine	1-2	0-0	0	2
Cunningham	1-1	2-2	1	4	Jones	4-10	3-4	0	11
Dandridge	9-13	1-4	6	19	Lee	2-6	0-0	11	4
Greacen	2-3	2-2	2	6	Lucas	4-11	1-2	7	9
McGlocklin	14-21	0-0	1	28	Mullins	2-8	0-0	0	4
McLemore	1-4	0-0	4	2	Ogden	1-4	4-4	3	6
Robertson	4-13	4-5	5	12	Portman	4-7	3-5	4	11
Smith	5-7	1-1	12	11	Thurmond	4-12	3-4	5	11
Winkler	0-3	0-0	0	0	Turner	0-3	4-6	3	4
Webb	1-4	2-2	0	4	Williams	5-13	3-4	3	13

Playoffs Round One: Game 5

Endnotes to Chapter 14

1) Rel Bochat, "Road Win Big Plus," *Milwaukee Sentinel*, March 29, 1971, pt. 2, p.1.

2) *Ibid.*

3) Phil Finch, "Milwaukee Takes Opener." *San Francisco Chronicle*, March 27, 1971. Sec C p.1.

4) "Bucks Hope UW Equals 2 More," *Wisconsin State Journal*, March 29, 1971, Sec. 3, p. 1.

5) Bob Wolf, "Warriors Discouraged, Giving Bucks Big Edge," *Milwaukee Journal*, March 29, 1971, pt. 2, p. 9.

6) Dick Friendlich, "Lew: Nate Still the Toughest," *San Francisco Chronicle*, March 29, 1971, p. 44.

7) Bochat.

8) Wolf.

9) Rel Bochat, "Road Win Big Plus," *Milwaukee Sentinel*, March 29, 1971, pt.2, p.1.

10) Rel Bochat. "Bucks Pin 2nd Loss on Warriors." *Milwaukee Sentinel*, March 30, 1971, pt. 2, p. 1.

11) Bob Wolf, "Warriors Last for a While, Then Roof Falls In Again," *Milwaukee Journal*, March 30, 1971, pt. 2, p.9.

12) Bochat.

13) Art Spander, "Bucks Surge By S.F., 104-90," *San Francisco Chronicle*, March 30, 1971, p. 44.

14) Rel Bochat, "Bucks Pin 2nd Loss on Warriors," *Milwaukee Sentinel*, March 30, 1971, pt. 2, p. 1.

15) Bob Hill, "Attles Oohs and Aahs," *Wisconsin State Journal*, March 30, 1971, section 3, p.1.

16) Rel Bochat, "Bucks Pin 2nd Loss on Warriors," *Milwaukee Sentinel*, March 30, 1971, pt. 2, p. 1.

17) *Ibid.*

18) *Ibid.*

19) Bob Hill, "Warriors Held at Bay," *Wisconsin State Journal*, March 31, 1971. Peach Section 2, p.1.

20) Art Spander, "Closer, but Bucks Beat Warriors," *San Francisco Chronicle Sporting Green*, March 31, 1971, p. 53.

21) Art Spander, "Why the Bucks Are Unstoppable," *San Francisco Chronicle*, April 1, 1971, p. 53.

22) Hill.

23) Bob Wolf, "Costello Wary but Bucks Set to Eliminate Warriors," *Milwaukee Journal*, April 1, 1971, pt. 2, p. 16.

24) Bob Wolf, "Attles to Fight to Last Man, Which Shouldn't Take Long," *Milwaukee Journal*, March 31, 1971, pt. 2, p. 19.

25) Rel Bochat,"Bucks Struggle to Third Win," *Milwaukee Sentinel*, March 31, 1971, pt. 2, p. 1.

26) Bob Wolf, April 1, 1971.

27) Bob Wolf, March 31, 1971.

28) Bob Hill, March 31, 1971.

29) Bob Wolf, April 1, 1971.

30) Bob Wolf, March 31, 1971.

31) Bochat.

32) Bob Wolf, "Ellis Shoots: Series Returns to Madison," Milwaukee Journal, April 2, 1971, pt. 2, p. 16.

33) *Ibid.*

34) Peach Sheet, "Far Out! Warrior Hero Admits," *Wisconsin State Journal*, April 3, 1971. sec. 3, p. 1.

35) Bob Wolf, April 2, 1971.

36) Rel Bochat, "'Have to Hold Down Lucas To Wrap It Up': Costello," *Milwaukee Sentinel*, April 3, 1971, pt. 2, p. 1.

37) Dick Friendlich, "Warriors Win in Final Second," *San Francisco Chronicle*, April 2, 1971, p. 51.

38) Rel Bochat, April 3, 1971.

39) Bob Wolf, "Hammer Falls, Bucks Roll," *Milwaukee Journal*, April 5, 1971, pt. 2, p. 10.

40) *Ibid.*

41) Art Spander, "Warrior Finale: 50-Point Loss," *San Francisco Chronicle*, April 5, 1971, p. 47.

42) Rel Bochat, "Bucks Eliminate Warriors," Milwaukee Sentinel, April 5, 1971, pt. 2, p. 1.

43) Spander.

44) Wolf.

45) Bochat.

46) Wolf.

CHAPTER 15

WESTERN CONFERENCE FINALS: BUCKS VS. LAKERS

GAME 1—BUCKS' LATE SURGE SWAMPS LAKERS: BUCKS 106, LAKERS 85

The Bucks did great at their "home away from home" in Madison, but it was nice to host the first game of the Western Conference Finals in the Milwaukee Arena. The Bucks' opponent was the Los Angeles Lakers who, despite losing starting forward Elgin Baylor and All-Star Jerry West to a season-ending knee injury on March 2, defeated the Bulls, four games to three in the first round. On Friday, April 9, after a very slow start, the Bucks took a 1-0 lead in the series with a 106-85 win.

After having as much as a seven-point lead, the Bucks led 26-21 at the end of the first quarter. The Bucks shot poorly, hitting only 34.7 percent of their shots in the first half, 25 percent in the second quarter, and trailed 44-43 at halftime. It could've been much worse. The Lakers should've had a bigger lead, and they could blame their four of 16 from the foul line, including eight free throws missed by Chamberlain, for not having a bigger lead. After the game, Lakers' Coach Joe Mullaney talked about the first half.

"I thought we should have been leading by more in the first half. I thought they didn't look so good in the first half. I thought we hurt them with our defense. Maybe we helped a little bit with that 34 percent shooting."[1]

Jon McGlocklin gave his reasons for the Bucks' lackluster first half.

"Our bad start was partially our fault. We came out a little sluggish. We hadn't played in five days, and sometimes a layoff does that to you."[2]

Two minutes into the third quarter, on the short end of a 50-45 score, the Bucks got going. McGlocklin, after having only one basket in the first half, sank four straight, two of them off fast breaks, and the game was tied at 53. After ties at 55, 57, and 59, the Bucks ended the quarter outscoring the Lakers 13-7, taking a 72-66 lead at the end of the third quarter.

Costello, obviously, was happy the Bucks got going.

"They played sort of a slow tempo. Sometimes when you play like that, it lulls you into the same style of play. We just didn't have any spark in the first half, but in the second half, we started moving the ball better and shooting better."[3]

McGlocklin agreed.

"The first half we were pushing ourselves and we didn't run. We came out determined the second half, and we created situations by playing our game. When the ball starts dropping through, you're on the way."[4]

Early in the fourth quarter, the Bucks opened the lead to 80-69, but the Lakers came back, cutting the score to 82-

75. Robertson answered with three baskets, added a couple of steals, and with five minutes remaining, the Bucks led 90-81. They outscored the Lakers 16-4 to end the game, holding the Lakers scoreless for four minutes en route to the 106-85 victory. The Bucks shot 75 percent in the fourth quarter, outscoring the Lakers 34-19.

Alcindor led the Bucks with 32 points and 22 rebounds. Robertson had 19 points and ten assists, and McGlocklin added 18 points. Despite going two of 10 from the free throw line, Chamberlain led the Lakers with 22 points along with 20 rebounds. Hairston connected on eight of 12 shots from the field, scoring 20. Gail Goodrich, who had a huge series against the Bulls, averaging 31, had only 16, only four points in the second half.

Costello was proud of his team's performance.

> *"When we did get going, Oscar did a great job leading the break. Defensively we did a good job on Goodrich all the way with Jon and Allen working on him, and in the last quarter we kept Wilt from dunking or dipping. We like to let him take those outside shots."*[5]

The atmosphere was different in the Lakers' locker room. Harold ("Happy") Hairston talked about not having Jerry West available.

> *"I hate to keep harping on it, but when we used to go flat as we did in the fourth quarter we always had number 44 to pull us out of it. He would always rise to the occasion."*[6]

Keith Erickson commented about the Lakers' play after the game.

"We've just got to take it to them. We were tight in the first half and they acted like they didn't want the game. We've got to run more on them and I think we showed that we could run on them tonight."[7]

Elgin Baylor, who suited up for the game but was unable to play because of the Achilles tendon injury, added his observations.

"We quit doing the things that had us on top at the half. We stopped moving the ball; we stopped going to Wilt, who was having success against Alcindor, and we started going one on one."[8]

GAME 2—BUCKS LASH LAKERS:
BUCKS 91, LAKERS 73

On Easter Sunday, April 11, in front of another sellout crowd at the Milwaukee Arena, in spite of an outstanding performance by Wilt Chamberlain, the Bucks defeated the Lakers in a defensive battle, 91-73, to take a 2-0 lead in the Western Conference finals.

The Lakers, who were already playing without two of their starters, (Elgin Baylor and Jerry West), lost another one before the game. Early on the morning of the game, Keith Erickson was suffering stomach cramps. He checked into Lutheran Hospital and ended up undergoing surgery for the removal of his appendix and would be unable to play for the remainder of the series.

The Bucks came out hot, taking a 7-1 lead. The Lakers had eight turnovers in the first quarter, and that was a big factor in allowing the Bucks to take a 24-15 lead at the end of the quarter.

Outstanding defense, in particular by Chamberlain, who was doing a great job rebounding and blocking shots, including some by Alcindor, allowed the Lakers to make it a 34-31 game with 5:32 left in the half. The Bucks took a 44-37 lead into the locker room at halftime.

Costello had a theory why the Bucks were so sluggish.

> *"Sometimes I think these guys sleep too long. They get out of the sack at 10:30 or 11 o'clock and may still be groggy by the one pm tip-off. Maybe I'll have to talk to management and see if we can afford more steak and eggs breakfasts together."*[9]

He also was not pleased with their performance on offense.

> *"We were walking through our offense, we weren't moving, we weren't cutting. We came up with a lot of steals, but we weren't doing anything with them. We'd get 10 or 12 points up and then relax. We got to get more hungry."*[10]

Lakers' coach Joe Mullaney was happy the Lakers kept the first half close.

> *"We worked hard defensively and it helped us hang in there although we shot only 34 percent the first half and had a lot of turnovers."*[11]

The Lakers trailed just 61-56 with three minutes remaining in the third quarter. They had two opportunities to cut the lead to three points, but they came up empty each time. Dick Cunningham tipped in a missed shot, and the Bucks ended the quarter outscoring the Lakers, 5-1, to take a 68-57 lead into the fourth quarter.

The Bucks finally got their offense in high gear in the fourth quarter and jumped ahead, 76-63, midway through the quarter. They outscored them 15-10, in a 91-73 victory. The Lakers' 73-point total was the lowest point total in a playoff game since April 7, 1955, when Fort Wayne beat Indianapolis, 74-71.

After the game, Mullaney downplayed the absence of Erickson.

> *"You hate to lose any player, but that wasn't the overriding factor why we lost. What's wrong with our offense? How much time do you have to listen to me?"*[12]

Chamberlain wasn't a fan of Mullaney's game coaching.

> *"I don't want to demean the coach, but our guys just ran out of gas. We're five guys against their eight or nine. We're lucky to be where we are. I was tired before the game started. We have a bench and I think we should play it. Isn't that what they're getting paid for?"*[13]

The low-scoring game was the result of both teams playing good defense. Costello talked about the defensive strategy used by the Bucks.

> *"Frankly, we're double-teaming and triple-teaming Wilt and Goodrich every chance we get. I'd rather see the ball go out, even to an open man, than to give either of those two guys a shot. Our defense won it for us. I think we're going to play better. I don't think we've played our best game yet. I think we are due for an offensive explosion."*[14]

After the game, Mullaney talked about the Bucks' defense on Goodrich.

> *"The Bucks' style of defense forced him into giving up the ball more often than he has. He wasn't getting the kind of shots. Most of them were off balance. Even when they played him one-on-one*

instead of doubling up, he'd penetrate and still
wind up against two of them. If he were getting his
kind of shots and missed 13 of 15 I'd be concerned,
but their defense was responsible."[15]

Lakers' forward Happy Hairston had high praise for the
Bucks' offense, and in particular Alcindor.

"Lew passes off, and Wilt isn't that mobile. That's
not a knock, just a fact. You turn your head from
Dandridge or Smith and Lew will spot one of them
under the basket and hook a pass for an easy
layup. Wilt is strictly a strength player, and Lew is
a finesse player. When people compare them, that's
the difference. Why, Lew even went down on the
fast break a couple of times, and that's amazing.
He's got to be the player of the seventies; the
century, for that matter."[16]

Costello was unhappy with the Bucks' offense.

"We're ready for an offensive explosion. Our offense
has been very poor, but our defense has been our
salvation. We're not taking advantage of fast-break
opportunities. Our offense should be sharper. We
get a lead and then we can't open it up."[17]

Why did the Bucks, who were ahead most of the time by
five or seven points, take so long to get a bigger lead?
Costello answered,

"They kept turning over the ball. We kept stealing it
with great defensive play, but we didn't turn those
chances into baskets. We should have won this one
in a waltz. We couldn't put things together. We
couldn't break it open."[18]

Chamberlain had a big game for the Lakers, pacing them
with 26 points along with 22 rebounds. The only other

Alcindor and the Big O. (Author's collection)

Lakers in double figures were Pat Riley with 13 and Gail Goodrich, who connected on only two of 15 shots from the field, with 10. Alcindor led the Bucks with 22 points and 10 rebounds. McGlocklin had 15 points, and Bob Dandridge scored 14 along with 11 rebounds.

GAME 3—LAKERS REBOUND:
LAKERS 118, BUCKS 107

On Wednesday, April 14, the series shifted to Los Angeles for a game at The Forum. The Lakers, decimated by injuries, suited up only eight players for the game. Larry Costello remarked,

*"You look up and see only eight guys on their bench
when we've got 12, and they introduce only three
men before they get to the starting lineup. After that
you think you just have to go out and walk through
your game and you've got it made. It could have
been a psychological move."*[19]

If the move was psychological, it really paid off as the
Lakers routed the Bucks, 118-107, cutting the Bucks' lead
in the series to two games to one.

The teams played a close first quarter. The Bucks
trailed early, but three baskets in a two-minute span by
McGlocklin gave the Bucks a 15-12 advantage. Two dunks
by Chamberlain helped the Lakers take an 18-17 lead.
Late in the first quarter, Alcindor scored his first basket,
and the Lakers led 28-27 at the end of the quarter.

The Bucks opened the second quarter outscoring the
Lakers 10-2, taking a 37-30 lead. The Lakers came back
on a pair of baskets by Chamberlain and a Gail Goodrich
jumper, making it 41-38. Riley's layup and basket tied the
game at 49, and the Lakers led, 56-55, at the half.

The Bucks were plagued early in the third quarter as
Alcindor, Dandridge, and Smith were called for their third
fouls. With the Bucks behind 65-59, a three-point play by
Dandridge and an Alcindor hook shot narrowed the score
to 65-64. The Lakers scored the next seven points and
took a 72-64 lead with 6:50 left in the quarter. Pat Riley
scored 11 of his 24 points in the third, hitting five of five
shots. The Lakers outscored the Bucks 34-22 in the
quarter, taking a 90-77 lead into the fourth quarter.

Riley talked about the Lakers' performance.

*"When Wilt clears the boards for us like he did
tonight and gets the ball out for fast breaks, we can*

*run with anybody. They call us methodical and
slow, but we didn't look slow tonight."*[20]

Lakers' coach Joe Mullaney gave credit to his defense.

*"Sure, we like to run when we can, but we didn't
say, 'We're going to run tonight.' The defense forced
them into awkward situations and we caught them
off balance."*[21]

Early in the fourth quarter, paced by five points from
Dandridge and baskets by Alcindor and Robertson, the
Bucks outscored the Lakers 12-5, cutting the Lakers' lead
to 95-89 with 7:17 left in the game. After a time-out the
Lakers surged again, outscoring the Bucks 12-1 on the
way to a 118-107 win.

What was the reason for the big difference from the
first two contests played in Milwaukee? Lakers' forward
Jim McMillian had a theory.

*"Two days of workouts really helped us. We were
more ready for their press and trap defense. We
probably should have won the first game, and even
though we were miserable in the second, they
didn't run away with it. We still have a chance to
beat them."*[22]

Riley also noticed a different Bucks team.

*"Milwaukee is a great pro team. To be honest, I
didn't think they were as mentally ready for us
Wednesday night as they were in the first two
games. I think we'll see a different team Friday
night."*[23]

The Bucks also had an injured player. Robertson, slowed
by a pulled stomach muscle, only scored 11 points. Joe
Mullaney talked about how the Lakers' defense changed.

"Oscar runs their offense, and we felt that with Riley overplaying him, McGlocklin would have to handle the ball more, and we would gain two ways. Oscar wouldn't get the ball as much, and McGlocklin wouldn't get as many shots."[24]

Riley agreed with the Lakers' defensive strategy.

"We knew Robertson was physically under the weather, so we figured if we could hold him up at midcourt by putting defensive pressure on him, their offense would be only 50 percent as effective."[25]

Costello was critical of the Bucks' performance, in particular Smith and Dandridge.

"In the whole first half they got us a total of three rebounds, and Smith didn't get any. We didn't get any boards, and you can't play when you don't have the ball, and when we did have it, too often we didn't do anything with it. We threw it away too much. Wilt was getting every defensive rebound and on offense he was stuffing in rebounds or earning them second and third shots. He's playing like he's 25 instead of 35, like he wants to prove something."[26]

Four Lakers, Chamberlain, Goodrich, Hairston, and Riley, shared scoring honors, each with 24 points. Chamberlain also had 24 rebounds, helping the Lakers to a 54-45 advantage over the Bucks. Dandridge led the Bucks with 25 points. McGlocklin added 22 points, and Alcindor had 20 points and 19 rebounds.

After the game, Costello talked about the rest of the series.

"We've got our work cut out. This isn't going to be a cakewalk. That's for sure. We've got to make some adjustments and we've got to get tough. Everybody came through for them last night. We won't double up on them as much because that's hard to do when they're spread out. We'll go back to playing them hard, head to head, and put Oscar Robertson on Gail Goodrich. Maybe being down 2-0 and nobody expecting them to beat us, made them looser and helped their game. Our guys should know that if you don't come out to play it gives the other team life and you're in trouble. The Lakers are tough at home, and we don't want to come out here Monday."[27]

GAME 4—BUCKS CELEBRATE ALCINDOR'S BIRTHDAY WITH A WIN: BUCKS 117, LAKERS 94

After their loss in game three, the question was, did the Bucks get a wake-up call? Jon McGlocklin noticed in the locker room before Game Four, things seemed different.

"There was an undercurrent of determination before the game."[28]

On April 16, 1971, Lew Alcindor celebrated his 24th birthday with a superb game in front of a capacity crowd of 17,505 at the Forum, helping the Bucks take a 3-1 lead in the Western Conference finals with a 117-104 win.

Alcindor tallied 17 points in the first quarter, scoring on a variety of baskets, jump shots, banks, and his hook shot, pushing the Bucks to a 30-22 lead at the end of the first quarter. Two baskets by Dandridge and a reverse layup by Alcindor helped give the Bucks a 36-23 lead early in the second quarter. Chamberlain and Goodrich brought the Lakers back to within eight, 40-32.

For four and a half minutes, Rick Roberson came off the bench replacing Chamberlain, but the Lakers lost little ground, trailing 51-42 with four minutes left in the quarter. Goodrich had a great first half, scoring 19 points. The Bucks shot a torrid 67.5 percent from the field in the first half, paced by 23 points from Alcindor, and led 62-51 at halftime.

After the game, Alcindor talked about Chamberlain's defensive game plan.

> *"He doesn't play you defensively like most centers in the NBA. He'll step back, make you commit yourself, and try to block your shot with his great jumping ability. I tried to take the ball to him, then bring him out, which took him out of his best shot-blocking position."*[29]

Costello commented on Alcindor's play.

> *"All of Lew's moves and fakes before he shoots catch Wilt off balance, and that's very important when you're up against Wilt. You can't go muscle-to muscle against him."*[30]

The Lakers, behind Hairston and Riley each scoring three baskets, cut the lead to 68-67 with 8:11 minutes left in the third quarter. The Bucks responded with baskets on a Smith layup, a Robertson jumper, a free throw by Dandridge, and a tip-in by Alcindor, taking a 75-68 lead. Boozer scored eight points in the third quarter, the Bucks' last eight points of the quarter, and the Bucks were on top, 92-74, at the end of three.

Costello talked about Boozer's role in opening up a comfortable lead for the Bucks.

> *"Happy Hairston got hot in the third quarter. Booz came in and cooled him off and hit some key hoops himself."*[31]

Obviously, Boozer was happy with his performance.

> *"I went out to take the jump shot away from Hairston and take the spark out of them, and I blocked five shots in the process. Being an offensive player as I have always been my 10 years in the league, when the ball goes in the hole it makes my whole game. As far as overall contributions are concerned, this was one of the best playoff games I've ever had."*[32]

The Bucks stayed hot in the fourth quarter, opening up a 20-point lead with less than two minutes to go on the way to a 117-94 win.

The Bucks were led in scoring by Alcindor's 31 points and 21 rebounds. Balanced scoring was big for the Bucks. Dandridge had 20 points, Robertson 19 points, hitting on eight of 12 shots, and Boozer had 16 points and seven rebounds in 25 minutes off the bench. Goodrich had 25 points to lead the Lakers. Riley had 17 points, and Chamberlain had 15 points and 16 rebounds.

Costello was pleased with the Bucks' performance.

> *"We ran at them tonight instead of them at us. We had better movement and did things when we got the ball. Oscar's defensive work was a big key. We put him on Gail Goodrich because they were running the stack offense. We figured it was better to shut off some of the other guys and not have four of them with 24 points (which had happened in the previous game). A big thing on offense was that we got the ball in to Lew in good position, in close."*[33]

Lakers guard Gail Goodrich agreed with Costello's assessment.

> "They were just too tough—wow! Sixty-one percent shooting for the game! They got it inside to Lew too much, and when you let anybody do that, it's all over."[34]

Coach Joe Mullaney knew things would be difficult if the Bucks got their fast break going.

> "When they get us into a running game, we're in trouble. We were running more than usual Wednesday night, but that wasn't by design. Well, they run by design and they're quicker and faster than we are, so they got good percentage shots and we didn't."[35]

After the game, Alcindor said,

> "It was just a case of wanting to win. If we had lost this game, we would have been in a bad position."[36]

Costello hoped that the impressive performance would carry over to the next game.

> "You can only hope you can win if you play this well again. I know one thing: none of us wants to come back here again."[37]

GAME 5—BUCKS HAMMER LAKERS, WIN SERIES:
BUCKS 116, LAKERS 98

Coach Costello had spoken on a number of occasions about not wanting to fly back to Los Angeles for Game Six. On Sunday, April 18, in front of another sellout crowd at the Milwaukee Arena, he got his wish as the Bucks won the Western Conference Finals best-of-seven series, four games to one, defeating the Lakers, 116-98. They would have to wait until Monday evening, after Game 7 of the Bullets-Knicks series, to see who they would be playing against for the NBA championship.

With the score tied at 13, the Bucks outscored the Lakers 8-2 to take a 21-15 lead. Despite the Bucks connecting on 10 of their first 12 shots, the Lakers only trailed 30-29 going into the second quarter. The first quarter also featured a number of disagreements about the officiating of Jack Madden and Don Murphy. Robertson was called for a technical foul, and Alcindor expressed his opinion about missed goal-tending calls and rough play under the basket. McGlocklin noted,

"We let the calls get to us."[38]

Costello also drew a technical but he said,

"At the end of the first quarter I told them to forget about the officials and just to play our game.
Nothing was going to help us but our own play."[39]

Alcindor struggled in the first half, going more than 14 minutes without scoring, and he hit on only one of his first seven field goal attempts. Chamberlain also blocked four of his shots. The Bucks led, 55-49, at halftime

Paced by McGlocklin, who scored nine points with outside shooting, and Bob Dandridge's eight points off inside play, the Bucks went on a run and took a 67-53 lead. The Lakers had eight turnovers and only scored 17 in the quarter as the Bucks boosted their lead to 81-66 at the end of the third quarter. They maintained their lead with a lot of fast breaks in the final quarter, winning 116-98.

When Chamberlain left the game with 2:25 remaining, he got a standing ovation from the sellout crowd. He was very touched by the crowd's appreciation of his performance, commenting,

> *"It was wonderful. I can't remember if this ever*
> *happened to me before. You give whatever you*
> *have to give, and that's all that can be expected,*
> *and when it's appreciated, it's gratifying. It shows*
> *you that basketball fans have come a long way,*
> *just like the players."*[40]

Alcindor talked about how it is to go up against Chamberlain.

> *"Playing against Wilt is simply hard work. It's*
> *exhausting because you don't shove him around.*
> *He's immune to that. As for the ovation he got, the*
> *fans here are more decent than they are in New*
> *York. They appreciate the effort that you put out."*[41]

Chamberlain had a defensive strategy to use on Alcindor.

> *"I just try to force Lew to take shots that aren't easy*
> *for him to make. I try to keep him from shooting a*
> *high percentage like 70 or 80 percent, and outside*
> *of one night I think I did."*[42]

Costello was impressed with Chamberlain's performance.

> *"I just thought Wilt played fantastic. Here's a guy*
> *33-34 years old and he just played beautifully."*[43]

Lakers coach Joe Mullaney also had high praise for his center.

> *"To me, Wilt's endurance this series was surprising.*
> *He had to go longer and harder than at any time*
> *this year. I'm amazed he maintained it that long.*
> *We have the best matchup in the league with Wilt*

*against Lew, but we have to spend too much time
helping on Alcindor. Their other guys hurt us then.
Oscar has given them poise, and you can't rattle
them like you could last year.*[44]

Despite losing the series, the Lakers were proud of their
performance. Coach Mullaney said,

*"I'm proud of the way we played in the entire
playoffs. As for today, it was just a struggle to try
to stay close."*[45]

Chamberlain observed,

*"We always seem to run out of gas because we all
have to go 40 minutes (of the 48 in a game). We go
out with our heads high. We were a little bit out-
manned."*[46]

Costello talked about the Lakers' effort in the series.

*"They kept coming at us all the way. When they lost
Keith Erickson, our team thought they could just go
through the motions and win. They found out
differently. The mental aspect of the game is
unbelievable."*[47]

Lucius Allen commented,

*"They played hard all the way. They didn't roll over
and die. As for Chamberlain, that's the best I've
ever seen him play. I didn't see him in person in his
younger years, but he couldn't have played much
better."*[48]

The Bucks shot 48 percent on 49 of 102 while the Lakers
hit on 38 of 90 for 42.2 percent. The Bucks, led by Dandridge and Alcindor with 15 each, won the battle of the
boards, 60-46. For the first time in 262 games as a Milwaukee Buck, Greg Smith led the team in scoring, 22

points in just 23 minutes, connecting on nine of 14 from the field. He sat out most of the second and the entire third quarter because of foul trouble.

> *"I felt light out there today. That's when I get a lot of fouls, also a lot of rebounds, but lead the scoring? No way. That's the first time I've done that since I was in high school."*[49]

Dandridge and Alcindor each scored 20, McGlocklin added 19, and Robertson had 16 points and 12 assists. Happy Hairston led the Lakers with 27, and Chamberlain, who played 46 minutes, added 23 along with 12 rebounds.

Costello had good vibes before the game.

> *"I felt we could win today, but I'd be a genius if I said I knew how things would go. Unlike Friday's game, the Lakers didn't come back at us this time. Today I told our guys at halftime that we should be up by 14 (actual score was 55-49). The second half we got the boards. Dandridge was really jumping. In the first half we'd get men open down court, but the damn ball went off our fingers. The second half we cleared it out and ran, which is what we do best."*[50]

Bucks	FG-FGA	FT-FTA	Rebs.	Pts	Lakers	FG-FGA	FT-FTA	Rebs.	Pts.
Alcindor	7-23	6-8	15	20	Chamberlain	10-21	3-9	12	23
Allen	2-3	0-2	1	4	Goodrich	6-15	6-9	5	18
Boozer	4-11	3-4	9	11	Hairston	10-16	7-11	9	27
Cunningham	0-1	0-0	2	0	Hetzel	1-3	2-2	2	4
Dandridge	10-20	0-1	15	20	Killum	0-0	2-3	0	2
Greacen	1-1	0-0	0	2	McCarter	3-7	0-1	4	6
McGlocklin	9-13	1-1	2	19	McMillian	5-12	0-0	4	10
McLemore	0-0	0-0	1	0	Riley	3-12	0-0	1	6
Robertson	6-15	4-5	6	16	Roberson	0-4	2-2	9	2
Smith	9-14	4-6	9	22					
Webb	1-1	0-0	0	2					

Playoffs Round Two: Game 5

After the game, the question in the Bucks locker room was, who would you rather play for the championship, New York or Baltimore? Costello said,

> *"I'd just as soon play New York. They're the champs, and I like to go against the best."*[51]

McGlocklin thought,

> *"If you don't beat the Knicks, they're never going to acknowledge us in the East."*[52]

It didn't matter to Robertson.

> *"Who cares whether they acknowledge us. It will be in the books, won't it?"*[53]

Endnotes to Chapter 15

1) Bob Hill, "Bucks Upstage LA," *Wisconsin State Journal*, April 10, 1971, sec. 3, p. 1.

2) Bob Wolf, "Bucks Run in 2nd Half," *Milwaukee Journal*, April 10, 1971, pt.1 p. 14.

3) Mal Florence, "Sound Familiar? Bucks Too Good for Lakers," *Los Angeles Times*, April 10, 1971, pt. 3, p. 5.

4) Bob Wolf, April 10, 1971.

5) Rel Bochat, "Bucks' Late Surge KO's Lakers," *Milwaukee Sentinel*, April 10, 1971, pt. 2, p. 1.

6) Mal Florence, April 10, 1971.

7) *Ibid.*

8) Bob Wolf, April 10, 1971.

9) Rel Bochat, "Bucks Stifle Lakers," *Milwaukee Sentinel*, April 12, 1971, pt. 2, p. 1.

10) Bob Wolf, "Lakers Reserves Too Scanty," *Milwaukee Journal*, April 12, 1971, pt. 2, p. 11.

11) Rel Bochat, April 12, 1971.

12) Mal Florence, "Fading Lakers Lose Erickson—and Game to Bucks, 91-73," *Los Angeles Times*, April 12, 1971, pt. 3, p. 1.

13) *Ibid.*

14) Glenn Miller, "Bucks Show Some Muscle, 91-73," *Wisconsin State Journal*, April 12, 1971, pt. 3, p. 1.

15) Rel Bochat, April 12, 1971.

16) Bob Wolf, April 12, 1971.

17) Mal Florence, April 12, 1971.

18) Glenn Miller, April 12, 1971.

19) Bob Wolf, "Empty Bench Fools Bucks," *Milwaukee Journal*, April 15, 1971, pt. 2, p. 17.

20) *Ibid.*

21) Mal Florence, "Lakers Alive and Kicking-118-107," *Los Angeles Times*, April 15, 1971, pt. 3., p. 1.

22) Wire services, "Lakers Are Fewer, So Are the Laughs," *Wisconsin State Journal*, April 16, 1971, pt. 2, p. 1.

23) *Ibid.*

24) Bob Wolf, April 15, 1971.

25) *Ibid.*

26) Rel Bochat, "Costello Grim, the Party's Over," *Milwaukee Sentinel*, April 16, 1971, pt. 2, p. 1.

27) *Ibid.*

28) Bob Wolf, "Hungry Bucks Enjoy Feast," *Milwaukee Journal*, April 17, 1971, pt. 1, p. 17.

29) Mal Florence, "Lakers Just a Birthday Cake for Lew (117-94)," *Los Angeles Times*, April 17, 1971, pt. 3, p. 1.

30) *Ibid.*

31) Rel Bochat, "Bucks Crush Lakers, 117-94," *Milwaukee Sentinel*, April 17, 1971, pt. 2, p. 1.

32) Bob Wolf, April 17, 1971.

33) Rel Bochat. April 17, 1971.

34) Mal Florence, April 17, 1971.

35) Bob Wolf, April 17, 1971.

36) *Ibid.*

37) Mal Florence, April 17, 1971.

38) Rel Bochat, "Bucks Would Rather Face Knicks," *Milwaukee Sentinel*, April 19, 1971, pt. 2, p. 1.

39) *Ibid.*

40) Bob Wolf, "Smith Leads Bucks: He's Shocked, Too," *Milwaukee Journal*, April 19, 1971, pt. 2, p. 13.

41) Mal Florence, "Lakers Fight but Fail- Series and Season Over, 116-98," *Los Angeles Times*, April 19, 1971, pt. 3, p. 1.

42) Bob Wolf, April 19, 1971.

43) Bob Hill, "Laker Win Woke Up Bucks," *Wisconsin State Journal*, April 20, 1971, pt. 3, p. 1.

44) Rel Bochat, April 19, 1971.

45) Mal Florence, April 19, 1971.

46) Bob Hill, "Bucks' Parting Shot Unfurls LA," *Wisconsin State Journal*, April 19, 1971, pt. 3, p. 1.

47) Mal Florence, April 19, 1971.

48) *Ibid.*

49) Bob Wolf, April 19, 1971.

50) Rel Bochat, April 19, 1971.

51) *Ibid.*

52) Bob Wolf, "Smith Leads Bucks: He's Shocked, Too," *Milwaukee Journal*, April 19, 1971, pt. 2, p. 13.

53) *Ibid.*

CHAPTER 16

WORLD CHAMPIONS!

GAME 1—BUCKS TAKE DOWN BULLETS:
BUCKS 98, BULLETS 88

Everyone had to wait until Monday evening's seventh and deciding game to find out if the Bucks would be playing the Baltimore Bullets or the New York Knicks for the NBA Championship. In a thriller at Madison Square Garden, the Bullets won, 93-91. The game wasn't decided until Bill Bradley missed a desperation, off-balance shot from the corner in the closing seconds.

Most experts thought that the finals would be the Knicks versus the Bucks, but the Bullets played great against the Knicks, and their play drew praise from Larry Costello.

> *"The Bullets are a different team than they were in the regular season, especially defensively. They were always explosive on offense, and now they're playing tough defense too. That's how they beat the Knicks."*[1]

Bullets' guard Kevin Loughery sensed that they were a team of destiny.

> *"I've been eight years in Baltimore. The feeling I get is that this is our year. The Bucks are a great ball club, but they can be had. We don't fear them. How can you fear any team after you knock off the world champs in the Garden?"*[2]

Bullets' coach Gene Shue saw things differently.

> *"There's no way we can be prepared for a new series. There's no way we can be emotionally ready. Milwaukee is sitting back like a bunch of caged lions while we're just savoring this victory."*[3]

Two players from the Knicks liked the Bullets' chances in the Finals. Walt Frazier said,

> *"If the Bullets play the Bucks the same way they played us, they can beat them."*[4]

Knicks captain Willis Reed observed,

> *"The thing with Lew is you can't hope to stop him, you just contain him to a degree. If you keep him to 30-35 points a game, you're doing okay. You can win. I don't think Milwaukee is such a cinch against Baltimore. The Bullets have a guy like Monroe and you know he's going to get his. Unseld plays Lew fairly well. I think they could give the Bucks a good run."*[5]

The Bullets were hampered with Gus Johnson having problems with his knees throughout the playoffs but got some minutes off the bench in the final two games in the New York series. He was unable to suit up for the opening game of the finals because of re-injuring his right knee in Game 7. Johnson talked about his knees.

> *"My main trouble is on the outside of both knees. They were getting stronger and I was moving pretty well, but I discovered today that something had happened to the inside of the right knee. I hope to be able to play the rest of the games, but I'm going to have both knees operated on after this is over."*[6]

In most cases, the first two games of a playoff series are played in the venue of the team with the better record.

This would not be the case in the 1971 NBA Finals. The Wonago Rodeo was booked for the Milwaukee Arena from Thursday, April 22, through Monday, April 26, so the home court would alternate with every game.

On Wednesday, April 21, 1971, in front of a Milwaukee Arena sellout crowd of 10,746 and a national television audience, the Bucks overcame a lackluster performance and having to play most of the first half without Alcindor due to foul trouble to take a 1-0 lead in the Finals with a 98-88 win.

Before the game, Bob Boozer noticed a different pre-game locker room.

> *"We had a very business-like attitude before the game. We had a job to do and we knew what it was."*[7]

Greg Smith agreed.

> *"It was very quiet before the game. There was no joking or cutting up like we usually do. Everybody kind of realized what we had to do. We were anxious to play the Knicks because we knew we could beat them. We forgot about the regular season, when they beat us four out of five times."*[8]

Unseld picked up two fouls in the game's first two minutes, the Bucks had five steals, four of them by McGlocklin, and after four minutes the Bucks led 14-6. Alcindor was charged with three fouls, two of them offensive, in a two-minute span in the first quarter, and with 5:20 minutes left in the first quarter he went to the bench. Unhappy with the calls, Alcindor stormed to the bench and slammed his warmup jacket to the floor. He sat out the rest of the quarter, but the Bucks led 28-22 at the end of the first quarter.

Alcindor started the second quarter, but because of his foul situation, he went to the bench with 10:13 left in the quarter and stayed there for the remainder of the half. He scored eight points and had one rebound in the first half. Baskets by John Tresvant and Jack Marin helped make it a two-point game at 30-28. The Bucks opened a 36-28 lead, only to have a comeback behind hot shooting by Monroe and Unseld cut the deficit to two, 44-42. After scoring the last six points of the quarter, and Baltimore finishing the half missing their last seven shots, the Bucks led 50-42 at the half.

Coach Shue talked about his team's performance in the first half.

> *"Boy, I'll tell you, when we were down by eight at halftime, I told the team we were lucky we weren't down by 20. I thought we were emotionally and physically drained. There was very little response in the huddle. We looked like we were making a run, but even then, we weren't playing well. We played like a YMCA team, handing the ball off to the other team."*[9]

Shue had high praise for Oscar Robertson.

> *"Oscar did a great job running the show when Alcindor was sitting out most of the first half. He played beautiful basketball. He does what he has to do."*[10]

Dick Cunningham talked about filling in for Alcindor when he was on the bench with foul trouble.

*"I remember thinking if he [Alcindor] gets one more
foul it will be my time, then bang there it was. I
tried to approach it as just another game. I've
gotten myself psyched up real high in the past, and
it's hurt me. I didn't want that to happen again. Our
offense changes when Alcindor isn't in there. We
pick and roll a lot and go for the fast break. I don't
think I was especially sharp, but I did my job."*[11]

Alcindor came out hot for the third quarter, with eight
baskets in the quarter, three on tip-ins, two off rebounds,
and three by way of his famous sky hook. The Bucks
opened up a 79-62 lead with a minute and a half left in
the quarter. After a television time-out, the Bullets scored
six straight points and trailed 79-68 at the end of the third
quarter.

After the game, Alcindor talked about the third quarter.

*"I got a chance to play, and that's what I have to
do. The fouls I got called for were for things they
didn't call that tight in the regular season. I thought
the fouls were questionable, but I'm not the official.
I just had to make adjustments."*[12]

The Bullets cut the lead to 84-78 with 7:50 remaining in
the fourth quarter. Then the Bucks outscored the Bullets
9-2, holding them scoreless for three minutes, taking a 93-
80 lead with 3:24 remaining. Alcindor picked up his fourth
and fifth fouls in a one-minute span with three minutes
remaining, but the Bucks won 98-88.

After the game, Coach Costello talked about his team's
performance.

*"It was a strange game. I just can't put my finger on
it. Lew was in foul trouble early, and we couldn't
set the pace as we wanted to. Our defense was all*

right, but it can be better and our passing wasn't good at all. I know we can play better, and I think Baltimore can too."[13]

Costello praised his bench.

"If Baltimore had taken over the lead, I'd have had Lew back in there in a hurry, but the other guys came through. We made a few defensive changes like keeping Marin off the baseline. When Lew was in our main objective was to get the ball to him. Dick is not an offensive center, but he did a good job on defense and we built up an eight-point lead while he was in. That's how important your bench can be."[14]

In the visitors' locker room, Shue gave the media his thoughts.

"I'm not disappointed that we didn't take advantage of Alcindor being out, I'm just disappointed we didn't get the win. He wound up with 31 points, but they still got only 98. Our players just couldn't do it tonight, that's all. We wanted to win badly, but we couldn't respond. We were just emotionally and physically let out after the Knicks' series. I could tell that in the huddles. The players were standing there listlessly, they weren't involved. We didn't have any basic problems we could point to. We just lost."[15]

Bullets' guard Kevin Loughery had high praise for the Bucks.

"That team is so damn powerful. They're so good. No matter what you try to do they know what it is and they stop you. And you can't fall off on them. They run patterns like figure skaters and they play like they're writing a textbook. I don't know if we

*can even take one game from these guys, even
when we get home. I want to win just one game.
Something for my pride. But I don't know if we
can.*"16

Despite being on the bench because of foul trouble most of
the first half, Alcindor wound up with 31 points and 17
rebounds. Robertson played 45 of 48 minutes, scoring 22
points along with seven assists. Dandridge added 15
points and 12 rebounds. The Bullets, who shot a frigid
36.4 percent from the field, were led by Earl Monroe with
26 points. Jack Marin scored 18, and Wes Unseld had 16
points and 10 rebounds.

After the game, Alcindor was asked if the Bucks could
win the series in four or five games. He replied.

*"Possibly, but I don't want to say we'll beat them in
four or five. They were a little down in the first
game after that tough series with New York, and I
think their play is going to pick up."* 17

GAME TWO—BUCKS DEFENSE HELPS CRUSH BULLETS: BUCKS 102, BULLETS 83

Both teams had four days' rest before game two. Coach
Shue believed this would benefit his team after only one
day off when they beat the Knicks.

*"We'll have a completely different team out there
Sunday. We know the things we have to do. We'll
just wait and see how the game turns out. There
are very few professional basketball players who
can be stopped. They have to be contained or
controlled. Lew had everything his own way. The
next game, we won't let him score as many
points."*18

Wes Unseld grabs the rebound. (Author's collection)

There was also a possibility of the Bullets having the services of Gus Johnson for the second game. Wes Unseld commented about Johnson being able to play.

> *"If Gus is there, the Bucks won't be getting that second shot. In the first game, they were getting five shots sometimes before we could get a rebound."*[19]

On Sunday, April 25, before a sellout crowd of 12,289 at the Baltimore Civic Center, the Bucks played tenacious defense, routing the Bullets 102-83, giving them a 2-0 lead in the NBA Finals.

The first quarter ended tied at 26. Early in the second quarter, the Bullets scored only one basket in a five-minute stretch, and helped by three baskets by Robertson, the Bucks outscored Baltimore 19-9 during the first eight minutes and opened up a 45-35 lead.

Earl Monroe sparked a comeback, scoring eight points in a two-and-a-half-minute span as the Bullets outscored the Bucks 10-4, cutting the Bucks' lead to 49-45 at the half. Alcindor had a big half for the Bucks with 14 points and 14 rebounds. Unseld had 11 and Monroe 10 for the Bullets in the first half.

The Bucks put the game away early in the third period. After a basket by Jack Marin opened the quarter, making it a two-point game, the Bucks answered with two baskets by Alcindor and one by Dandridge. After another basket by Marin, with the score 57-51, the Bucks scored 13 straight points, jumping to a 70-51 lead. They sank 14 of 20 shots in the third quarter, while the Bullets only hit three of their first 13 shots in the quarter, and the Bucks led 79-61 heading into the fourth quarter. There was no letdown in the fourth quarter. Their biggest lead was 100-74 with two minutes left, *en route* to a 102-83 win.

After the game, Robertson talked about the Bucks' great second half.

> *"We talked at halftime and got together in the second half. We ran our patterns better, and that's the key."*[20]

McGlocklin seconded Robertson's analysis.

> *"We didn't move the ball well early. Their defense was better, but in the second half we were moving*

*the ball better. We played straight, head-on de-
fense—that's the key to getting our offense going."*[21]

Not only was the Bucks' offense running great in the
second half, but their defense and rebounding played a big
part in the win. Jack Marin was very frustrated.

*"How can you win if you can't get any layups?
Every time you make a move to the hoop, you run
right into that giant oak tree in the middle. You just
can't make any penetration and you can't beat
anybody by taking 20-footers all night."*[22]

Bullets assistant coach Bob Ferry agreed with Marin.

*"Alcindor's defense was more a factor than his
offense. We have mostly guys that shoot inside—
Unseld, Gus Johnson, and Tresvant, but he takes
away our inside game."*[23]

The Bucks' defense had great outings in the first two
games. Costello asked rhetorically,

*"Can you imagine holding a high-scoring team like
this to 88 and 83 points in two straight games? But
we still didn't stop Jack Marin. He got 22 points
today, and that's 40 in two games. We've got to do
something about him."*[24]

Costello, obviously, was happy with the Bucks' performance.

*"We took away what they wanted to do. Their
offense was all screwed up. They couldn't get
anything at all inside or set anything up. All they
had was Marin, moving laterally and going one on
one for some long outside shots. Our forwards
played real defense in the third quarter, and Lew
Alcindor was never better at controlling the boards.*

*That's Baltimore's big thing, but Lew grabbed
everything in sight."*[25]

Costello talked about the important role Alcindor plays for
the Bucks.

*"When Lew goes the way he went in Sunday's
game, nobody else is going to get anything off the
board. That's the whole thing. You can't run if you
don't get the ball."*[26]

After the game, Gene Shue talked about his team's performance.

*"This wasn't like the first game in Milwaukee when
our players weren't really involved in what was
going on after the New York series, but we were
more involved today. You can say we lost because
of the good Milwaukee defense, but it was also a
matter of everybody trying to do it on his own."*[27]

Alcindor led the Bucks with 27 points and 24 rebounds.
Robertson added 22, Dandridge had 16, and McGlocklin
connected on seven of eight shots from the field for 14.
Marin was the leading scorer for Baltimore with 22 points.
Unseld had 13 points along with 20 rebounds, only three
in the second half. Gus Johnson, who had shots in both of
his knees before the game, played 30 minutes, scoring 10
points and grabbing eight rebounds. The Bucks connected
on 44 of 87 for 50.6 percent while Baltimore shot a frigid
37 percent on 36 of 97 from the field.

The Bucks' impressive win in Baltimore gave them a
2-0 lead in the series, and with Game 3 scheduled in
Milwaukee, discussion began about a possible sweep.
Oscar Robertson thought,

*"Some of the guys are thinking four straight, but
me? Not really. We're still only half way home."*[28]

Costello agreed with Robertson.

> *"Two down and two to go. Now all we've got to do is tie the knot. We can't let them get off the hook now."*[29]

Jon McGlocklin was very happy about the position the Bucks were in.

> *"I don't even want to think about it, because I get excited. Yes, I'm thinking about it. It would be nice to get next Sunday off, and the next three months besides."*[30]

GAME 3—BUCKS PREVAIL, TAKE 3-0 LEAD IN SERIES: BUCKS 107, BULLETS 99

On Wednesday, April 28, in front of a sellout crowd of 10,746 at the Milwaukee Arena, the Bucks held off numerous Bullets' rallies in the second half to take a commanding 3-0 lead in their best-of-seven series for the NBA title with a solid 107-99 win. Most of the fans in attendance had a feeling that this would be the last game in Milwaukee for the series.

The Bullets, in particular Earl Monroe, who scored nine points on three baskets and three free throws early, came out hot and grabbed a 9-8 lead. The Bucks came back strong, opening the lead to 10 on three different occasions and taking a 30-22 lead at the end of the quarter. Early in the second quarter, though, the Bullets failed to score for three minutes, and the Bucks jumped to a 46-30 lead. The Bucks took their turn with a scoring drought of two-and-a half minutes, and the Bullets scored nine straight, making it a 46-39 game. The Bucks led 54-46 at halftime.

The Bucks went up, 68-52, with 7:30 left. Robertson went to the bench with four fouls with 6:26 left in the third quarter. The Bucks went scoreless again for more than four minutes and, led by Kevin Loughery, the Bullets outscored the Bucks 16-2, making it a 70-68 game with 2:10 in the quarter.

Alcindor talked about Baltimore's comeback.

> *"The Bullets made some steals and we took some bad shots. They made three fast breaks and we tightened up."*[31]

Two free throws by Allen made it 72-68 with 1:58 left in the quarter. Robertson returned to the lineup, and his three-point play with 27 seconds left in the third helped the Bucks to a 79-69 lead going into the final period.

After the game, Costello talked about the Bucks' performance in the third quarter.

> *"They got back in the ball game because we had to take Oscar out. I had to bring him back in earlier than I wanted to. Our offense wasn't sharp. We didn't dribble or pass well. I think Baltimore is working harder now. I think in the playoffs you see better defense because you can't afford to lose a game."*[32]

Alcindor agreed with his coach.

> *"It was quite obvious to me that Oscar started things for us again at that point. When he's out there, he makes things happen."*[33]

Robertson talked about his game plan when he returned to action.

> *"When I went back in, my idea was to work plays that get us good shots. That's experience. After you*

play a while, you have plays that you think will work. Some of the younger guys can't always do that."[34]

Led by Lucius Allen and Oscar Robertson, the Bucks opened an 87-73 lead early in the fourth quarter. Allen talked about giving the Bucks some breathing room.

"I had to do something right. I was helping Baltimore cut down those 16-point leads, missing easy shots and having the ball stolen. Actually, if I'd known the game was that close, I might not have taken some of the shots I did."[35]

Monroe and Loughery helped the Bullets cut the lead to 100-93 with 2:10 left, but two baskets by Dandridge helped put the game away. Costello took Alcindor out with 50 seconds left, and Robertson 10 seconds later. Each of them received a standing ovation as the Bucks took a 3-0 lead with the 107-99 victory.

Dandridge, who connected on 13 of 20 shots from the field, led the Bucks with 29 points and also grabbed 10 rebounds. Alcindor was right behind with 23 points and 21 rebounds, and Robertson added 20 points along with 12 assists. Jack Marin led the Bullets with 21, Wes Unseld scored 20 and grabbed 23 rebounds, and Kevin Loughery chipped in with 19 points.

Coach Costello talked about being close to clinching the NBA title.

"Yeah, I feel pretty good tonight, but I'll feel great when it's all over. There's still one big win to go. If we get that one, it will be a dream come true. We never really could put it away. I don't know if they played much better, or if we just weren't sharp. Our guys wanted to win so badly, and sometimes when

you want to do things out there, you just can't. We still haven't had a real sharp offensive game in this series, although the defense has been good.[36]

Alcindor gave his thoughts on the Bucks' win.

"We beat them mainly on hustle and defense. They've adjusted well to our offense now. They're clogging the passing lanes, so we have to improvise."[37]

Robertson talked about the Bullets' performance.

"I think it was a good game for us. You can say we didn't ever put them away, but when you go up 16 points on a team, they close the gap, and you shoot out ahead again, that kind of thing breaks their back. Remember, we've played these guys quite a few games over the course of the season, and when you play a team a lot, it gets tougher every time."[38]

In the Bullets' locker room, guard Kevin Loughery talked about the game and Alcindor.

"We tried, that's all I can say. We were running, but the shots just wouldn't drop. That's the name of the game. That big guy [Alcindor], he's proved it to me. He's the greatest, well, maybe Bill Russell in his prime, but Lew is so smooth he doesn't turn the fans on. They don't know how good he is. The way he moves, he could play guard. Those easy shots we missed early, you can give him part of the credit. He just makes you change your shot."[39]

Bullets' coach Gene Shue gave his thoughts to the media.

"Alcindor was playing a zone, but then he always is. He's not guarding anyone, just hanging back there in the middle and that hurts guys like Earl (Monroe) who drive to the hoop. The referees called

*zone against Milwaukee once when it was so
obvious, but I don't want to use that as an alibi
why we lost. I think we played a terrific game, but
they had their best game in the series. We got hurt
by Dandridge and Smith a lot tonight and we
shouldn't allow that to happen."*[40]

When asked if the Bullets could make a comeback, Shue
responded,

*"No, I won't say it's impossible for us. Let's just say
it's very difficult. But I've always told the team, you
have to win four games and that still stands. I'd
say we played the best game of the three tonight.
We did a lot of good things. We were getting wide
open shots, which is what we have to do, but we
were missing the shots. The thing is we dug a hole
for ourselves early, and we were playing catch-up
all night. You can get by with that against mediocre
teams, but you can't do that with the Bucks. They
can get the easy basket on you very quickly. They
could work for layups and we had to hit 17-foot
jump shots."*[41]

Bullets' trainer Skip Feldman talked about Monroe's
condition.

*"He's extremely tender right now. It's his abductor
muscle, commonly known as the groin muscle. It's
tender now and we won't know until the doctor
looks at him tomorrow how bad it is."*[42]

Lucius Allen was pleased with the way the Bucks' quest
for the championship was going.

*"It feels beautiful. It just seems the way the series
is going it's supposed to happen to us. We lost our
stride for a while when they started to catch up, but*

we called time-out, talked it over, and then we were on our way again."[43]

Costello was confident going into Game Four.

"I expect to win it Friday. I think our guys want it to end. I want it to end. Our guys want a vacation."[44]

Jack Marin shakes hands with Lew Alcindor after the Bucks take a commanding 3-0 lead in the 1971 NBA Finals. (Lulloff collection)

GAME 4—SITTING ON TOP OF THE WORLD
BUCKS NBA CHAMPS:
BUCKS 118, BULLETS 106

With a commanding 3-0 lead in the series, Lew Alcindor was asked if he was getting excited as the Bucks drew closer to the title. Alcindor replied,

> *"No, I'm much too involved to get excited. You do that after it's over. When you get excited, you start to lose. Right now it's a lot of hard work."*[45]

Things were different for the team down 3-0. Kevin Loughery thought,

> *"I'd sure like to win one game from these guys. I know they want to win four straight, but we're representing the Eastern Conference and we just have to show a lot of pride and win one game. Just to do that would be a pleasure against a great team like Milwaukee."*[46]

On Friday, April 30, with a less-than- capacity crowd of 11,842 at the Baltimore Civic Center and a national television audience, the Bucks, in only their third year of existence, won the NBA title in a 4-0 sweep of the Bullets with a 118-106 victory. The Bucks' 12-2 post-season record surpassed the George Mikan-led Minneapolis Lakers' 10-2 mark recorded in 1950, and it was the first sweep in the finals since 1959, when the Celtics swept the Lakers.

The Bullets took a 15-10 lead only to see the Bucks outscore them 21-7 in the last six minutes of the first quarter to take a 31-22 lead. There were also two physical exchanges in the first quarter. One was between Earl Monroe and Jon McGlocklin, and the other between Jack

Jack Marin and
Bob Dandridge
sparring.
(Author's collection)

Marin and Bob Dandridge. Gus Johnson helped end the Marin fight by bodily carrying away Dandridge from the encounter. After the game, Marin talked about the fight.

> *"He pushed me and I elbowed him back. We didn't hurt each other, but it was a better fight than the one between Anderson and Foster for the light heavyweight title."*[47]

In the second quarter, the Bucks opened a 19-point lead before the Bullets narrowed it to 60-47 at halftime. Robertson scored 21 points in the first half.

Baltimore scored the first six points in the opening 55 seconds of the third quarter, tightening things, 60-53. Costello was upset and called a time-out.

> *"I told the guys they had to realize we had to keep playing. They had that big lead at halftime and figured it was going to be easy. Believe me, nothing comes easy in this game."*[48]

Costello's motivational speech worked as the Bucks answered with a 10-0 run paced by two baskets by McGlocklin, and one each from Dandridge, Smith, and Robertson that helped the Bucks grow their lead to 82-64 with four minutes remaining in the quarter. The Bullets answered with a run of their own, narrowing the gap to 89-77 going into the fourth quarter.

Monroe's groin injury was a factor for the Bullets. Bullets' trainer Skip Feldman talked about the injury.

> *"I don't know how he played as much as he did [22 minutes]. I took him in and taped him up in the third quarter and got five more minutes out of him, but he was really hurting."*[49]

The closest to which the Bullets narrowed the lead to in the fourth quarter was 12 points, and with 2:30 minutes left in the game and the Bucks comfortably ahead, 112-95, Costello pulled his starters as the Bucks won with a final score of 118-106.

The Bucks shot 56.1 percent from the field led by Robertson, who scored 30 points, hitting on 11 of 15 from the field and contributing nine assists. Alcindor was close behind with 27 points and 12 rebounds, and Dandridge added 21 points and 12 rebounds. The Bullets, who shot an ice-cold 41 percent from the field, were led by Fred Carter's 28 points. Loughery added 18, Marin and Monroe had 12 each, and Unseld scored 11 along with 23 rebounds.

In the locker room, some of the Bullets talked about the playoffs. Earl Monroe said,

> *"We never really got ready to play the Bucks. We played two really physical seven-game series against Philadelphia and New York and that took so much out of us. Milwaukee came along at the right time and played good ball."*[50]

Wes Unseld noted,

> *"It wasn't all of us that were down, but I know Earl Monroe was. He won both of those series for us (against Philadelphia and New York), and he was spent. I bet he doesn't weigh 175 pounds now."*[51]

Gene Shue gave credit to the Bucks' other starters.

> *"We didn't do a good job on the other guys (Dandridge, Smith, and McGlocklin), that's what beat us."*[52]

The Bucks' title victory earned each player $17,666.67, and Alcindor was voted the series MVP, earning him a Dodge Charger.

After the game, there was some discussion about the MVP award. Bullets coach Gene Shue thought,

> *"It should have been Robertson. He was the leader, he controlled the offense, he hit the open man, and he played tremendous defense. I said when they got him they would be the best team in basketball."*[53]

Bucks' coach Larry Costello said,

> *"Oscar and Lew, if I had to choose I'd have to make them co-MVP's. I don't know how to draw the line."*[54]

Teammates and opponents alike had high praise for Robertson. Gene Shue said,

> *"I've always been an admirer of his. Nothing he does surprises me. The moves he put on Carter (guard Fred Carter) were super."*[55]

Carter, who defended Robertson, had an observation.

> *"I told Bob Ferry (Bullets GM) the other day that a healthy Eddie Miles could probably do a better job of stopping Oscar. But Ferry told me, 'Oscar has been making jump shots over Elgin Baylor, Gus Johnson, and even Wilt Chamberlain the past 10 years. That's why he's averaged 30 points for his career. And you know, he's right."*[56]

Alcindor talked about having Robertson as a teammate.

> *"Oscar has made my job much easier than it has ever been. It's just great to have somebody there who you know can do the job every time. That, of course, is no reflection on anyone we had at guard last season. It's just that Oscar is the greatest. No one can compare with him."*[57]

Bucks reserve forward Bob Boozer talked about the title victory.

> *"This is the ultimate. I've had many a thrill in basketball—playing in the Olympics, making All-American—but this has to be the greatest. I broke in with Oscar at Cincinnati and I've seen him at his greatest. He really let it all out tonight."*[58]

When Robertson was asked if this was his biggest moment in basketball, he said,

> *"I can't compare different stages— high school, college, pro. They are all different plateaus."*[59]

Holding a glass of champagne, he said,

> *"You know, this is the first champagne I've ever had, and it tastes mighty sweet. We won the title in high school, but it was soft drinks then. This is the big leagues, man."*[60]

Later in his life, Robertson said that after he was traded from the Royals, he knew that an NBA title was going to happen.

> *"When I joined the Bucks, I knew we were going to win the championship that year as soon as I got there. Destiny, confidence. I just knew we were going to win."*[61]

Costello's dad, Hubert, of Minoa, New York, was with his son after the game and said it was...

> *"...one of the proudest moments of my life. Now Larry has won it both as a player and as a coach. He won with Philadelphia four years ago. I don't know which was a bigger thrill."*[62]

Greg Smith was elated over the Bucks' series sweep.

> *"I'm so happy I can't explain it. This is a long way from a small town in Kentucky, Princeton's the name, man, and be sure to spell it right. I started out just wanting to make the team. I figured if I could last a year, I'd be happy. This is too much for me to believe it's true."*[63]

Lucius Allen had experienced winning a championship in college. He commented,

> *"This is even better than winning the NCAA title for UCLA. You get paid for this, and it's more exciting. But I personally feel that I still have to prove myself, so I'm still going to be a hungry player next year."*[64]

Mid-season acquisition McCoy McLemore was in awe.

> *"It's like the dream of a lifetime. It's the thrill of my whole career just to be able to play with two of the greatest players at their position in the world. And to go from last place to the championship—well, call it luck or just being in the right place. Yet after seven years in this league, I feel that I've paid my dues."*[65]

Reserve guard Jeff Webb, who played his high school basketball at West Milwaukee High School before attending Kansas State, beat huge odds.

> *"I was a 1,000-to-1 shot when I walked into the office for a tryout. And to end up on a championship team in my home town is still a dream to me. I'm proud just to be known by these guys."*[66]

Wes Unseld had high praise for the Bucks.

> *"They were just too much for us. This is the best team I've seen since I've been in the league."*[67]

Gus Johnson foresaw a bright future for the Bucks.

> *"They'll be there for a long, long time. As long as Lew and Oscar can produce, I don't know who can stop them."*[68]

When Alcindor was asked about a potential Bucks' dynasty, he responded,

Bucks	FG-FGA	FT-FTA	Rebs.	Pts	Bullets	FG-FGA	FT-FTA	Rebs.	Pts.
Alcindor	10-16	7-11	12	27	Carter	14-24	0-0	2	28
Allen	2-6	0-0	3	4	Gus Johnson	4-12	3-3	7	11
Boozer	2-3	1-2	4	5	Geo. Johnson	0-2	0-0	4	0
Cunningham	0-1	0-0	1	0	Loughery	8-14	2-2	0	18
Dandridge	9-16	3-5	12	21	Marin	5-17	2-3	4	12
Greacen	0-1	0-0	0	0	Monroe	6-14	0-0	2	12
McGlocklin	4-9	4-5	0	12	Murrey	0-0	0-0	1	0
McLemore	2-5	1-2	7	5	Tresvant	4-10	0-2	5	8
Robertson	11-15	8-9	3	30	Unseld	3-12	5-8	23	11
Smith	6-9	2-3	7	14	Zeller	2-7	2-2	2	6
Webb	0-0	0-0	0	0					
Winkler	0-1	0-0	0	0					

The Bucks' Final Game

"I don't know about dynasties, but right now we're on top of the world."[69]

Jon McGlocklin recalled the victorious Bucks' return home the afternoon after the championship.

"At the time, there were no parades. The city and the state did nothing officially for us. But the fans did. We heard estimates of 10,000 fans showed up at the airport when we got back from Baltimore. They had to take us through a different path than we normally took through the airport. It took four policemen to get my wife and I and our son to my car. When we got home, there were signs in our yard and the neighbors came out to greet us."[70]

Bucks radio announcer Eddie Doucette has unforgettable memories of the Bucks.

"The great thing about it was that I worked with people here who said, 'I don't know how you are going to do it, but let's create some excitement. You figure it out.' They allowed me to do whatever I had to do, and it was a creative smorgasbord for me. It was a great era in Milwaukee Bucks basketball. It was wonderful to be involved in it. Man, we had fun!"[71]

World Champions! (Author's collection)

Alcindor looking over the Dodge Charger he won for being the MVP of the Finals.
(Author's collection)

Endnotes to Chapter 16

1) Bob Wolf, "Bullets Destined to Win? They Think So," *Milwaukee Journal*, April 21, 1971, pt. 2, p. 22.

2) Rel Bochat, "It's a Brand New Game for Bucks," *Milwaukee Sentinel*, April 21, 1971, pt. 2, p. 1.

3) Press Dispatches, "Bullets Win: Shue Looks Into Future," *Milwaukee Journal*, April 20, 1971, pt. 2, p. 11.

4) Bochat. April 21.

5) *Ibid.*

6) Bob Wolf, "Ragged Bucks Too Sharp for Weary Bullets, 98-88," *Milwaukee Journal*, April 22, 1971, pt. 2, p. 19.

7) Bob Hill, "Bucks Gave Bullets the Business," *Wisconsin State Journal*," April 22, 1971, sec.2, p. 1.

8) *Ibid.*

9) *Ibid.*

10) Alan Goldstein, "Big O Almost A Bullet Helps Bucks Rise To Top," *Baltimore Sun*, April 24, 1971, p. B1.

11) Dale Hofmann, "Bucks Just Couldn't Set the Pace-Costello," *Milwaukee Sentinel*, April 22, 1971, pt. 2, p. 1.

12) Bob Wolf, April 22.

13) Dale Hofmann, April 22, 1971.

14) Bob Wolf, "Alcindor's Big 3rd Kills Bullets," *Milwaukee Sentinel*, April 22, 1971, pt. 2, p. 1.

15) Dale Hofmann, April 22, 1971.

16) Eddie Doucette, "The Milwaukee Bucks and the Remarkable Abdul-Jabbar." (Englewood Cliffs, NJ. Prentice-Hall Inc.. 1974) p. 29

17) Bob Wolf, "Bucks Too Strong, Alcindor Maintains," *Milwaukee Journal*, April 25, 1971, pt. 3, p. 1.

18) Wire Service, "Bullets' Rest Ends," *Wisconsin State Journal*, April 25, 1971, pt. 3, p.1.

19) Bob Wolf, April 25, 1971.

20) Ed Winsten, "Big O's Performance Difference In Second Game," *Baltimore Sun*, April 26, 1971, p. C1.

21) *Ibid.*

22) Alan Goldstein, "Bucks Rout Bullets, 102-83, As Alcindor, Robertson Star," *Baltimore Sun*, April 26, 1971, p. C1.

23) *Ibid.*

24) Bob Wolf, "Bucks No Longer Deny Their Goal: Clean Sweep," *Milwaukee Journal*, April 26, 1971, pt. 2, p. 9.

25) Rel Bochat, "Can't Let 'Em Off Hook," *Milwaukee Sentinel*, April 26, 1971, pt. 2, p. 1.

26) Rel Bochat, "Bucks Try to Make It 3-0," *Milwaukee Sentinel*, April 28, 1971, pt. 2, p. 1.

27) Alan Goldstein, April 26, 1971.

28) Bob Wolf, April 26, 1971.

29) *Ibid.*

30) *Ibid.*

31) Glenn Miller, "Costello Wants a Vacation," *Wisconsin State Journal*, April 29, 1971, pt. 2, p. 1.

32) *Ibid.*

33) Dale Hofmann, "Bucks Coolin' It With 3-0 Lead," *Milwaukee Sentinel*, April 29, 1971, pt. 2, p. 1.

34) Dave Anderson, "Bucks Win 3rd in Row, 107-99," *New York Times*, April 29, 1971, p. 53.

35) Bob Wolf, "Bucks On Verge Of Sweep," Milwaukee Journal, April 29, 1971, pt. 2, p. 17.

36) Dale Hofmann, April 29, 1971.

37) Bob Wolf, April 29, 1971.

38) Dale Hofmann, April 29, 1971.

39) Ed Winsten, " ' We Tried,' Said Loughery, ' But the Shots Wouldn't Drop' ", *Baltimore Sun*, April 29, 1971, p. B1.

40) Alan Goldstein, "Bucks Close In On Title With 107-99 Victory," *Baltimore Sun*, April 29, 1971, p. C1.

41) Dale Hofmann, April 29, 1971.

42) Ed Winsten, April 29, 1971.

43) Rel Bochat, April 29, 1971.

44) Glenn Miller, April 29, 1971.

45) Dale Hofmann, April 29, 1971.

46) Bob Wolf, April 29, 1971.

47) Staff Correspondence, "Bucks' Cup Bubbleth Over," *Milwaukee Journal*, May 1, 1971, pt. 1, p. 20.

48) Bob Wolf, "Big O+ Big A Do= Title," *Milwaukee Journal*, May 1, 1971, pt. 1, p.18.

49) Staff Correspondence.

50) Alan Goldstein, "Alcindor, Oscar Set Pace; Carter Nets 28 For Bullets," *Baltimore Sun*, May 1, 1971, p. B1.

51) Bob Wolf, May 1, 1971.

52) Alan Goldstein, May 1, 1971.

53) Staff Correspondence.

54) Wire Service, "Oscar Had No Doubts," *Wisconsin State Journal, Sports Peach*, May 1, 1971, sec. 3, p. 1.

55) Paper of Record. *The Afro-American*, May 4, 1971 p.17.

56) Alan Goldstein, May 1, 1971.

57) Alan Goldstein, April 24, 1971.

58) Staff Correspondence, "Bucks' Cup Bubbleth Over," *Milwaukee Journal*, May 1, 1971, pt. 1, p. 18.

59) Bob Wolf, May 1, 1971.

60) *Ibid.*

61) Eric Nehm, *100 Things Bucks Fans Should Know & Do Before They Die.*" (Chicago, IL. Triumph Books LLC, 2018) p. 4.

62) Staff Correspondence.

63) *Ibid.*

64) *Ibid.*

65) *Ibid.*

66) *Ibid.*

67) Alan Goldstein, May 1, 1971.

68) Staff Correspondence, "Bucks' Cup Bubbleth Over," *Milwaukee Journal*, May 1, 1971, pt. 1, p. 20.

69) Alan Goldstein, May 1, 1971. *Championship in the Making Part Four. 2010-11 Milwaukee Bucks Tip-Off*. p. 52.

70) *Ibid.*

71) *Ibid.*

CHAPTER 17

NO REPEAT

<hr/>

THE FUTURE LOOKED PROMISING FOR the 1971-72 Milwaukee Bucks. The only notable changes were the retirement of forward Bob Boozer, and no Lew Alcindor. What? Not having Lew Alcindor available isn't a notable change? He changed his name to Kareem Abdul-Jabbar during the off-season.

On December 9, 1971, the Bucks traded starting forward Greg Smith and a 1973 third-round draft choice to the Houston Rockets for forward Curtis Perry and a 1972 first-round draft pick. Many people were not happy with the departure of Smith. In addition to being a close friend of Smith, Abdul-Jabbar considered him a very important part of the team.

> *"Greg was a key ingredient in the special chemistry that made us champions. His selflessness, his continual movement, his leaping and defense, all were blended into a team that knew exactly how to win. We had become close as a team on and off the court largely because of his bright and affable personality. We'd just become champs; why break us up?"*[1]

The Los Angeles Lakers had a super season in 1971-72, posting a 69-13 regular season record, which included a 33-game winning streak. On January 9, 1972, the Bucks ended the Lakers' streak in front of a capacity crowd at the Milwaukee Arena with a 120-104 win.

In the playoffs, the Bucks defeated the Golden State Warriors, four games to one, and next up were the Lakers, who defeated the Chicago Bulls, four games to one. After winning the opening game on the road, the Bucks lost four of the next five to the Lakers and were eliminated.

The Bucks finished the 1972-73 season with a 60-22 record, tying the Lakers for the best record in the Western Conference. The Bucks were the first NBA team to compile three straight 60+ win seasons. After winning their last 14 regular season games, they appeared poised for the playoffs.

Despite defeating the Golden State Warriors, their first-round opponent, five out of six games during the regular season, the Bucks lost the series, four games to two. It was obviously very disappointing.

The training camp for the beginning of the 1973-74 season was held at Carroll College in Waukesha, Wisconsin. Oscar Robertson was in the best shape of his career and was hoping to win another title before retiring.

Numerous injuries plagued the Bucks during the season. Robertson injured a groin muscle and missed some games in the middle of the season, but on March 15, 1974, a major injury happened in Detroit. Lucius Allen slipped on a Pistons warm-up jersey left on the sideline and suffered a season-ending injury. He tore a ligament and was out for the rest of the season. The Bucks still posted the NBA's best regular-season record, 59-23.

The first-round opponent for the Bucks was the Los Angeles Lakers, whom the Bucks eliminated, four games to one. The next series was against their rivals to the south, the Chicago Bulls. It was a "sweep" time for the Bucks as they eliminated the Bulls in four games. Next up were the Eastern Conference champion Boston Celtics.

The home court advantage meant very little in the championship series as the home team prevailed in only one game. The Bucks had a big win in the sixth game. Facing elimination, down by one point in the second overtime with seven seconds left, Abdul-Jabbar's hook shot gave the Bucks a 102-101 victory. Game Seven back in Milwaukee did not go well, with the Celtics winning, 102-87.

One of the reasons for the Celtics' success in the series was their pressing defense on the Bucks' guards. One could speculate how things might have gone differently if the Bucks had Lucius Allen available.

Before the 1974-75 season began, two big events changed the Bucks. Oscar Robertson retired, and after being poked in the eye and hitting the basket support in frustration during a pre-season game, Abdul-Jabbar broke his hand.

Abdul-Jabbar returned after missing 16 regular-season games, in which the Bucks posted a 3-13 record. Another change was that after returning to the roster, Abdul-Jabbar would be wearing goggles to protect his eyes.

It was difficult for the Bucks to overcome that disastrous start, and they finished the season with a 38-44 record, out of the playoffs.

Abdul-Jabbar expressed to the Bucks' management that he wanted to be traded. On June 16, 1975, the Bucks traded him and reserve center Walt Wesley to the Los Angeles Lakers for center Elmore Smith, hot-shooting guard Brian Winters, and two highly-regarded rookies, Dave Meyers and Junior Bridgeman.

Endnote to Chapter 17

1)   Kareem Abdul-Jabbar and Peter Knobler, *Giant Steps: The Autobiography of Kareem Abdul-Jabbar* (New York: Bantam Books, 1983), p. 254.

NICKNAMES:

- Abdul-Jabbar: "The King"
- Lucius Allen: "The Rabbit"
- Bob Boozer
- Dick Cunningham: "The Cement Mixer"
- Bob Dandridge: "The Grayhound"
- Gary Freeman
- Bob Greacen
- Jon McGlocklin: "Johnny Mac"
- McCoy McLemore: "The Real McCoy"
- Oscar Robinson: "The Big O"
- Greg Smith: "Captain Marvel"
- Jeff Webb
- Bill Zopf

CHAPTER 18

WHERE ARE THEY NOW?

HEAD COACH LARRY COSTELLO: Larry Costello coached the Bucks until the beginning of the 1976-77 season. The team had a 3-15 record when he was fired. He returned to the sidelines again, coaching the Chicago Bulls for 56 games in the 1978-79 season and was terminated after posting a 20-36 record.

It was back to Milwaukee for Costello, as he accepted the head coaching position for the Milwaukee Does of the Women's Professional Basketball League for part of the 1979-80 season.

Bill Byrne, founder and president of the Women's Professional Basketball League, introduces Larry Costello as the Milwaukee Does' coach. (Bud Lea collection)

His final coaching assignment was at Utica College, where he coached until his retirement in 1987.

Costello died of cancer on December 13, 2001, at the age of 70.

ASSISTANT COACH TOM NISSALKE: After serving as assistant coach for the Bucks' championship season, Nissalke accepted a head coaching job with the Dallas Chaparrals

Tom Nissalke coached the ABA San Antonio Spurs. (Author's collection)

of the ABA. He was named the ABA Coach of the Year. It was back to the NBA, coaching the 1972-73 NBA's Seattle Supersonics. After he was fired, he returned to the ABA as a coach for the San Antonio Spurs in 1973-74, and the Utah Stars from 1974-76.

Nissalke returned to Texas and the NBA, coaching the Houston Rockets from 1976-79. The 1976-77 team posted a 49-33 record and lost in the Conference Finals. Nissalke won the Coach of the Year award, giving him the rare distinction of being named coach of the year in both the NBA and ABA.

Later coaching assignments included the Utah Jazz from 1979-82 and the Cleveland Cavaliers from 1982-84.

After retiring, Nissalke owned a number of health clubs in Texas, was co-owner of Green Street, a bar-restaurant in Salt Lake City, and was very involved with the YMCA of Utah, serving as Chairman of the Board and interim CEO.

KAREEM ABDUL-JABBAR: Since Abdul-Jabbar announced his retirement at the conclusion of the 1989 season, he has been involved in a variety of projects.

His first involvement with basketball was in 1998 when he was a volunteer assistant coach at Alchesay High School on the Fort Apache Indian Reservation located in Whiteriver, Arizona. His salary was $1. He later wrote a book about this experience titled *A Season on the Reservation: My Sojourn with the White Mountain Apaches.*

He also has written other books, which include his autobiography, *Giant Steps, Black Profiles in Courage: A*

The author and
Abdul-Jabbar
(Photo courtesy of
Yvonne Kemp)

Legacy of African-American Achievement, On the Shoulders of Giants: My Journey Through the Harlem Renaissance, and *Coach Wooden and Me.*

Abdul-Jabbar remains involved in journalism, contributing as a columnist for *The Guardian* and *The Hollywood Reporter.* In 2017 and again in 2018 he was the recipient of the Columnist of the Year Award, given by the Southern California Journalists.

Many people have enjoyed seeing Abdul-Jabbar in the movies as well. Those films include *Fletch, Airplane,* and *Troop Beverly Hills.* Television series in which he has appeared are *Everybody Loves Raymond, Different Strokes,* and *21 Jump Street.*

Abdul-Jabbar has also held a number of different positions in the NBA. In February 2000, he was hired as an assistant coach for the Los Angeles Clippers and later served in that role for the Seattle Supersonics. In 2002, he was the head coach for the Oklahoma Storm of the United States Basketball League (USBL), who won the league championship that season. The next job he had was working as a scout for the New York Knicks. On September 2, 2005, he joined Phil Jackson's staff with the Lakers as a special assistant, working with the team's centers.

His tireless efforts to change various issues that plague humanity resulted in him being awarded the Presidential Medal of Freedom, the United States' highest civilian honor, from President Obama on November 21, 2016.

President Obama said,

> *"The reason we honor Kareem is more than just a pair of goggles and the skyhook. He stood up for his Muslim faith when it wasn't easy and wasn't popular. He's as comfortable sparring with Bruce*

Lee as he is advocating on Capitol Hill or writing
with extraordinary eloquence on patriotism."

LUCIUS ALLEN: After retirement, Allen worked five years for Columbia Savings and Loan in Los Angeles.

"I used my contacts with agents and players and
invested their dollars," he said. "I was not a stock-
broker but a money manager."

Allen later formed his own construction company, which carried out a lot of federal, county, and state work. "It did very, very well until the savings and loan industry, where I was getting most of my loans from, failed," he said.

He also worked part-time as an analyst for Kings games in the franchise's final year in Kansas City (1984-85) and first three in Sacramento. "Having that time made my retirement a lot easier," he said. "I could stay close with basketball, which is my first love."

Allen has remained close to the game he loves, first as a long-time Lakers and UCLA season ticketholder and then through his older sons. Kahlil graduated from the University of California-San Diego in 1996 and now attends law school. Bakir, an honorable-mention All-American at the University of California-Santa Barbara, graduated in 1997.

BOB BOOZER: Boozer retired following the 1970-1971 season. And when his playing days were over, he returned to his hometown, Omaha, Nebraska. He worked as an executive for Bell Systems, a position he held for several years late in his playing career, working in a management-training program. Later, Washington D.C. became home for Boozer, where he worked 10 years as a federal lobbyist.

A month after Bob retired in 1997, Nebraska Governor Ben Nelson appointed him to the State Board of Parole. He spent a lot of volunteer time working for Boys' Town, a home for troubled youth. He also made a strong commitment to help inner-city youth in North Omaha.

His wife of 46 years, Ella, was at his side when he died in a hospital in Omaha, Nebraska on May 19, 2012 at the age of 75 due to a brain aneurysm.

DICK CUNNINGHAM: After basketball, Cunningham and his wife Carole moved to Florida.

He returned to school and learned the golf industry. He helped design some of the courses in Sarasota, Florida. On the last course he helped design, he worked with Jack Nicklaus. He's now totally retired and enjoying life.

Dick Cunningham.

BOB DANDRIDGE: After a 12-year NBA career, which included winning the 1978 NBA World Championship with the Baltimore Bullets, Dandridge was not done with his involvement with basketball. He served as an assistant coach at Hampton University from 1987 to 1992, and later opened basketball camps.

He has a special talent communicating with the attendees and athletes who wanted to improve their skills. He told attendees where he would take them on the floor and where he would shoot from, all the time ensuring

Bob Dandridge.

The author and
Bob Dandridge at
a Bucks
fundraising event.

them there was no way they would contain him and therefore, would have to foul him.

In 1992, he was elected to the Virginia Sports Hall of Fame.

GARY FREEMAN: Freeman, who said he thought being traded would give him more time on the court, not less, played just 47 minutes in 11 games for the Cleveland Cavaliers. He will go down in history as the Cavs' original number 23, a number made famous by LeBron James. "I never even considered," said Freeman, 66, who was a financial advisor in Albany, Oregon. He has three kids, including a son who plays professional basketball in France. Freeman played professionally in Holland and Belgium after his one NBA season and still plays twice a week for fun.

BOB GREACEN: After his two seasons with the Bucks (1969 to 1971), he played half a season for the New York Nets in the ABA. From 1972-74, Greacen was a graduate assistant coach at the University of Utah, where he also earned a Master's Degree in Education. From 1974 until 2009, he taught European and World History at Parkland High School in Allentown, Pennsylvania, and also coached the boys' basketball team from 1974-86.

Greacen currently resides in Washington Crossing (Bucks County), Pennsylvania with his wife of 49 years, Lynn. They have three grown children and seven beautiful granddaughters.

Bob Greacen. (photo courtesy of Bob Greacen)

JON MCGLOCKLIN: Retirement means take it easy? Not for Jon McGlocklin, who stayed busy since his last season in the NBA in 1975-76. The same day he retired, McGlocklin and Bucks' radio announcer Eddie Doucette founded the MACC Fund.

MACC is an acronym for Midwest Athletes Against Childhood Cancer. Doucette's son, Brett, was diagnosed with cancer at the age of two. The group is still in existence, and it helped finance the construction of the MACC Fund Research Center at the Medical College of Wisconsin (MCW). It also supports the never-ending battle against childhood cancer.

In June of 2004, after spending 18 years serving as a Trustee for the MCW, McGlocklin was named a Trustee Emeritus.

Partnering with former major league ballplayer Sal Bando, he co-founded an investment group, the Bando-McGlocklin Investment Co. Inc. From 1997-2001 Jon was the president and owner of Healy Awards Inc, a company in Menomonee Falls, Wisconsin, that markets

Jon McGlocklin and friends.

athletic awards and sports recognition items. He also served on the Board of Directors for the Wisconsin Chapter of the Fellowship of Christian Athletes and was involved with Athletes for Youth, the Wisconsin Society to Prevent Blindness, and the Wisconsin Easter Seal Foundation.

Did he stay involved with basketball? You better believe he did. McGlocklin has served as a color analyst for Bucks TV telecasts, and has also done radio broadcasts since 1976.

Jon and his wife live in Hartland, Wisconsin.

McCoy McLemore: Before transferring to Drake University, McLemore played two seasons at Moberly (MO) Junior College. He averaged 21.3 points and 21.3 rebounds his sophomore season. In 2011, McLemore was inducted into the National Junior College (NJCAA) Basketball Hall of Fame.

He concluded his NBA career with the Houston Rockets after the 1971-72 season. He was a color analyst for the Rockets television broadcasts on Home Sports Entertainment in the late 1980s.

He died on April 30, 2009 after a battle with cancer. He was 67.

Oscar Robertson: Robertson wasn't off work very long. After retiring at the end of the 1973-74 NBA season, he worked as a color analyst for CBS-TV.

In 1981, putting to use the skills he learned when he studying for his B.S. degree from the University of Cincinnati in 1960, he founded Orchem (Oscar Robertson Chemical) Company. The chemicals its manufactures are utilized to clean equipment for major companies. Kraft,

Pepsi, and Anheuser Busch were some of Orchem's customers.

Oscar continues his involvement helping minority business owners and gives seminars on leadership development.

He was very involved helping his fellow NBA players with their negotiations with ownership. He served as President of the National Basketball Players Association from 1965 until his retirement. In addition, he filed a class action anti-trust lawsuit on behalf of the players, and in a court settlement in 1976, known as the Oscar Robertson Rule, NBA players were the first professional athletes to gain free agency.

In 1992, Robertson was one of the people taking a lead role in forming the National Basketball Retired Players Association. They are instrumental in maintaining and improving pension benefits and healthcare for former players.

Probably the biggest gift he made happened in 1997 when he donated a kidney to help save the life of his daughter, Tia, who was suffering from lupus. He continues his fight against diseases and is deeply involved with the National Kidney Foundation, and the International Prostate Cancer Foundation.

With his wife Yvonne, he founded provide The Oscar and Yvonne Robertson Scholarship Fund at the University of Cincinnati, which annually provides assistance to students.

In 1998, Robertson wrote and published *The Art of Basketball*, a book stressing fundamentals of the game for young players. In 2010 , he wrote his autobiography, *The Big O: My Life, My Times, My Game.*

GREG SMITH: After retiring from the NBA at the age of 29 at the conclusion of the 1976 season, Greg was hired in April, 1976 by King Broadcasting Company, headquartered in Seattle, as an account executive in broadcast sales on 620/ KGW, the station's affiliate in Portland, Oregon. He's currently employed in broadcast sales by Salem Communication and has 43 years of service in various positions dealing with sales.

Greg Smith.
(photo courtesy of Greg Smith)

His NBA career might have been done, but Greg continued playing on some city league teams that had talented college and former pro players. He, along with some former Portland Trailblazer players, formed a Blazer Alumni team that played against non-profit groups in Oregon and southwestern Washington. He attended Blazers games as an ambassador to the Blazer organization, which included visiting suite sponsors and attending marketing functions.

Greg and his wife, Linda, have five children and 12 grandchildren from age 21 to 10 months (as of this writing) and enjoy taking getaway trips to Mexico, Hawaii, Las Vegas, and resorts in Oregon and Washington.

Not enough can be said about Greg's first NBA coach. As Greg wrote, "I would be remiss if I did not say how grateful I am to the late coach Larry Costello for giving me the chance and opportunity to play in the NBA with the Milwaukee Bucks, and later with the Houston Rockets and Portland Trailblazers."

JEFF WEBB: Born and raised in Milwaukee, Wisconsin, Jeff Webb has called Texas home for the last 23 years. Working primarily in Economic Development, collaborating with Texas cities, counties and state officials. After retiring in 2016 from a Texas lobbying firm, Webb now resides in Dallas, Texas

Jeff Webb. (photo courtesy of Jeff Webb)

with his wife of 28 years, Deborah. They have three grown children and two beautiful grandchildren.

BILL ZOPF: Zopf graduated from Duquesne University, which is located in Pittsburgh, and was the second round pick of the Bucks in the 1970 draft.

Yes, the Vietnam War was still going on in 1971, and it impacted Billy Zopf. Zopf was in the Army Reserves, and was called up for 16 weeks to serve his active duty. As a result, he missed the remaining 17 games of the regular season and the playoffs. After his active duty, Zopf returned to the Bucks for training camp before the 1971-72 season. Unfortunately, he was one of the final cuts.

His next stop was the Pittsburgh Condors (ABA) for a practice session. Zopf recalls that things were a little unusual in Pittsburgh. "So I went out to their practice, and frankly, they were in disarray. I got there for the first practice, nobody was there on time. You know if you weren't on time in Milwaukee you were fined X dollars for every minute. To make a long story short, they basically ran out of money and dissolved the team." (*Phone interview 2/19/2014*)

There was another option for Zopf. Tom Nissalke, the Bucks' assistant coach during their championship season, was now the head coach of the ABA's Dallas Chapparals. Nissalke offered Zopf an opportunity to play for Dallas. Zopf made his decision. "I opted not to go down to Dallas, and I went back and got my degree in Master's of Business Administration. I ended up at PNC Bank for nine years, left PNC, and started up an independent finance company in 1981. To this day we still exist." The company's name is Laurel Capital Corporation. Zopf serves as its CEO and loves his job.

Basketball remained in Zopf's activities. He coached AAU basketball for 17 years. He began by coaching boys but also coached girls. Two of his players were his son, Billy, who later played at Washington & Jefferson, and his daughter, Annie, who played at Fordham University.

Zopf and his wife Patty live in Wexford, Pennsylvania, and are blessed with one grandchild.

EDDIE DOUCETTE: Eddie Doucette was the original radio and television voice of the Bucks for their first 16 seasons. On September 7-8, 2013, Doucette was given the Curt Gowdy Media Award and was inducted into the broadcasting wing of the Naismith Memorial Basketball Hall of Fame.

Announcer Eddie Doucette, the original "Voice of the Bucks.

Doucette currently lives in the San Diego area and is the Relationship Manager for Homer Sports Flooring. He's actively involved with the MACC Fund and the Naismith Memorial Basketball Hall of Fame.

He still does occasional college games and voice-over work. He and Ted Davis, the Bucks current announcer, did a Bucks broadcast on March 6, 2013 for a game against the Los Angeles Clippers.

Eddie mentioned that he loves spending time with his family and watching his grandchildren compete in their school and athletic endeavors.

ACKNOWLEDGMENTS

THERE ARE SO MANY PEOPLE who helped me with this book.

First, I'd like to thank Kira Henschel and HenschelHAUS Publishing, Inc., who did a fantastic job of getting this book out to the public.

My wife, Debbie, was very understanding and patient about the time I spent researching and writing.

I want to thank the Bucks team from that championship season. Without that great season, which culminated with an NBA title, I wouldn't have as great a story. I'd especially like to thank Dick Cunningham, Bob Dandridge, Bob Greacen, Jon McGlocklin, Greg Smith, Jeff Webb, and Billy Zopf. Bucks' radio announcer Eddie Doucette was also very helpful, as was the Bucks' current Executive Vice President of Operations, John Steinmiller.

The Golda Meir Library, located on the University of Milwaukee–Wisconsin's campus, where I did most of my research, has a great staff.

Bob Buege did a fantastic job editing the book and is a big reason why this book, hopefully, is a good read.

Richard Lulloff provided a large number of pictures from his collection that are really unique and nostalgic.

Dennis Sell and Cornelius Geary were invaluable in directing me to the publisher and proofreading.

Thank you all!

ABOUT THE AUTHOR

RICK SCHABOWSKI IS A RETIRED machinist from Harley-Davidson who is currently teaching for the Wisconsin Regional Training Partnership in Milwaukee. He is also President of the Wisconsin Old-Time Ballplayers Association, President of the Ken Keltner Badger State Chapter of Society of American Baseball Research (SABR), and a member of the Hoops Historians. He has contributed to a number of book projects for SABR and the Pro Football Researchers Association. He and his wife Debbie live in Saint Francis, Wisconsin.